MORNING & EVENING
DEVOTIONAL

From the
Rising
of
the Sun

DEVOTIONS OF PRAISE
AND THANKSGIVING

BroadStreet
PUBLISHING

From the rising of the sun

to the place where it sets,

the name of the LORD

is to be praised.

PSALM 113:3

Introduction

Morning and evening, God is worthy of all our praise!

The circumstances of life may have you feeling overwhelmed, frustrated, discouraged, or even depressed. But God's love isn't dependent on your situation. Because his love for you is unchanging and his promises are true, you can choose to believe that today will be a good day from the minute you wake up to the moment you lay down to sleep.

Find the hope, joy, and strength that is abundant in God as you reflect on these devotional entries, scriptures, and prayers *twice* a day.

No matter what comes your way today, you can choose a heart of praise and thanksgiving for your Creator who loves you deeply.

Give thanks to the LORD, for he is good!
His faithful love endures forever.

PSALM 136:1 NLT

Continual Praise

From the rising of the sun to its going down
The LORD's name is to be praised.

PSALM 113:3 NKJV

What would it look like to be a woman who praises God from the time she awakens each morning until the time she falls asleep each night? Not only would we be pleasing God as we worship him constantly, but we would also effect an incredible change in our personal outlook.

As we go about our day, we can look for reasons to praise God. Out of an overflow of a heart of thankfulness, we will share God's goodness with those around us and give them a reason to praise his name as well.

God, I praise you for your love for me. Help me to be a woman who praises you all day, every day. Cultivate in me an appreciation of your goodness and a longing to worship you constantly.

Everywhere—from east to west—praise the name of the LORD.

PSALM 113:3 NLT

Intentional, continual praise can only naturally result in intentional, continual joy. When we choose to look at each moment as a moment in which to be thankful and worshipful, then we will find in each moment beauty, joy, and satisfaction.

As we reflect on the day, let us do so with a heart of praise. Let us choose to remember how God's goodness echoed in everything around us.

God, I see your goodness all around me. Tonight I choose to remember all that I have to be thankful for. I choose to see your beauty and grace in all circumstances. You alone are worthy of my praise, and I direct my heart of thanksgiving toward you now. Be praised in my life, God!

Take a moment to reflect on the goodness of God shown to you today.

Something New

"I am about to do something new.
See, I have already begun! Do you not see it?
I will make a pathway through the wilderness.
I will create rivers in the dry wasteland."

ISAIAH 43:19 NLT

Whether you have generated a color-coded list of goals, dreams, and an execution plan for this year, or you've banned resolutions and vowed to make this just another year, the clean slate represented by a new year is filled with an undeniable air of expectation. Deep down inside, there is a part of us which thinks, "This could be my year!"

Guess what? It *is* your year. This day, and every one that follows, is yours. It is yours to choose who and how to love, to serve, and even to be. And the choice you made in spending time with God represents the choice to take this journey in his company. That is a beautiful place to start.

Heavenly Father, I give you this year. I ask that you would help me keep you in the forefront of my mind as I make decisions and plans. I want to seek your advice in everything I set my hand to.

Behold, I am doing a new thing;
now it springs forth,
do you not perceive it?
I will make a way in the wilderness
and rivers in the desert.

ISAIAH 43:19 ESV

The excitement of a new bauble or gadget pales in comparison to the promise of a new beginning. What a blessing to know you can start over each year, each month, each day with a God who makes a way in your wilderness. He creates refreshing rivers in your desert.

Watch closely for the new things God is bringing into your life this year. Choose to spend time gleaning wisdom and encouragement from his Word each day.

God, you have new things for me this year, and I trust you to reveal them to me in your perfect time. As I go to sleep tonight, help me rest peacefully, knowing your plans for me are good.

What new things can you imagine God doing for you this year?

Fresh and New

Therefore, if anyone is in Christ, the new creation has come:
The old has gone, the new is here!

2 CORINTHIANS 5:17 NIV

When we accept Christ as our Savior, we get to start over,
as if from scratch. Our old, ugly lives and selfish ways are
forgotten, and we are brand new. Oh goodness, aren't you
thankful for it?

We all have plenty of days we could happily erase: memories
of bad choices we made and poor decisions followed through.
But we can give those regrets to God and start again—every
day if we need to!

Lord, I'm once again in awe of the depth of your love for me.
Thank you for the gift of forgiveness and for making me fresh and
new. Help me to live today differently than I did yesterday.

Anyone who belongs to Christ has become a new person.
The old life is gone; a new life has begun!

2 CORINTHIANS 5:17 NLT

Every day, we get to stand before our King and hold our heads up high, knowing we are forgiven and clean. There's no checklist of our sins and faults, no remembering the worst of our mistakes.

There is nothing in this world that can take away past regrets. Only the tender love of our Father's heart flowing down in abundance upon us, can make us new.

God, I receive your newness today. Thank you for washing me with your grace, filling me with your life, and giving me hope for an even better tomorrow. Watch over me as I rest tonight and fill me with your peace.

How do you feel when you think of God's love washing over you and making you new?

All in Love

Let all that you do be done in love.

1 CORINTHIANS 16:14 ESV

Humans are emotional beings. We are motivated and impacted by our feelings and those of others. We speak harshly in anger, embark on adventures because of curiosity, lash out when embarrassed, and give to those in need through empathy. Emotion is a gift, but if we allow ourselves to be overly driven by our human passions, they will misguide us.

As followers of Jesus, we can check our hearts and continually remind ourselves to act in love. Everything God does is motivated and backed by overwhelming love for us, and that's the example we should follow.

Lord, love doesn't come naturally to me in every situation. Thank you for enabling me to do all things out of love through your love in me. Help me to always check my heart before I react to any situation, so I respond and act in love.

Do everything in love.

1 Corinthians 16:14, niv

We can't trust our emotions to drive us—they are too
unpredictable. But we can choose to do everything in
love. Acting in love is always the right course of action; it
neutralizes any sinful attitude or motivation.

The positive effect of love on our lives is undeniable; love
brings us closer to God and more into his likeness. As we
become more like him, we are able to choose love over other
emotions that spring up so quickly.

*God, I know I can show love to those around me when I choose to
love like you do. It isn't always easy, but I know it's what you want
me to do. I choose love when I'm tired, stressed, annoyed, and
angry. I choose love this evening because you chose to love me.*

How do you take control over your emotions and choose to love?

Powerful Kindness

I will tell about the LORD's kindness
and praise him for everything he has done.
I will praise the LORD for the many good things he has given us
and for his goodness to the people of Israel.
He has shown great mercy to us
and has been very kind to us.

ISAIAH 63:7 NCV

The Bible says that the kindness of the Lord leads people to repentance: not his anger, not his wrath—his kindness. There is power in kindness: a power that moves souls and changes lives. We can subconsciously equate kindness with weakness, but it's the exact opposite.

We can trust God and turn to him often, confident that his mercy is present, even in suffering.

God, I sometimes miss your point. I assume that you're angry with me or that I've distanced myself too far from you, but your arms are always open wide to me. Help me to walk in this truth today.

I will tell of the LORD's unfailing love.
I will praise the LORD for all he has done.
I will rejoice in his great goodness to Israel,
which he has granted according to his mercy and love.

The Israelites turned their backs on God too many times to count. But what we see time and time again in their story is that God was still good. He showed them mercy; he gave them good things. He was kind to them.

Of course, Israel wasn't spared consequences and trials, but the people knew God's promises and trusted him. In the same way, we can trust God and turn to him often, confident that his mercy is present, even in suffering.

God, no matter how many times I turn my back on you, you're still constant in mercy. Thank you for your kindness and your unfailing love for me.

Can you see God's goodness in your life even through the consequences of your choices?

The Fear Factor

When I am afraid, I will put my trust in you.
I praise God for what he has promised.
I trust in God, so why should I be afraid?

PSALM 56:3-4 NLT

David did not hesitate to admit when he was afraid! King Saul was pursuing him and so great was his terror that he ran to the enemy's camp—an unlikely place to find refuge. It was bold and risky, but perhaps King Achish would not recognize him, or might consider him a deserter and an asset.

Unfortunately, David was found out, reported to the king, and, motivated by more fear, acted like a mad man and was sent away. Fear causes us to do things we normally would not. Think about that as you go about your day.

God, I am afraid today, but like David I am going to trust you! I don't have to worry about anything because I know that whatever you allow in my life is designed for my good. I rest in that knowledge today.

When I'm afraid, I put my trust in you.
I trust in God. I praise his word.
I trust in God. I am not afraid.

PSALM 56:3-4 NIRV

It wasn't long before David readjusted his thinking and put his trust once again in God. It is interesting that he says, "*When* I am afraid," not "*If* I am afraid." David knew he would experience fear again.

Fear is a human response, and unless counteracted by trust, is destructive at best. What are you afraid of this evening? Are you magnifying a concern into an impossible mountain of what ifs? Trust Jesus. Remember his promises to you. No matter the outcome, he is in charge!

God, your promises are good. I don't need to be afraid of anything because I trust in you. You are the powerful, all-knowing God so I have no reason to be afraid tonight. Help me to remember that when fear knocks at my door.

What are you afraid of today?
Can you choose to trust God instead?

Twirling with Joy

You changed my sorrow into dancing.
You took away my clothes of sadness,
and clothed me in happiness.
I will sing to you and not be silent.
Lord, my God, I will praise you forever.

PSALM 30:11-12 NCV

Abandoned, abused single mother finds love, purpose, and healing. That's a movie most of us would watch. Who doesn't love a good restoration story? When God heals broken places and redeems lost situations, our hearts swell with possibility. If he can restore her life, he can surely come in and fix mine.

It's true. The mourners will dance, clothed in happiness. Voices silenced by sadness will sing loudest songs of praise. And you, regardless of what you face today, will be there: twirling with joy, singing your heart out. You will be there.

Lord, like a dancer spinning with grace, you turn things around.
You restore what is broken and redeem what is lost. I praise you for
your goodness. Hear my voice, delight in my dance—it is all for you.

You turned my loud crying into dancing.
You removed my clothes of sadness and dressed me with joy.
So my heart will sing your praises. I can't keep silent.
Lord, my God, I will praise you forever.

PSALM 30:11-12 NIRV

When we give God a chance to change our outlook for the day, he will gladly step in and do it. We don't need to focus on our sadness. In fact, we should be shouting his praises from the ends of the earth.

Even when we feel surrounded by grief, we can trust God to change us into our party clothes! There is an abundance of joy in his presence. We just need to spend time there to find it.

God, tonight I choose to change into the party clothes you have laid out for me. I take off my sadness and put on your joy instead. I lift my voice to you now and proclaim your goodness. I twirl around in joy and thanksgiving for all you have done in my life.

Thank God for the joy he has dressed you with today.

Truly Awesome

By the word of the LORD the heavens were made,
their starry host by the breath of his mouth.
He gathers the waters of the sea into jars;
he puts the deep into storehouses.

PSALM 33:6-7 NIV

"These cookies are awesome!"

"Wow, you look awesome today!"

The word *awesome* has slipped into American speech so
thoroughly, we may have lost sight of its true meaning.
The cookies, though delicious, probably don't inspire
overwhelming reverence. Your friend looks gorgeous, but
you're not truly taken aback, knocked to your knees. Only
God does that.

Reread the Scripture above out loud, lingering over its
meaning. Ponder all he has done and will do.

Lord God, I am in awe of you. When I consider the universe,
formed by your breath, and the oceans as merely jars in your
storehouse, I can barely contain my amazement. Truly, you alone
are worthy of my praise.

The sky was made at the Lord's command.
By the breath from his mouth, he made all the stars.
He gathered the water of the sea into a heap.
He made the great ocean stay in its place.

Psalm 33:6-7 NCV

As you think about all the things you may have considered *awesome* today, compare each of those to the Creator of the Universe. They pale in comparison.

God, your Father, can hold an ocean in his hand, and yet he knows every hair on your head. He lovingly anticipates every move you make. He delights in *you*, and that is truly awesome.

God, you are awesome. There is no end to your goodness, your faithfulness, and your wisdom. The fact that you love me in all my imperfection is more than I can fathom. Let that thought rest over me as I wind down for the evening.

What have you seen today that you would consider truly awesome?

All Comfort

All praise to God, the Father of our Lord Jesus Christ. God is our merciful Father and the source of all comfort. He comforts us in all our troubles so that we can comfort others. When they are troubled, we will be able to give them the same comfort God has given us. For the more we suffer for Christ, the more God will shower us with his comfort through Christ.

2 Corinthians 1:3–5 NLT

There are many things in this world we tend to look to for comfort. Sometimes it might be food, a hot shower, an air-conditioned room, family, friends, television, a good book… the list is endless.

The Word of God says our merciful Father is the source of all comfort. His promise is to comfort us in all of our troubles. How often do we look elsewhere for comfort when our true comforter is the one who created us and knows our every need?

Oh Father, I pray that today I would look to you to be my source of all comfort. I pray you would teach me to receive my comfort from you and in turn be a comfort to others.

Praise be to the God and Father of our Lord Jesus Christ. God is the Father who is full of mercy and all comfort. He comforts us every time we have trouble, so when others have trouble, we can comfort them with the same comfort God gives us. We share in the many sufferings of Christ. In the same way, much comfort comes to us through Christ.

2 Corinthians 1:3-5 NCV

Many things may appear to offer us comfort throughout the day. But when we really stop and think about it, our only real comfort comes from the one who loves us unconditionally.

While some things may satisfy our need for comfort and peace in the moment, they never last, and we are once again on the lookout for a new source. If we can learn to go to God first, we will be comforted in a way that is undeniable, and lasting!

God, thank you for being my true source of comfort. I don't want to look anywhere else for that. You are always with me, ready to wrap me in your arms and show me your unfailing love.

What are you seeking comfort in today?

Beyond Your Sight

From the end of the earth I call to you
when my heart is faint.
Lead me to the rock
that is higher than I.

PSALM 61:2 ESV

Have you ever wandered through a maze? Even though you may be good at solving mazes on paper, moving through shrubbery or stalks of corn at ground level you are bound to run into a dead end or two. If only there were a place to climb up high, and see the way through.

So what can you do? Call for help. Follow the voice of someone who can see more than you. Today as you run into situations that require a better view, ask God to guide you. He loves to answer those prayers!

Lord, how wonderful it is to know that when I am lost, I can call
to you. Your voice will be my beacon and your hand will lift me up.
Will you be that for me today?

From the ends of the earth,
I cry to you for help
when my heart is overwhelmed.
Lead me to the towering rock of safety.

PSALM 61:2 NLT

When life feels like a maze, and you're faint from the exhaustion of running into walls, call out to God. Follow the sound of his voice to the next turn. Allow his hand to lift you up—beyond your own sight—and show you the way through.

Do you know that God is your towering rock of safety? He is always listening, waiting to guide you through the overwhelming situations in your life. Call out to him whenever you need help. He will not let you down.

Father, thank you for showing me what otherwise can't be seen.
You know what turns I need to take and when I should take them.
Help me to continue to listen for your perfect guidance in my life.
I trust you, God.

Do you find it easy to ask God for guidance?
Why do you think that may be?

Better than Life

Your unfailing love is better than life itself;
how I praise you!

PSALM 63:3 NLT

We've all heard about the dessert, or the necklace, or the dress that was "to die for." What is meant, of course, is delicious, beautiful, a perfect fit. As brownies, baubles, and body-flattering clothes go, they are the pinnacle.

Clearly, a girl's not about to throw herself in front of a moving train to get her hands on the perfect little black dress. Only one thing is truly better than life, and that's life with the Maker.

Lord, nothing compares to your love. On my worst day, I find
comfort in your promise. On my best, I marvel at the knowledge
that so much more awaits me in heaven. Help me to remember
that as I go about my day.

Because your love is better than life,
my lips will glorify you.

PSALM 63:3 NIV

Do we believe that God's love is better than life? *Can* we believe it this side of heaven? It may be easier on the days when life's not so great, but when things are going our way, when life couldn't be better, can we see how great God's promise is? What awaits us is *so much better* than anything we can ask or imagine here on earth!

His love never fails, and nothing compares to it. Regardless of the season we are in or the day we have had, let's acknowledge this beautiful truth from his Word.

God, you are bigger than life, you are better than life, and you are the love of my life. How I praise you. Oh, how I love you.

Can you believe in your heart that God's love is better than life itself?

Inherent Goodness

You, O Lord, are good and forgiving,
abounding in steadfast love to all who call upon you.

PSALM 86:5 ESV

We all approach God for different reasons, with different
matters on our hearts. Sometimes, we come to him in joy and
thankfulness. Other times, we come with our heads bowed
low, nearly crushed by shame and sorrow.

No matter how we come to God, he meets us the same way—
with goodness. As you move through your day today, make a
point of seeing God's goodness in your life.

Thank you, God, for your inherent goodness. I never fear
unfairness when I come to you. Thank you for your steadfast love
and for always responding to me in goodness.

You, Lord, are good, and ready to forgive,
And abundant in lovingkindness to all who call upon You.

PSALM 86:5 NASB

God is full of love for us, his children. He doesn't receive us with quick anger or frustration, but with a love that is steadfast and unchanging.

God isn't just good some of the time; goodness is his nature. Whether he is passing righteous judgment or granting undeserved grace, he is good. Because of his perfect character, we can wholly trust him.

God, help me understand your inherent goodness, so I won't hesitate to come to you first in every situation. Thank you for showing me your goodness today.

How did you see God's goodness manifested in your life today?

Heavenly Rewards

Be patient, therefore, brothers, until the coming of the Lord. See how the farmer waits for the precious fruit of the earth, being patient about it, until it receives the early and the late rains.

JAMES 5:7 ESV

There is a prevalent message in today's culture that whispers sweet and appealing lies: rights to luxury and self-indulgence. You deserve it, Christian! God wants you to have it and to be happy. This whisper takes away the sweet truth of a God who rewards us, and injects the poisonous lie that that enjoyment must be immediate.

God wants to reward you. That is truth. He promises rewards to the faithful, and he keeps his promises. Those rewards are often not on this earth, and why would we want them to be? Earthly rewards are enjoyable, but they can be destroyed by moth and rust. Heaven's treasures are eternal.

Develop patience in me, God! Grant me endurance to wait for the gifts you have in heaven and not be satisfied with temporary things.

Be patient as you wait for the Lord's return. Consider the farmers who patiently wait for the rains in the fall and in the spring. They eagerly look for the valuable harvest to ripen.

JAMES 5:7 NLT

To lean into the pull of God's kingdom instead of the tug of instant gratification, requires enduring patience. When you are tempted to give in to temporary satisfaction, remember the rewards that wait for you in heaven.

Know that your loving Father is waiting to give you more than you could think to ask for. Let that spur you on in your works and actions, motivating you to live with a kingdom-driven mind-set.

I want to be fully satisfied by you, God, and by the promise of eternal life with you. I patiently wait for your return, knowing you have blessed me with everything I need.

What do you find it most difficult to be satisfied with in your life right now?

What Defines You?

The believers were filled with joy and with the Holy Spirit.

ACTS 13:52 NLT

Do you ever try to describe someone to another person and then wonder how people describe you? Usually we start with physical features before throwing in a few characteristics. What about "Christian"? That simple descriptor has negative connotations in a lot of minds.

In Acts, the first Christians are described as full of joy and the Holy Spirit. The two go hand in hand. To be full of true joy, you must be full of the Holy Spirit.

God, help me to be full of joy. I want to be a good witness of your character to those who come in contact with me today. I know it won't be easy, but I want to choose joy. So help me, please.

The disciples were filled with joy and with the Holy Spirit.

ACTS 13:52 ESV

You choose to value God's presence in daily life. Joy is not circumstance based; it's an inner confidence in the sovereign control of Christ.

What defines you? Circumstances? Do waves and crashing waters shape you like a canyon void? Or is the Holy Spirit shaping you into fullness: a pillar of strength and a beacon for your family and community?

God, I don't want to be crashed around by the waves. Define and mold me with your Spirit. Open my eyes to whatever changes I need to make, and let your life live in me.

Would people describe you as being a joy-filled Christian?

A Greater Wonder

When I look at your heavens,
the work of your fingers,
the moon and the stars,
which you have set in place,
what is man that you are mindful of him,
and the son of man that you care for him?

PSALM 8:3-4 ESV

The God of all—the universe and everything in it—is the same God who gave his life to know us. The God who spoke the world into being is the same God who speaks quietly to our hearts. His love for us is as unsearchable as the heavens.

It's hard to believe that the Creator of the Universe is not only interested in us, but he is invested in us. His love for us knows no limits or boundaries. Let your mind ponder this throughout the day today.

Father, I don't understand why you love me the way you do when you are as great as you are. But I am so thankful you do.

I look at your heavens,
which you made with your fingers.
I see the moon and stars,
which you created.
But why are people even important to you?
Why do you take care of human beings?

PSALM 8:3-4 NCV

The greatness of our God is displayed majestically throughout his creation. When we look into the night sky at all the twinkling stars and the far-off planets, we realize almost instantly how small we are in his universe.

A greater wonder than the grandeur of God's capacity is his value for mankind. He is an incredible Creator who wants to be fully engaged with his creation.

God, thank you that you see me as being important. Thank you for giving me life and the choice to follow you. You are the greatest wonder that exists in all the universe.

Spend time pondering the majesty of God's creation and the wonder of his desire to be directly involved in it.

More than Gold

These troubles come to prove that your faith is pure. This purity of faith is worth more than gold, which can be proved to be pure by fire but will ruin. But the purity of your faith will bring you praise and glory and honor when Jesus Christ is shown to you.

1 PETER 1:7 NCV

We can waste much of our lives trying to answer the "whys" of our most difficult times. Most of the answers we seek will not be revealed to us until we meet the Lord in heaven, but Scriptures such as this one from Peter provide lovely encouragement while we wait.

We know gold is precious—so precious it's a universal standard for measuring the entire world's wealth. Here, we are told that faith that withstands troubled times is worth more than all the gold on earth. Be encouraged by that today!

Lord, I invite you to use my pain, present and future, as a proving ground for my faith. Allow my troubles to strengthen my trust in you; allow difficulty to increase my reliance on you.

These have come so that the proven genuineness of your faith--of greater worth than gold, which perishes even though refined by fire-- may result in praise, glory and honor when Jesus Christ is revealed.

1 PETER 1:7 NIV

Holding strong to God's promises regardless of what struggles we face affords us an invaluable reward: the praise, honor, and glory of Jesus himself.

This doesn't mean our difficulty is a test *assigned by* God, but the outcome—a faith that withstands the fire—is *used by* him to bless us beyond imagining.

Father, when you prove yourself faithful, as you always do, I grow to love you more and more. Thank you for being faithful to me as I walk through difficult times and seasons. I want my faith to be proven as genuine through all the tests.

What testing do you sense in your life lately? Can you determine to be proven genuine in your faith throughout the testing?

He Will Be Found

"I will be found by you," says the LORD. "I will end your captivity and restore your fortunes. I will gather you out of the nations where I sent you and will bring you home again to your own land."

JEREMIAH 29:14 NIV

Lost. It's an uncomfortable word. Being lost is unnerving, and losing something is unsettling. Losing someone: unbearable. Losing God? Unthinkable.

Though they were sent far away from him for many years, Jeremiah 29 contains God's beautiful words of comfort to his beloved Israel. "I will be found by you…I will bring you home again." Thank God that he can always be found.

Father, there are days I fear I've lost you. I know it isn't true, but I can't feel your presence or find your peace. I never want to be away from you, Lord. Find me, Father. Draw me near. Bring me home.

"I will be found by you," declares the LORD, "and will bring you back from captivity. I will gather you from all the nations and places where I have banished you," declares the LORD, "and will bring you back to the place from which I carried you into exile."

JEREMIAH 29:14 NIV

Many believers encounter a season where God might feel far away, or even lost. The relief of finding what we've misplaced is nothing—nothing—compared to the incomprehensible joy of reuniting with the Lord. He will be found!

God intends good for you. He adores you, and if you continue to seek his face and claim his promises for your life, he will bring you home again.

Father, you deeply care about me. Thank you that you always know where I am, and that you are never far from me. Wrap me in your arms tonight.

How do you draw near to the Lord when he seems far away?

I Am Yours

*He predestined us for adoption to sonship through Jesus Christ,
in accordance with his pleasure and will—to the praise of his
glorious grace, which he has freely given us in the One he loves.*

EPHESIANS 1:5-6 NIV

No matter what life gives to you, or what it takes from you,
one thing is sure. You are a child of God and nothing can
change that truth. He paid a high price for your soul.

Whether you feel worthy of his love or not, you're wrapped up
in it. Embrace it today and allow it to change the way you feel
about yourself and others.

*Thank you, God, that I am one of yours—that I am your child
and nothing can change that. Help me not to doubt your love but
instead to walk in the power of knowing who I am in you.*

Because of his love, God had already decided to make us his own children through Jesus Christ. That was what he wanted and what pleased him, and it brings praise to God because of his wonderful grace. God gave that grace to us freely, in Christ, the One he loves.

EPHESIANS 1:5-6 NCV

God is a good Father. He delights in being kind to you. He inhabits your praise and he enjoys your prayers. There is so much power in understanding your identity as a child of God.

As you dwell on the goodness of God tonight, remember that his heart is for you. There is no good thing in him that has not been extended to you through his Son.

Thank you, God, for being a good Father to me. I rest in your goodness this evening and thank you for the peace that brings to my heart.

How does knowing you are a child of God change the way you think about yourself?

Truly Special

You are a chosen people, a royal priesthood, a holy nation, God's special possession.

1 PETER 2:9 NIV

We all want to believe that we are special. Most of us grow up being told that we are, and it feels good to believe it. But over time, we look around us and realize that, really, we are just like everyone else.

Sometimes doubt creeps in, making us second guess ourselves and damaging our self-confidence. Choose to believe today that God has called and chosen you for something truly special.

Thank you, God, that you see me as special. I revel in that knowledge today.

You are a chosen people, royal priests, a holy nation, a people for God's own possession.

1 PETER 2:9 NCV

Long before you were even a wisp in your mother's womb, you were set aside and marked as special. You were chosen to be God's special possession, and that's a pretty amazing thing.

Of all the people in the world, God has chosen you to do something only you can do. Ask him to show you what he has for you as you continue to walk in his wonderful light.

Father, you have called me out of the darkness of the ordinary and have brought me into the light of the extraordinary. You have hand-picked me and you love me. I am so thankful.

Ask God to show you just how special you are to him.

Celebrate God's Blessings

For seven days celebrate the festival to the LORD your God at the place the LORD will choose. For the Lord your God will bless you in all your harvest and in all the work of your hands, and your joy will be complete.

DEUTERONOMY 16:15 NIV

When you hear the words *spiritual discipline*, what comes to mind? Usual responses include prayer, fasting, and meditating on Scripture. If someone mentioned celebrating, would you rebuke them? Is that answer unspiritual, irreverent?

Surprise! God actually commanded us to celebrate, rejoice, and have parties. Joy is overflowing exaltation. When you see a beautiful sunset, you want to grab someone and share it with them. It is right to celebrate the goodness of the Lord!

Thank you, God, for the abundance of blessing and joy in our lives! I celebrate you and the wonder of who you are. Let my rejoicing be a beacon for your glory.

Seven days you shall keep the festival to the Lord your God at the place that the Lord will choose; for the Lord your God will bless you in all your produce and in all your undertakings, and you shall surely celebrate.

DEUTERONOMY 16:15 NRSV

Celebration causes joy to overflow into the world around us. What if you heard a joyous celebration and found out people were praising the Lord? It would be difficult to not join in. It's okay to laugh, dance, and celebrate what God has done in our lives. He is a good father!

Gather around a campfire and sing your lungs out. Take your partner's hands and spin around the kitchen floor. Delight in a warm meal with true friends. These things are pleasing to God. They bring him glory.

God, thank you for creating special occasions for me to celebrate. I am so grateful for the many blessings you have showered on me. Help my celebration to be a light to those around me—leading them to you.

What can you celebrate today?

Our Rock

There is no one holy like the LORD,
Indeed, there is no one besides You,
Nor is there any rock like our God.

1 SAMUEL 2:2 NASB

Most of us have been blessed by special relationships in our lives. We are surrounded by friends and family that love us. These are people we can turn to in times of trouble and pain. And it can be tempting to allow these people to feel like a rock: a stabilizer. As soon as something happens, we run to them and ask for their strength to get us through.

The Bible tells us that there is no rock like our God. He's the best; there's no one else that can take his place. Run to God today when you need strength.

Father, I give you my burdens. I'm so thankful that you are my rock and my daily source of strength. Help me to turn to you first in all that I do.

No one is holy like the LORD!
There is no one besides you;
there is no Rock like our God.

1 SAMUEL 2:2 NLT

When we start to worry, become afraid, or experience difficulty, our first source of comfort should be the Lord. He is so good to us! No matter what we are going through, he will be there for us. There is simply no one like him.

As the day comes to a close, let God the Rock be the place you rest. Let him take all of your worries and fears away.

God, my Rock, there is none like you. Thank you for being the only place I can turn to for real, lasting peace. I trust you for that this evening.

Can you trust God to be your first source of comfort?

Mind Games

Let the peace that Christ gives control your thinking, because you were called together in one body to have peace. Always be thankful.

COLOSSIANS 3:15 NCV

Our minds can be a baseball field with baseball-like thoughts hurtling every which way. Maybe you have your mitt out, ready to catch, or maybe you get hit with a thought out of left field.

Instead of allowing your thoughts to be set statements of truth, take thoughts as information, and then determine your response. Your response should be considered through this lens; earlier in Colossians, Paul says you are a new creation. As a new creation, learn to quiet your thoughts; don't let them knock you over.

Lord, help me to guard my thoughts and surround me in truth. Lead me through sometimes muddy fields, that I may know what is truth and what is not.

*Let the peace that comes from Christ rule in your hearts.
For as members of one body you are called to live in peace.
And always be thankful.*

SMALL>COLOSSIANS</SMALL> 3:15 NCV

Are your "baseball thoughts" God-honoring? In God's eyes, you are dressed in the righteousness of Christ. Accept that thought as truth and act on it.

Dismiss wrong thoughts as a part of your old, sinful nature. Desire peace with other Christians, viewing them as new creations too. Allow your thoughts about them to promote peace among you. Trust God's promise that his peace can control your thoughts.

Your Word is truth, and I desire it more than anything else. Help me tonight to quiet my thoughts. I submit them to you and ask for your peace to rule my mind. I am so thankful for your peace, God.

What's the best way for you to let the peace of Christ rule your mind?

God's Constancy

All the ways of the LORD are loving and faithful
toward those who keep the demands of his covenant.

PSALM 25:10 NIV

There is a phrase used to describe warmth, happiness, and melancholy: a bittersweet mix of emotions—*all the feels*. If you only read this one verse for your devotion today, you would assume that things were going pretty well for the Psalmist.

Open your Bible and read the whole psalm. In verse 25, David states his current condition: lonely, afflicted, distressed, and full of troubles. It doesn't feel quite the same, does it? You can choose today to believe that God is always loving and faithful regardless of your emotional state, just as David did all those years ago.

God, my circumstances may swirl and crumble around me, but you are faithful! Surround me in your love, and keep my eyes lifted to you.

The LORD leads with unfailing love and faithfulness
all who keep his covenant and obey his demands.

PSALM 25:10 NLT

God is more than whatever situation you are in. Circumstances ebb and flow, but God is constant. He is constantly righteous, constantly just, and constantly loving. This is the essence of his being; there is nothing temporary in God.

You can know unfailing love and faithfulness by knowing God. Because Christ's life is lived out in you, it does not matter what your circumstances are. You remain on paths of love, knowing God's faithfulness.

Thank you, God, that you are greater than my circumstances. You are constant and steady. I surrender my will to yours and ask you to help me keep the demands of your covenant.

How can you draw near to God today in the middle of your circumstances?

In Sunshine and Storm

When times are good, be happy;
but when times are bad, consider this:
God has made the one as well as the other.
Therefore, no one can discover
anything about their future.

ECCLESIASTES 7:14 NIV

It's easy to feel happy on a sunny day, when all is well, the birds are singing, and life is going along swimmingly. But what happens when waters are rougher, bad news comes, or the days feel just plain hard?

God wants us to feel gladness when times are good. He has made each and every day. We are called to rejoice in all of them whether good or bad. Make today a good day just because you know God loves you.

God, I don't want my happiness to be determined by my circumstance. Help me discover true joy in you today.

In the day of prosperity be joyful,
and in the day of adversity consider;
God has made the one as well as the other,
so that mortals may not find out
anything that will come after them.

ECCLESIASTES 7:14 NRSV

Happiness is determined by our circumstances, but true joy comes when we can find the silver linings, hidden in our darkest hours—when we can sing God's praises no matter what.

We don't know what the future holds for us here on earth, but we can find our delight in the knowledge that our eternity is set in the beauty of full relationship with our heavenly Father.

Father, give me a deep and abiding satisfaction in each day that goes beyond human understanding. Help me to rest in your joy this evening.

Do you trust God with your future?

Delightful

The LORD takes delight in his people;
he crowns the humble with victory.

PSALM 149:4 NIV

If ever there was something to lift your spirits and get you through the toughest of days, it's the knowledge that the Lord our God takes delight in you. He tells you so in his Word!

God takes pleasure in your very existence. Your heavenly Father created you to be in relationship with him, and he gets great joy out of it. Take that delightful thought with you throughout your day.

Father, it makes me smile to know that you delight in me. I lift up others who haven't experienced your delight, and pray that they'd come to know you in a deep and real way. You are truly glorious, and I'm amazed by you!

The LORD delights in his people;
he crowns the humble with victory.

Revel in the knowledge of God's delight for the rest of the evening and into tomorrow. Embrace the fact that there is one who loves you and is truly captivated by you.

God loves spending time with you; he wants to get closer to you each day. Allow him to take you deeper! Dive in and experience his delight for yourself.

God, thank you for loving me and wanting me to draw closer to you! Help me to embrace your delight and walk in your victory each day.

Did you feel God's delight in you today?

Pieced Together

Praise the LORD!
It is good to sing praises to our God;
it is good and pleasant to praise him.
He heals the brokenhearted
and bandages their wounds.

PSALM 147:1, 3 NCV

Whether you are carrying pain and suffering from past abuse or tragedy, or you've more recently been hurt, run toward the one who heals.

It will take constant communion with God to remind you of his healing power, but he will glue you back until you are whole. Sing praises to God today in spite of your pain. It is good to acknowledge him at every turn.

Father God, I am in need of your healing power. I release
everything I am holding on to and ask for you to heal my wounds.

Praise the LORD.
How good it is to sing praises to our God,
how pleasant and fitting to praise him!
He heals the brokenhearted
and binds up their wounds.

PSALM 147:1, 3 NIV

No matter how broken you feel, there is no requirement or need too great; God can piece you back together.

Broken souls, broken bodies, broken hearts, be reminded of his power in your pain-filled moments and do not turn away from his love. Sing praises to the God who heals.

God, I praise you tonight even though I may not feel like it. I acknowledge that you are good and perfect. Heal my brokenness as I give glory and honor to you.

Do you believe that God can heal you and make you whole?

The Greatest Investment

We also have joy with our troubles, because we know that these troubles produce patience, and patience produces character, and character produces hope.

ROMANS 5:3–4 NCV

Gordon B. Hinckley once said, "You will come to know that what appears today to be a sacrifice will prove instead to be the greatest investment that you will ever make." In the financial world, a risk-free investment is too good to be true.

Spiritually speaking, there is such a thing. What is painful to give to God? Whatever you just can't release your grip on, go ahead and let go. You are not just giving up for the sake of giving up—you are investing. You can give confidently, knowing that God will make a greater return than you ever could.

God, I trust you! You are good. I rest in the truth that you have good in store for me.

We can rejoice, too, when we run into problems and trials, for we know that they help us develop endurance. And endurance develops strength of character, and character strengthens our confident hope of salvation.

ROMANS 5:3–4 NLT

In your hard times, God is returning patience. When you feel like your patience is measured small, he is returning character for your life! When your character is being tried, what's coming back to you is hope—beautiful, joyful, love-inspired hope, and hope in God never disappoints.

Don't be like a child who has a stick and refuses to trade it in for the prize they cannot see or imagine, when a new bike is around the corner. Trust in the investment that God wants to make in you.

God, thank you for investing in me. Thank you for turning my struggles into strength and building my character. You have given me continued hope and I am so thankful.

Can you see the investment God is making in your life right now?

Eternal Gift

The lovingkindness of the LORD is from everlasting to everlasting on those who fear Him,
And His righteousness to children's children,
To those who keep His covenant
And remember His precepts to do them.

PSALM 103:17-18 NASB

Today, always, and forevermore, the Lord's love will be with you if you only allow him in. He is sheer mercy and grace. Isn't that amazing?

We don't deserve his love. We fall short daily, and we will never live up to a life of perfection. Yet he continually doles out more and more of his abiding love for us.

Father, I am amazed by your love and how you give it readily.
I do not deserve it, but you still give it freely. Thank you.

The love of the LORD remains forever
with those who fear him.
His salvation extends to the children's children
of those who are faithful to his covenant,
of those who obey his commandments!

PSALM 103:17-18 NLT

God's love is always available to us when we choose to follow his ways and seek a relationship with him. Turn your face to him tonight. Let that deep love of his soak in and wash over you. He knows you inside and out, and he calls you beloved despite your flaws.

Take joy in his love! It's an eternal, precious gift.

God, I pray I'd never take your love for granted. Help me to follow you all the days of my life.

How do you see God's everlasting love in your life today?

Hope in His Word

You are my hiding place and my shield;
I hope in your word.

PSALM 119:114 NCV

Hope. It isn't a big word, but there is so much meaning behind those four letters. Hope is a feeling of expectation. It's a desire for a certain outcome.

We are designed to live with hope. And thankfully, we can put our hope in someone greater than ourselves—our God. His Word is truth, and all of our expectations and desires can rest in that knowledge.

Father, I praise you for being my refuge and shield. Thank you for giving me your Word.

You are my refuge and my shield;
your word is my source of hope.

PSALM 119:114 NLT

God is our refuge. He loves us, protects us, and wants the best outcome for us. He gave us his Word, the Bible, as a promise. We can go to it at any time. When hope begins to waver, and doubts creep in, his truth is still there.

We have hope for a future because God is our past, present, and forever Lord. Take that promise with you tonight and allow it to bring hope to your current situation.

God, help me turn to you with my every desire and live expectantly, knowing that I can put my hope in you.

Where do you place your hope?

Not a Quitter

Give thanks to the LORD, for he is good
his love endures forever.

1 CHRONICLES 16:34 NIV

We've all been there before—times get hard, life gets rough, and we just want to say, "I quit!" It's only natural. But there is one who never quits on us.

God never gives up on his love for us. For him, it's natural to keep on loving. He loves us with a never-ending, everlasting, beautiful, forever love that sees us through everything.

Father, thank you for your enduring love that sees me through thick and thin. Help me remember your love when I feel lost and lonely.

Oh give thanks to the LORD,
for he is good;
for his steadfast love endures forever!

1 CHRONICLES 16:34 ESV

Isn't it extraordinary that no matter what, God loves us. He doesn't sit on his throne in heaven and say to himself, "Ugh, how annoying! There she is again, off on her own, making poor choices and not listening to me. I'm done with her!" He won't give up on you; you are never alone.

Remember God's goodness tonight and remind yourself that he doesn't ever quit loving you.

God, I give you all the praise because you are such a good God!
I know you will never quit loving me, and for that I am so
incredibly thankful.

Thank God for his steadfast love that never quits!

Abundant Rain

Be glad, O children of Zion,
and rejoice in the LORD your God,
for he has given the early rain for your vindication;
he has poured down for you abundant rain,
the early and the latter rain, as before.

JOEL 2:23 ESV

Our Lord is so good and faithful. He provides us with everything we need if we only look to him for it.

When our lives are in drought, parched from our daily grind, he sends us rain in abundance, to nourish our souls and keep us from drying out spiritually. The fields that are our lives begin to green up again after a season of becoming brown. We feel refreshed as his showers of love pour down over us.

Lord, thank you for protecting me from drying out. You give me everything I need to flourish, and for that I give you all the praise.

Rejoice, you people of Jerusalem!
Rejoice in the LORD your God!
For the rain he sends demonstrates his faithfulness.
Once more the autumn rains will come,
as well as the rains of spring.

JOEL 2:23 NLT

Let's celebrate and be glad! Our God in heaven cares for us so much. He wants to see us bearing good fruit, and he will continue to give us what we need to nourish and grow.

Turn to him when you are feeling parched, and he will give you rain for the exact season you are in. He always knows just what you need.

God you know which rain I need in which season. I rejoice in you because you are faithful to care for me just the way I need to be cared for.

What kind of refreshing rain do you need today?

Rest Easy

Blessed be the LORD, who daily bears our burden,
The God who is our salvation.

PSALM 68:19 NASB

There may be times when life's problems begin to feel
overwhelming. Do you know you can always rest in the
knowledge that the Lord will carry your burdens for you?

God knows it all. He loves you. He is for you. He saves you.
He wants to rescue you. Allow him to do that for you today.

Lord, I am amazed by your power and might! When I am
struggling, you are there to see me through. I know you will rescue
me when I am in need, and I praise you for it.

Praise be to the Lord, to God our Savior,
who daily bears our burdens.

PSALM 68:19 NIV

Close your eyes and feel God's love surrounding you. Permit him to come in and take over every fiber of your being. Feel him wash over you, filling you up with his love.

You can hand over each of your trials to God, knowing that you cannot carry the load on your own. The Father is strong enough to take them all. So let him.

God, thank you for being strong enough to carry the weight of my burdens. I give them to you tonight and ask you for rest and peace.

Picture yourself handing your heavy load to God. Let it go and be free.

His Love Song

The LORD your God is in your midst,
a mighty one who will save;
he will rejoice over you with gladness;
he will quiet you by his love;
he will exult over you with loud singing.

ZEPHANIAH 3:17 ESV

One of the most popular reasons people buy puppies is so that there is always someone excited to see them when they get home. A puppy forgives quickly and loves to spend as much time with its owner as possible.

Even better than the feeling you get from being with a dog is the delight that your Father in heaven takes in you. He actually rejoices over you and sings you a love song! Let him sing over you today.

Lord, thank you for loving me. I don't deserve it, but you take delight in me anyway. Help me listen for your song with each and every waking moment, joining in the chorus and praising you all the while.

The LORD your God is living among you.
He is a mighty savior.
He will take delight in you with gladness.
With his love, he will calm all your fears.
He will rejoice over you with joyful songs.

ZEPHANIAH 3:17 NLT

Is it hard for you to imagine that God is living with you? When we begin to believe that, we can understand why our fears are calmed and a spirit of joy presides in our homes. God is with us and he saves us.

Smile! The Lord loves you fiercely. Your mighty warrior wants to save you from yourself. He gets great joy from his relationship with you. Join in his beautiful song and rejoice with him tonight.

God, the thought of you being near to me always gives me courage and joy. I want to hear the song of delight that you sing over me. Open my ears to hear it tonight!

Can you hear your mighty warrior singing over you with his love?

Shout His Goodness

Give thanks to the LORD and proclaim his greatness.
Let the whole world know what he has done.
Sing to him; yes, sing his praises.
Tell everyone about his wonderful deeds.
Exult in his holy name;
rejoice, you who worship the LORD.

1 CHRONICLES 16:8-10 NLT

When something great happens, sometimes we want to shout it on the mountain top, telling everyone who will listen. That's how we should feel about our relationship with Christ!

By dying on the cross, taking away our sin, and loving us through our worst, he's done something incredible. We should be broadcasting it for all to hear. Let your praise for God be evident today.

Lord, thank you for all that you've done for me. My life would be nothing without you! I pray that I would be one who is willing to share your glory with those around me.

Give praise to the LORD, proclaim his name;
make known among the nations what he has done.
Sing to him, sing praise to him;
tell of all his wonderful acts.
Glory in his holy name;
let the hearts of those who seek the LORD rejoice.

1 CHRONICLES 16:8-10 NIV

God is the epitome of good. He has done so many wonderful things for us. Let's rejoice in that tonight, glorify his name to all who will listen, and praise him without ceasing.

Revel in God's goodness this evening. Dwell on the many wonderful things he has brought into your life and thank him for them as you think of them. He is worthy of your praise, and he loves to be thanked for his goodness.

God, there are not enough words in a day to thank you for all the blessings you have poured out on my life. I know there have been difficult times as well, but you have always been faithful and that just gives me another reason to praise you tonight.

Begin listing all the ways God has blessed you and proclaim his goodness today!

Fruit from Pain

To all who mourn in Israel,
he will give a crown of beauty for ashes,
a joyous blessing instead of mourning,
festive praise instead of despair.
In their righteousness, they will be like great oaks
that the LORD has planted for his own glory.

ISAIAH 61:3 NLT

Pain is real. Whatever grief has met you on this journey of life, it does no good to suppress that pain, run from it, or nourish it. It will overtake who you are. Trials, pain, and suffering will come; let God move mightily for good.

Let the pain be soil that nourishes a life full of the fruit of the Spirit! Let God be your gardener, growing love, joy, peace, and gentleness out of unlikely situations. The Lord has planted you for his glory. He wants to complete his good work in you by making you a shelter for others.

I release my pain and grief to you, God. Use it as soil in my life. I love you, I trust you, and I know you are working good within me.

I will give them a crown to replace their ashes,
and the oil of gladness to replace their sorrow,
and clothes of praise to replace their spirit of sadness.
Then they will be called Trees of Goodness,
trees planted by the LORD to show his greatness.

ISAIAH 61:3 NCV

Let grief and pain do more than just subside over time. Use it to bring glory to God. Grow into the love of Christ and spread your roots wide, so that you may be tall to the world outside, a beacon of the hope and glory of God.

God will grow strong gentleness and love in you through what you have suffered, so you can share his glory with others. Let them know they are not alone—there is a God who loves them deeply.

God, I choose this evening to use my pain as a way to help others through their pain. Thank you for the hope that is in you. You will replace my sadness with joy. I want to share that with other hurting people around me.

Can you see good fruit coming from the hardships you have suffered?

Look for Blessings

Oh, how great is Your goodness,
Which You have laid up for those who fear You,
Which you have prepared for those who trust in You,
In the presence of the sons of men!

PSALM 31:19 NKJV

Nothing moves us quicker out of our worldview, swirling around the god of self, than thankfulness to the true God. We can step outside of our world and into thoughts of him, by examining the goodness he shows in the world, from big to small, A to Z. It is then that we see God touching every area of our lives.

God is not boxed up in the praise of our Sunday mornings or set down at the end of our Bible reading time. He is fluid and available, large and in motion, touching, moving, and breathing into the joints and ligaments of everyday life. Feel him with you today in this way.

Thank you, Lord, for the sunrise and the beauty of the world around me. Thank you for the food you have given me, the roof over my head, and the clothes on my back. I choose to walk in thankfulness today.

How great is your goodness
that you have stored up for those who fear you,
that you have given to those who trust you.
You do this for all to see.

PSALM 31:19 NCV

It creates an outworking of goodness in our lives when we acknowledge the goodness God has bestowed on us. We are moved to compassion when we thank him for moving in compassion toward us, and gratefulness stirs our hearts until it overflows.

Spend time this evening in gratefulness and praise. Start little, start big. It doesn't matter. Position yourself outside of your world to see God at work around you.

God, there really is no end to your blessings and your goodness.
The more I think about what I am thankful for, the more there is to
be grateful for. You are worthy of all my praise.

How does being thankful change the way you view your day?

Ask Confidently

Let us come boldly to the very throne of God and stay there to receive his mercy and to find grace to help us in our times of need.

HEBREWS 4:16 TLB

It's hard to ask for help sometimes, isn't it? There's something truly humbling about admitting that we can't do everything on our own. God wants to help you, so approach him with joy and take the help he offers.

You are a precious child of God. He loves you deeply and wants the best for you. That means that it gives him joy to be able to help you in times of need.

Lord, thank you for your willingness to help me. I'm humbled by your grace, and I'm walking in confidence that I can approach you with my needs.

Let us, then, feel very sure that we can come before God's throne where there is grace. There we can receive mercy and grace to help us when we need it.

HEBREWS 4:16 NCV

When we let others know that we aren't as super human as we've been letting them believe, it's like a piece of us crumbles and our confidence drags.

But in the kingdom of heaven, it's an entirely different story! We're told that we should hold our head up high when we ask for God's help. Swallow that pride and turn to him. He will always help you, and you won't regret asking him.

God, I come to you boldly and ask you to help me. I acknowledge my great need for you. Thank you for being merciful and gracious toward me every time I come to you.

What do you need God's help with today?

Wildest Dreams

To him who is able to do far more abundantly than all that we ask or think, according to the power at work within us, to him be glory in the church and in Christ Jesus throughout all generations, forever and ever.

EPHESIANS 3:20-21 ESV

Picture the greatest thing you could ever imagine actually coming to fruition in your life. Your wildest dream realized. Your greatest hope come true.

Guess what? It's all possible through our God. He can accomplish more than you could ever think to ask for. And you know what else is true? He wants to do it through you. Ask him to give you snippets of his plan for you throughout your day. Prepare to be amazed.

Father, you really are good. Thank you for using me to attain greatness for your kingdom. I know that I'm able to accomplish so much more with you than I ever could on my own.

All glory to God, who is able, through his mighty power at work within us, to accomplish infinitely more than we might ask or think. Glory to him in the church and in Christ Jesus through all generations forever and ever! Amen.

Ephesians 3:20-21 nlt

The Lord has given us the gift of the Holy Spirit living within us, guiding us, pressing us on toward achieving great things. He deserves all the glory and all the credit for the good we see around us.

Let's praise him together and give him the honor. He places dreams and desires on our hearts and then gives us everything we need to accomplish them. He is so good to us!

God, thank you for giving me big dreams and allowing me the chance to participate in doing great things. Thank you for giving me confidence to do all that you ask me to do.

Can you see God beginning to stir up big dreams in your life? Chase after them!

Effortlessly Good

The LORD is good;
his steadfast love endures forever,
and his faithfulness to all generations.

PSALM 100:5 ESV

The Lord is good, always and forever. The list of ways in which he loves us is endless. Every day there is reason to rejoice because we serve a God who is the very essence of good.

Have you ever tried to be good, all the time? It's an impossible task for us. But God makes it look easy, and it truly is easy for him. Ask God to help you reflect his goodness to everyone who surrounds you today.

Father, I am amazed by who you are. You are effortlessly good, and I am thankful to be a recipient of your everlasting love and mercy.

The LORD is good and his love endures forever;
his faithfulness continues through all generations.

PSALM 100:5 NIV

Our good, good God loves us so much and tells us so hundreds of times throughout the pages of the Bible. He forgives us over and over again. He shows us mercy and grace.

God's goodness will stand the test of time and last forever throughout the ages. It's a promise we can count on. His Word says that his faithfulness will continue through all generations.

God, help me to remember your enduring love each time I begin to falter or doubt you. You are always faithful and good.

Is it hard for you to grab hold of the goodness of God? Trust him today!

Stand Your Ground

Stand firm. Let nothing move you. Always give yourselves fully to the work of the Lord, because you know that your labor in the Lord is not in vain.

1 CORINTHIANS 15:58 NIV

There are times in which we all grow weary. It can be hard to live for the kingdom, following the straight and narrow path we're called to walk on. But we are told to stand firm, to stand our ground.

There is a reward coming that is greater than anything you can imagine. It's worth the work and the extra effort! Stick to the narrow path—stand strong where you are.

Lord, I am confident in what I do because you give me joy. Thank you for loving me through the hard days. I pray that I'd sense your presence at every turn and through every difficulty.

Be strong and immovable. Always work enthusiastically for the Lord, for you know that nothing you do for the Lord is ever useless.

1 Corinthians 15:58 nlt

Take a deep breath. Breathe in his life and his love this evening. He will give you what you need to continue on your path.

Your labor is not in vain, and it doesn't go unnoticed. Unspeakable joy is your gift for the taking. Be confident that nothing you do or say for his glory is a waste of time or energy.

God, help me to continue to work enthusiastically. You are the best boss in the universe and I can fully trust that you see everything I do.

Have you lost your steam? Ask God to give you enthusiasm for the work set before you each day.

You Can Always Pray

I urge you, first of all, to pray for all people. Ask God to help them; intercede on their behalf, and give thanks for them. Pray this way for kings and all who are in authority so that we can live peaceful and quiet lives marked by godliness and dignity.

1 TIMOTHY 2:1-2 NLT

Ever feel like your hands are tied and there's nothing you can do about a certain situation? Rest assured that is never the case. You can always pray.

We are encouraged to pray about every situation, in every way we know how. We are even told to pray for our country's leaders regardless of whether or not we agree with the decisions they make. Spend time today praying for situations that seem hopeless. God is a god of hope and he listens to you.

Father, thank you for listening to me when I pray. You deserve all the praise and glory for answering prayer the way you do even when it's not the way I had hoped for.

I urge, then, first of all, that petitions, prayers, intercession and thanksgiving be made for all people—for kings and all those in authority, that we may live peaceful and quiet lives in all godliness and holiness.

1 TIMOTHY 2:1-2 NIV

Daily conversation with God is the key to living a joy-filled life. Lifting others up, interceding for them, and giving God thanks are all a huge part of the regular discussions we should be having with our Creator.

When you feel as if there is nothing you can do, stop everything and begin to pray. God has his ear tuned in to your station and he's waiting for you to talk.

Father, our conversations give me joy! Thank you for caring enough to listen to me. I know I don't always make sense, but you understand my heart and you answer my prayers in the very best way.

Is there a seemingly hopeless situation in front of you? Pray about it today and believe God for the best.

Sufficient Grace

God is so rich in mercy, and he loved us so much, that even though we were dead because of our sins, he gave us life when he raised Christ from the dead. (It is only by God's grace that you have been saved!)… God saved you by his grace when you believed. And you can't take credit for this; it is a gift from God. Salvation is not a reward for the good things we have done, so none of us can boast about it.

EPHESIANS 2:4-5, 8-9 NLT

There is no greater education in the amazing grace of God than his own words. When the impact of his grace has saved you, these words have a particularly powerful and humbling effect.

We have done nothing, yet we have everything. We were dead but now we have life. We didn't pay with money, flesh, or enslavement. We just believed. Allow your mind to dwell on God's sufficient grace today. It will change the way you view yourself and the way you look at others.

Thank you, God, for your undeserved gift of grace.
I am in awe of you.

God's mercy is great, and he loved us very much. Though we were spiritually dead because of the things we did against God, he gave us new life with Christ. You have been saved by God's grace. I mean that you have been saved by grace through believing. You did not save yourselves; it was a gift from God. It was not the result of your own efforts, so you cannot brag about it.

EPHESIANS 2:4-5, 8-9 NCV

We cannot boast in our salvation, but we can sing praises from the rafters for God's amazing gift of grace. Sing long and loud, for grace is the one and only gift we will ever need. And we can share it, without losing an ounce of our portion. It multiplies over and over, as long as we are willing to give it away.

We can know beyond a shadow of doubt that his grace is sufficient for us. It has been from the moment we first believed!

God, your gift of grace is astounding. My mind cannot comprehend it. Help me to extend grace toward the many people who cross my path each day.

Express your thanksgiving to God for his abundant, sufficient grace.

Piece by Piece

Do you see people skilled in their work?
They will work for kings, not for ordinary people.

PROVERBS 22:29 NCV

Building a large Lego set takes skill. You have to read the instructions, follow them exactly (even for tiny gray pieces that appear to have no purpose), patiently build layer upon layer, and have a vision for how the pieces will come together.

If you put a Lego piece in the wrong spot, take a breath, ready your teeth and nails, and pry them apart. It takes patience, endurance, and confidence. With a little work, you could end up creating a masterpiece.

God, thank you for giving me endurance for hard work. I thank you for these piece-by-piece opportunities. Help me to keep you in the forefront of my life, whatever I'm working on.

Do you see someone skilled in their work?
They will serve before kings;
they will not serve before officials of low rank.

PROVERBS 22:29 NIV

Hard work feels good! When you put your heart and soul into something and see positive results, you feel joy in your accomplishment.

The glory of hard work belongs to God. He often asks us to do things, and when we put our best effort forward, the reward is beautiful and fulfilling. Praise God for the work he gives you!

God, thank you for the opportunity to grow in so many areas. You have placed me where you want me and I rely on you to help me with all the work that needs to happen.

Thank God for the work he has provided you with today.

Praise Him

I will praise you with an upright heart,
when I learn your righteous rules.

PSALM 119:7 ESV

The Lord is deserving of so much praise. There is nothing we have that he hasn't provided for us. Doesn't it make your heart sing to think of all his wonderful ways? He is so good to us.

If we live by his law, and make the choice to follow him, we can praise him with an unburdened, pure heart. Ponder what it means to praise with an upright heart today.

Father, I choose you! I praise you today because you are worthy of all the glory and honor.

As I learn your righteous regulations,
I will thank you by living as I should!

PSALM 119:7 NLT

It is a choice to love God, isn't it? He doesn't force us into it. Instead, he leaves it up to us. We can opt to walk away, to follow our own path and forge our own way. Alone, afraid, and unsure, we can blaze a trail of our own.

But we could choose instead to obey him in finding righteousness, joy, and life. We thank God for his righteousness by living according to his Word. And when we do that, we are blessed!

Thank you, God, for providing your Word and your laws as a roadmap to living a righteous life. You are a righteous God and I want to live for you.

Can you understand the goodness of God's regulations?

Light of Love

How priceless is your unfailing love, O God!
People take refuge in the shadow of your wings.

PSALM 36:7 NIV

Whenever you start to doubt the love that God has for you, simply turn to his Word and be reminded of the truth. He picked you! He chose you as his special possession.

God wants a relationship with you, and he wants you to work with him to draw others into the light of his kingdom. Dive deep into your relationship with the Father today. Out of a place of connection with God, you will draw others into his love.

Lord, thank you for choosing me as your special possession. I can scarcely believe that you'd want me, but I'm so grateful that you do!

How precious is your unfailing love, O God!
All humanity finds shelter in the shadow of your wings.
PSALM 36:7 NLTV

Before we knew Jesus as our Savior, we lived in darkness.
Now life is bright! Jesus is the lamp that illuminates the path
ahead of us, directing us where to go and what to say and do.

Even in the darkness of the night, we are surrounded by his
illuminating presence. Let's declare his praises together, and
stay in the brilliance of his light.

God, with you my darkness has gone. Help me to live only in the
light of your love.

Can you see the brilliance of God's love even when
surrounded by darkness?

Rich Promises

Mercy, peace, and love be yours richly.

JUDE 1:2 NCV

To be rich is to have plenty, to want nothing, and to be full of all you've ever desired. This verse in Jude is powerful because God has desires for us. He really does!

He desires us to feel his perfect mercy, peace, and love, and to feel them all richly. Not just a little, not just a sprinkling—no, a flood of gifts, absorbed into who we are. Notice the rich promises of God throughout your day and thank him for them.

God, thank you for being a God of redemption. Take this broken life of mine and fill it with your mercy, peace, and love.

Mercy, peace and love be yours in abundance.

JUDE 1:2 NIV

You can feel God's rich promises daily through hope in Jesus. It doesn't mean you won't have hard moments, tough situations, or trying times, but Jesus has promises of redemption—of mercy, peace, and love.

There is the promise of true joy that comes each morning, of the purposeful path that he puts you on, and the guarantee that he will never abandon you. His desires are for you to feel these things richly, fully, and often.

God, I don't want to fill my life with temporary riches that don't matter; I want to be full of matters of the heart. Guide me in this journey, to find them through your Son.

Make a list of God's rich promises in your life and be sure to thank him for them.

Much Stronger

Be strong in the Lord and in his mighty power.

EPHESIANS 6:10 NIV

You have a strength you may not know you possess. Sure, there are days when it's a battle just to get up, when it seems like the world is pitted against you and you're not certain you'll be able to fight your way through.

But you've got a secret power. The Holy Spirit is ready to give you his strength when you no longer have any of your own. Ask for strength today and be strong in God's mighty power.

Lord, I'm in awe of your power and might. I'm so thankful that you make me strong—so much stronger than I am on my own!

Be strong in the Lord and in his great power.

EPHESIANS 6:10 NCV

Thank goodness we don't have to stand in our own power. How exhausting it would be, slogging through the daily grind by ourselves.

On our own, we are repetitively lifting those puny one-pound weights, going nowhere. But with Christ, we become Olympic-ready weight lifters, throwing a heavier load on each time and hardly exerting ourselves. God is mighty, and he gladly shares his strength with us.

God, thank you for being willing to share your strength with me. I know I am weak and I ask you humbly for help in my weakness. Thank you for your promise of strength.

Is there something you need God to be strong for you in tonight?

Working with Joy

Whatever you do, do your work heartily, as for the Lord rather than for men.

COLOSSIANS 3:23 NASB

We are each called to do different work, whether it's behind a desk, caring for children, cleaning a home, or selling products. Sometimes work can be exhausting. You may not want to work wholeheartedly. Perhaps you just want to get through the day and be done.

Let's put our minds to working with joy. Let's work with thankful servant hearts, knowing that our effort is seen and appreciated. When we think about the reward of hard work, it helps us to push through.

Lord, I want to serve you! Help me to put my efforts into working with my whole heart while I wait for my reward.

In all the work you are doing, work the best you can. Work as if you were doing it for the Lord, not for people.

Colossians 3:23 NCV

When you serve a heavenly master, there's a greater reward than a paycheck waiting for you. We are promised an inheritance that's better than anything we can imagine.

When we work, we are serving one who loves us beyond comparison. Think about God watching you work and being pleased with your efforts. You'll be surprised at how changing your mind about work can change your life.

God, I'm excited to receive my inheritance from you. I know I have to continue to work hard. Help me to have a good attitude toward the work you have blessed me with.

Can you work with your whole heart today?

Refreshment Source

O God, You are my God; I shall seek You earnestly;
My soul thirsts for You, my flesh yearns for You,
In a dry and weary land where there is no water.

PSALM 63:1 NASB

When we are thirsty, our body lets us know. If we go too long without quenching our thirst, we slowly begin to shut down. We don't function properly. Our thirst is at the forefront of our mind, and we wonder when we are going to get something to satisfy our need.

This is how we should feel when we go too long without daily conversations with God. We should feel as if we just can't function properly because a vital part of what we need to fuel ourselves is missing from our system. Make sure you quench your thirst for God today.

Father, I thirst for you. Fill me up with your living water today,
refreshing my soul and satisfying every part of me.

You, God, are my God, earnestly I seek you;
I thirst for you, my whole being longs for you,
in a dry and parched land where there is no water.

PSALM 63:1 NIV

There are definitely times when we feel parched. Maybe we've been running around for too long without stopping to drink in the rest and peace of God.

Thankfully, the landscape of our lives needs not feel like a desert. We don't have to thirst for God for long. He is available to us whenever we need him. We can simply turn to him, and drink in his love. It's a never-ending source of refreshment.

God, help me pay attention to when I'm getting thirsty. I want to quench my thirst with you. Help me come to your well of rest and peace often!

Sit for a while and drink in the abundant refreshment from God.

Shelter and Refuge

Let all who take refuge in you be glad;
let them ever sing for joy.
Spread your protection over them,
that those who love your name may rejoice in you.

PSALM 5:11 NIV

Have you ever been caught in a horrible storm and needed to find shelter? As a child, maybe your parents had to pull over under a bridge to protect your car from hail. Maybe you were caught in a tornado warning and went down to the basement to stay safe.

God says he is our refuge in times of trial. He is our safety net, always willing to catch us and put us back down safely. He gives us shelter, yes, but he also gives protection and guidance. Walk confidently in the shelter of God's protection today.

God, I praise your name today for the way you have rescued me!
I rejoice and sing for the love you have for me and the protection
you give me. Thank you, Father God, thank you!

Let all who take refuge in you rejoice;
let them sing joyful praises forever.
Spread your protection over them,
that all who love your name may be filled with joy.

PSALM 5:11 NLT

"Taking refuge" is another way of saying "seeking shelter." You may have encountered situations in your life where you had to seek a safe shelter—emotionally, physically, mentally, or even spiritually.

It's important that we realize who our true protection comes from. God is the source of our security and comfort. Not only does he protect us, he fills us with joy in the process. There's really nothing in this world that can compare to that.

God, tonight as I run to you for safety, fill me with your joy. I am so thankful that you take delight in being my protector. I love you and praise you this evening.

Do you trust God to be your refuge?

Celebrating Promises

It was a time of happiness, joy, gladness,
and honor for the Jewish people.

ESTHER 8:16 NCV

In this verse in Esther, the Jewish people are celebrating! It was a great time of joy because God's promise was delivered to them. They could see that faithfulness and devotion to God had allowed them to prosper, as he said they would.

God's promises are evident when we follow his commands, when we live a life worthy of him, and when we are faithful. Choose to live that way today and be blessed with gladness.

God, I desire to live a life worthy of you! I want to seek you first.
Let my life be a celebration of you.

The Jews were filled with joy and gladness and were honored everywhere.

ESTHER 8:16 NLT

Celebrations are beautiful. No matter who or what you are celebrating, being in a room full of people smiling and laughing together over a happy event is good.

You can probably envision a moment like that now: the delicious food, the fancy attire, the happy noise, the beautiful toasts, and the togetherness that comes with being united in one room for a purpose. Now think forward to the wonderful celebration awaiting us at the return of Jesus. It is really something to get excited about!

God, I know that your promises come true, and I trust in them. Help me to see joy in all you've given and entrusted to me. Help me to be patient as I await the wonderful celebration you are preparing for all those who believe in you.

How can you celebrate your relationship with God tonight?

Many Rewards

"Rejoice in that day and leap for joy,
for surely your reward is great in heaven."

LUKE 6:23 NRSV

There are many rewards in this life. Acknowledgment for a job well done at work. A diploma after years of study. A smile from a stranger. An unexpected "I love you" from a child. A salary increase. A miraculous healing.

Still, none of these can compare to the reward in heaven. They don't even scratch the surface of a life of eternity with Jesus. Yet at times, we put more work into these earthly rewards than we put into the greatest heavenly one. Spend some time today on building your heavenly reward.

Jesus, I want to remember that you promise a life with you if I follow you. I want to set my eyes and focus on eternity.

*"Rejoice in that day and leap for joy,
because great is your reward in heaven."*

Luke 6:23 niv

It becomes normal to prioritize the immediate rewards we work for here on earth and forget what life is really all about. We focus on what we need to do to earn favor, status, honor, and wealth and we forget that our best reward lies in eternity with our heavenly Father.

Remember to live in thankfulness every day. Think about all that God has blessed you with and all that he still has in store for you. Live for your eternal reward today.

God, I love this life you've given me here, and I want to do it well, but I want to make sure my priorities are with you first. Help me to focus on my heavenly reward tonight.

Can you think of earthly rewards that are consuming you right now? Begin working on your greater value rewards tonight!

A Beautiful Sound

"To choose life is to love the LORD your God, obey him, and stay close to him. He is your life, and he will let you live many years in the land, the land he promised to give your ancestors Abraham, Isaac, and Jacob."

DEUTERONOMY 30:20 NCV

We were created to enjoy hearing beautiful things. We listen to music, we smile at the sound of children's laughter, and the birds chirping on a crisp spring morning is a sweet melody. But the most beautiful sound of all is the sound of the Lord's voice speaking to us.

God is life. He is the source of everything. Let's sing with him together, a new song of redemption and love, for all who have ears to hear.

Father, thank you for your voice. Help me choose to obey you when you call to me, and hold fast to your teachings.

"You can make this choice by loving the LORD your God, obeying him, and committing yourself firmly to him. This is the key to your life. And if you love and obey the LORD, you will live long in the land the LORD swore to give your ancestors Abraham, Isaac, and Jacob."

DEUTERONOMY 30:20 NLT

We can hear God if we listen. He talks to us in many different ways: through prayer, music, reading the Word, and being in fellowship with others. When we choose to obey his teachings and cling to him, it's like we're singing an incredible song of joy back to our Savior.

Listen for his voice this evening. He is calling to you with a sound of pure beauty.

God, sometimes it's hard to hear your voice. Help me to listen for you in the quiet, and in all the other places you speak to me. I love you, and I commit myself to you again this evening.

How do you usually hear God's voice?

Place Your Hope in God

Guide me in your truth and teach me,
for you are God my Savior,
and my hope is in you all day long.

PSALM 25:5 NIV

When you are at your wit's end, who do you look to for help? If you are putting your hope in God, then you will never be let down.

You have hope for a future, because he is your past, your present, and your everything from here on out. Put all your hope in him, and you will see the reward.

Lord, I'm putting my hope and trust in you. Guide me in your truth. Teach me your ways. You are my Savior, and I'm so thankful for that!

Guide me in your truth,
and teach me, my God, my Savior.
I trust you all day long.

PSALM 25:5 NCV

When you hang onto God's truth and allow him to teach you, it's easy to put your hope in him. He lives in you each day and stokes the fire in your soul, keeping hope alive in your body and spirit.

It can be hard to trust people—whether we know them well or not at all. Because God is truth, he is trustworthy. As you lie down to sleep tonight, take great comfort in that thought. God can be trusted with every detail of your life.

Father, thank you that you are good and true. You can be trusted with everything. I confidently put my hope in you tonight.

What do you want to trust God with tonight?

Crowned with Love

Let all that I am praise the LORD;
with my whole heart, I will praise his holy name.
Let all that I am praise the LORD;
may I never forget the good things he does for me.
He forgives all my sins
and heals all my diseases.
He redeems me from death
and crowns me with love and tender mercies.
He fills my life with good things.
My youth is renewed like the eagle's!

PSALM 103:1-5 NLT

Everything we have is a gift from God. We would be nowhere without him. Nope, scratch that. We would be in the muck and mire, for all eternity, without him.

Let's praise him all the days of our lives. Let's raise our voices to the heavens and worship him. God has forgiven our sins so we can live with unending joy.

Father, thank you for your forgiving heart. I give you all the praise,
because it is from you alone that all good things flow.

Bless the LORD, O my soul;
And all that is within me, bless His holy name!
Bless the LORD, O my soul,
And forget not all His benefits:
Who forgives all your iniquities,
Who heals all your diseases,
Who redeems your life from destruction,
Who crowns you with lovingkindness and tender mercies,
Who satisfies your mouth with good things,
So that your youth is renewed like the eagle's.

PSALM 103:1-5 NKJV

God, in his infinite mercy, has pulled us out of our hopelessness. He took one look at our sorry selves and crowned us with love and compassion.

Meditate on this Scripture tonight and let it renew and refresh your body, mind, and spirit.

Oh God, you are so loving and kind. You are merciful and forgiving. You bring healing and redemption. I praise your wonderful name tonight.

Read today's verse out loud and let it sink in!

A Peaceful Place

Then Jesus said, "Let's go off by ourselves to a quiet place and rest awhile." He said this because there were so many people coming and going that Jesus and his apostles didn't even have time to eat.

MARK 6:31 NLT

Life gets crowded sometimes. It's not always easy to get away from the things that cause our anxiety—endless to-do lists, busy holidays, visits from family, work deadlines—life gets hectic and stress builds up.

Jesus shows us that there is a time and a place for refreshing. Like the disciples, we can and should *go off by ourselves to a quiet place and rest awhile*. Find time to do that today. You won't be sorry you did.

Jesus, you truly know my anxieties. Show me a peaceful place and meet with me there.

He said to them, "Come aside by yourselves to a deserted place and rest a while." For there were many coming and going, and they did not even have time to eat.

MARK 6:31 NKJV

When life's troubles begin to press in, take Jesus' advice. If he and his disciples needed to get away from the crowds for a while, it certainly makes sense for us to do the same.

If only for half an hour, spend time in prayer, read God's Word, or sing his praises. Acts of worship bring relief from stress and anxiety, and in today's crazy world, that's what we desperately need.

Father, calm my anxious heart and give me your quiet rest. Help my sleep to be sweet tonight—not filled with busy thoughts and endless worries. You give me peace and I thank you for it.

Find a moment today to quiet your heart and mind.

Quiet Beauty

Your beauty should come from within you—the beauty of a gentle and quiet spirit that will never be destroyed and is very precious to God.

1 PETER 3:4 NCV

Let's say a prayer of thanks that God sees our inner beauty and not just what we see in the mirror. Scars, wrinkles, droops, and stretched skin are invisible to his searching eye, but beautiful hearts are fully exposed.

While exposure may seem scary, we have to realize that God sees us with eyes of love and mercy. Try to look at yourself through his eyes as you make your way through this day.

Father, let the darkness of my inner heart be filled with the light of your glory as I reflect the gentle and quiet beauty that is so precious to you.

Let your adorning be the hidden person of the heart with the imperishable beauty of a gentle and quiet spirit, which in God's sight is very precious.

1 PETER 3:4 ESV

If you're nervous that your inner beauty doesn't measure up to God's gaze, take heart. The more time you spend with him, the more you will come to look, sound, and act like him. You can reflect his character more with each passing day.

As you prepare for the close of another day, reflect on how much more you resemble Jesus now than you did last year, or the year before that. Allow your spirit to be quieted as you sit in his presence.

Jesus, I want your beauty to shine through me. I want to look, sound, and act like you. Thank you for the steps I have taken to become more like you. Help me to continue on that path.

What does it look like to have a gentle and quiet spirit?

Joy Is a Choice

This is the day the LORD has made.
We will rejoice and be glad in it.

PSALM 118:24 NLT

It's fair to say that some days are harder than others.
Sometimes the sun doesn't shine, the day ahead feels
daunting, and it seems almost impossible to get out of bed.
Thankfully the joy that God has rooted into our hearts is not
circumstantial.

Joy is a choice—a gift to embrace daily. In every situation,
good or bad, God has given it to us for the taking.

God, thank you that every day from you is a precious gift. Help
me see your unfailing goodness in every situation. Let your joy be
rooted in my spirit.

This is the day that the LORD has made.
Let us rejoice and be glad today!

PSALM 118:24 NCV

Joy is not dependent on our financial situation, our relationships with others, or our emotional state. It may take some effort, but it is his joy that calls us out of our hiding places. It is what allows us to see the beauty in the midst of chaos and turmoil. It causes us to rejoice, and praise him, even if the floor beneath us seems to be crumbling.

Did you choose joy today in the middle of your circumstances? Whether an easy day or difficult one, if you look for joy you will find it.

Lord, I want to see your joy in everything I encounter. I know in order to do that I have to look with a different view. Help me to rejoice in each day that you have made.

Can you accept the challenge to be glad today?

Faithful Companion

The heavens will praise Your wonders, O Lord;
Your faithfulness also in the assembly of the saints.

PSALM 89:5 NKJV

Have you ever had a dog? A dog that follows you around wherever you go and whines when you head for the door without her? A dog that jumps up and down in excitement when your key turns in the lock because he knows you're home and staying put? A dog that is so loyal, you know he would do anything to protect you?

God jumps in excitement when you spend time with him. He sings along with you when he hears your voice praising his name! He cries when you walk away from him and rejoices when you come crawling back, broken and ashamed. Walk confidently in his faithfulness today.

God, you are faithful, loving, and true. Your admiration of me is unfathomable, and I'm not worthy of this love. Thank you that through your Son you deem me worthy of your love.

All heaven will praise your great wonders, LORD;
myriads of angels will praise you for your faithfulness.

PSALM 89:5 NLT

Are you still having trouble seeing yourself as being worthy of God's faithful love? He is best thought of as a loving Father who picks you up off the floor, and wipes your eyes and slate clean. He whispers words of love and forgiveness into your heart and tells you that you are loved, cherished, beautifully made, and purposefully formed.

Take comfort in God's faithfulness today. Actively seek to understand it. It will bring incredible peace to your life when you finally accept it.

I'm so grateful for your faithfulness, God. I want to spend my life following you and understanding your great wonders.

Can you hear God's faithful love whispered over you today?

Jesus-Centered

You make him most blessed forever;
you make him glad with the joy of your presence.

PSALM 21:6 ESV

There is no sweeter place than the presence of Jesus. Life's trials take their proper place in the background when we rest in his embrace. God's Word says we should enter his presence with thanksgiving, praise, and worship. His Word also says that in his "presence there is fullness of joy" (Psalm 16:11 ESV).

Our cares lose their bite the moment we rest in God. Feast upon him, so your cares cannot feast upon you.

Heavenly Father, as we travel each day together, let me always seek deeper intimacy with you, worshiping you with a heart of gratitude and a song of praise.

You bestow on him blessings forever;
you make him glad with the joy of your presence.

PSALM 21:6 NRSV

Jesus is the King of Kings and Lord of Lords; he guides us in every situation, showing us which troubles to avoid and helping us withstand what must be passed through. He leads our lives well.

If we are continually feasting upon God's Word, seeking his face through thanksgiving and praise, and waiting on him to speak to us, we will never lack joy. We will ably assess life's trials from a heavenly perspective.

God, I want to live life with a heavenly perspective and a joy-filled heart. Give me eyes that focus on you in all situations.

Feast on God's Word, seek his face, and wait for him to speak to you today.

Faithful Reward

"The LORD rewards everyone for their righteousness and faithfulness."

1 SAMUEL 26:23 NIV

In 1 Samuel 26, David, future king of Israel, is running for his life from King Saul. When God gives David the upper hand, he does not kill Saul; instead, he trusts that the Lord would work out the situation for his good.

Following Jesus is grueling work. Convictions of the heart, persecution from loved ones, and misunderstanding make it difficult to remain pure in a sinful world. Remember the joy that is yours when you pursue Jesus and follow his lead! Do not grow weary; rest in Jesus, trust him, and watch as he rewards you for your faithful devotion to him.

God, I want to remain faithful to you even when it's difficult. I want to press in instead of leaning away, trusting in your eternal reward promised to me.

"The LORD gives his own reward for doing good and for being loyal."

1 SAMUEL 26:23 NLT

Our reward in heaven is filled with more than we can comprehend. Being loyal may not be praised in the world today, but it is very pleasing to God. When you feel like giving up, keep pressing on, knowing that God is pleased with your faithfulness.

Hold on to Jesus in the middle of a crisis, and remember the good he has promised you. This is only the beginning! The eternal reward is coming soon.

God, remind me that my faithful devotion to you is necessary and purposeful. I want to be pleasing to you because I love you. Thank you for the reward waiting for me as I choose loyalty!

Imagine the reward waiting for the loyal followers of God.

Deepest Contentment

He will keep in perfect peace
all those who trust in him,
whose thoughts turn often to the Lord!

ISAIAH 26:3 TLB

When we put our trust in God, and only in God, we find
peace that truly satisfies our distress. Scripture repeatedly
advises us to keep our thoughts on the Lord, with our eyes
focused on his promises, because it is in God that our deepest
contentment and joy are found.

Where are you looking for your contentment? Is true peace
eluding you? Try focusing your thoughts on God today, and
rest in the peace that floods your soul.

God, you are faithful to meet all of my needs. Help me to focus my
thoughts on you because the world has nothing for me!

You will keep in perfect peace
all who trust in you,
all whose thoughts are fixed on you!

ISAIAH 26:3 NLT

We can search our whole lives for pleasure, wealth, and success in the hope that peace and fulfillment will come, but only an intimate relationship with God can give us that.

The more we focus on ourselves, the more peace eludes us. The more we focus on God, the more his peace sustains us. Did you notice an increase of peace today as you let your thoughts drift toward the Lord?

Only in you, God, whose love and faithfulness never cease, will I find peace. Tonight I continue to fix my mind on you. Fill me with sweet peace as I lay down to sleep.

Do you sense God's peace when your mind is focused on him?

A Beautiful Day

I will recount the steadfast love of the LORD,
the praises of the LORD,
according to all that the LORD has granted us,
and the great goodness to the house of Israel
that he has granted them according to his compassion,
according to the abundance of his steadfast love.

ISAIAH 63:7 ESV

We can claim the truth of this verse each and every day, regardless of our circumstances or emotions. His goodness is plentiful; his steadfast love is abundant.

Show God how thankful you are by remembering his goodness and telling others about what he has done for you.

You are so good, God! Your goodness cannot be recounted in one day alone, but I will rejoice in attempting to remember as many blessings as I can. Thank you for your steadfast love and compassion.

I will tell of the kindnesses of the LORD,
the deeds for which he is to be praised,
according to all the LORD has done for us—
yes, the many good things he has done for Israel,
according to his compassion and many kindnesses.

ISAIAH 63:7 NIV

God's goodness never waivers and his love for you never decreases. Even if life seems like drudgery and today feels rotten, the list of blessings in your life is quite long.

Recall the steadfast love he has granted to you, his goodness and compassion, and know that according to those, this day has been beautiful.

Loving and kind Father, thank you for all you have blessed me with. You are full of compassion and you care for me deeply. I am amazed by your love and I want everyone around me to know about it.

How have you seen God's kindness in your life today?

Joy Always

Our hearts ache, but we always have joy.
We are poor, but we give spiritual riches to others.
We own nothing, and yet we have everything.

2 CORINTHIANS 6:10 NLT

It's easy to confuse joy with happiness; both bring to mind positive feelings, maybe even memories filled with laughter and smiles. But happiness is an emotion that comes and goes according to our circumstance; like sunshine on a cloudy day, it can be here one minute and gone the next.

The fullness of joy, however, is experienced in the heart. Regardless of one's surroundings or experience, the fullness of God's love pours forth a well-spring of unspeakable joy. Take that fullness of joy with you today.

Loving God, I pray that your joy would overflow in my life. Regardless of how happy I may feel, let joy pour out abundantly in my words and deeds so that those around me might know your loving salvation.

We have much sadness, but we are always rejoicing. We are poor, but we are making many people rich in faith. We have nothing, but really we have everything.

2 Corinthians 6:10 NCV

As God's beloved, you are given the gift of joy to keep you company no matter what trials life brings. You can always have joy. So, as the verse says, even in much sadness, you can rejoice.

You might not have a lot of earthly wealth to hand out, but you have the priceless treasure of faith that can be generously shared with everyone around you. Instead of thinking about what you are missing, focus in on the fact that you really have everything—because you have Jesus!

God, it's easy to dwell on hardships and lack. Help me instead to realize that I have everything because I have you. Give me an eternal perspective so I can rejoice even in hardship.

Having an eternal perspective means you can always rejoice.

One Step at a Time

To him who is able to keep you from stumbling and to present you blameless before the presence of his glory with great joy, to the only God, our Savior, through Jesus Christ our Lord, be glory, majesty, dominion, and authority.

JUDE 24-25 ESV

This race called life is a tiring one; sometimes the road gets long and our legs threaten to buckle underneath heavy burdens. How, then, do we persevere?

Hear this glorious news: God, whose majesty is matchless, is waiting to hold you up under the weight you are carrying. He lifts the burden to his own strong shoulders. He keeps you from slipping and falling away. He brings you into his presence! Rest a while in his presence today and draw strength from your time with him.

Father, whether the path is rugged or smooth, thank you for staying by my side, keeping me upright, and encouraging me with every step. I pray that I would hear your joyous voice today!

God is strong and can help you not to fall. He can bring you before his glory without any wrong in you and can give you great joy. He is the only God, the One who saves us. To him be glory, greatness, power, and authority through Jesus Christ our Lord for all time past, now, and forever. Amen.

JUDE 24-25 NCV

When the cold rains of sorrow or the sharp winds of discouragement are at our backs, how do we press on and finish the race?

Run your race listening to the encouragement of your heavenly Father—his mighty shouts of everlasting joy! Take it one holy step at a time. Keep your eyes on him, and you will finish victorious.

Lift me up, mighty God, when I stumble. Let me hear your whispers and shouts of encouragement along the way. I need your strength and your joy to be victorious in this life.

Listen for God's encouraging voice as you take one step at a time.

Sacrifice of Praise

Bring your petition.
Come to the Lord and say,
"O Lord, take away our sins;
be gracious to us and receive us
and we will offer you the sacrifice of praise."

HOSEA 14:2 TLB

Songs of praise and worship are sometimes the last thing we feel like singing. A lamentation or a dirge feels more appropriate if we feel lonely, disappointed, or angry. How can we continue to praise our worthy God when we cannot find anything worthy of praise in our lives?

First, recognize the little things that are truly blessings: air in your lungs, God's love pouring over you, the salvation you have in Jesus Christ. Begin with these truths today and see how it changes your outlook.

You alone, God, deserve my praise. Thank you for your mercy and every good thing in my life. I praise your holy name!

Take words with you,
And return to the LORD.
Say to Him,
"Take away all iniquity;
Receive us graciously,
For we will offer the sacrifices of our lips."

HOSEA 14:2 NKJV

Just as Hosea was instructed, sometimes we have to offer God the *sacrifice of praise*. Sometimes praise comes at the cost of humbling ourselves and giving God what he deserves. God restores hearts a hundred-fold when they are submitted to him.

Choose the sacrifice of praising God tonight. Even if you don't feel like it, he is worthy of your praise, and he will restore your joy.

You are always worthy. I am undeserving, yet you bless me. I am always falling, yet you lift me up.

Can you choose the sacrifice of praise tonight?

God's Family

To godliness brotherly kindness, and to brotherly kindness love.

2 PETER 1:7 NKJV

Everyone in the body of Christ is our brother or sister. We may not be related by blood, but we are all part of God's family. We are all precious to him, uniquely created, beautifully designed, and intricately, purposefully pieced together.

Our greatest purpose should be to shower love and kindness on our brothers and sisters so others ask, "Where does your joy come from?" It is such a simple, beautiful concept, and one we should constantly pursue.

God, I know it pains you to see us living separately from one another and apart from you. I want to shower my family with the supernatural love and kindness that only comes from you. Show me how, Jesus!

To godliness, mutual affection; and to mutual affection, love.

2 PETER 1:7 NIV

Our family is the family of God, united together under the name of Jesus Christ. We have an incredible promise of eternal life with God and his people. He desires to see unity among his children.

We have work to do. As believers, we live a different way of life, one radically filled with love. When others stop to wonder why we are so kind and loving, that glorifies our Father. Through our display of love, let us unify this family of God and draw others into it.

Father, help me to see everyone in your family as my brothers and sisters. Let me love them well and cause others to be drawn to you. I want to help expand your kingdom.

What can you do today to show love to a brother or sister?

Perfect Forgiveness

Be kind and compassionate to one another, forgiving each other,
just as in Christ God forgave you.

EPHESIANS 4:32 NIV

Showing others forgiveness is imperative to living a life with
less baggage. The weight of unforgiveness and ill feelings
toward others can drag you down, make you feel awful, and be
a hindrance to living your best life. Jesus Christ is our perfect
example of forgiveness.

Christ suffered for all of us, promising us freedom through
his blood. He forgives us, time and time again, when we let
him and others down. We certainly can forgive others in his
name.

Jesus, I praise your name for the countless times you've forgiven
me as I've walked in sin. I'm so sorry for the ways I let you down
when temptation gets the best of me. Give me wisdom about how to
forgive as you do.

Be kind to one another, tenderhearted, forgiving one another, as God in Christ forgave you.

EPHESIANS 4:32 ESV

When we think of the way we sin, our humanness, the reasons treat others unkindly, we need to remember Jesus. He suffered torture and abuse, was yelled at, spat on, nailed to a cross, and left to die—for us. Jesus showed us the ultimate act of forgiveness, taking all of our sin on himself and dying in our place because he loved us. We didn't deserve that at all.

Sometimes others don't deserve our forgiveness either—but we have to extend it because God extended his forgiveness to us. As you accept God's forgiveness tonight, start choosing to forgive those around you.

Jesus, thank you for thinking of me when you died on the cross, for doing the hard work for me, so I can live a life of freedom and grace. Help me extend that same grace to others.

Is there someone who needs your forgiveness today?

He Is All I Need

Happy are those
who do not follow the advice of the wicked,
or take the path that sinners tread,
or sit in the seat of scoffers;
but their delight is in the law of the Lord,
and on his law they meditate day and night.
They are like trees
planted by streams of water,
which yield their fruit in its season,
and their leaves do not wither.
In all that they do, they prosper.

PSALM 1:1–3 NRSV

Thanks to a modern diet of technology and social media, women today can feast on heaping portions of gossip, envy, boastful pride, and selfishness. It is not a nourishing diet, but it is deviously sweet.

What sicknesses are we susceptible to when we replace time with our Father with time in front of a screen? Can you choose today to spend time in God's Word and be refreshed by the rich promises found there?

God, I admit that at times I am underfed on your Word. I'm malnourished from overeating at the modern-day buffet of social media and entertainment. Help me get rid of these unhealthy habits and embrace you more fully each day.

Blessed is the man
Who walks not in the counsel of the ungodly,
Nor stands in the path of sinners,
Nor sits in the seat of the scornful;
But his delight is in the law of the LORD,
And in His law he meditates day and night.
He shall be like a tree
Planted by the rivers of water,
That brings forth its fruit in its season,
Whose leaf also shall not wither;
And whatever he does shall prosper.

PSALM 1:1-3 NKJV

Praise God for his nourishment! His Word is as relevant for us today as it was for David thousands of years ago. Meditate on these words, and hear his voice calling to you.

When we spend time with God and read his Word, we are on the path to joy and delight. Under his nourishment we yield delicious fruit without the threat of withering. We prosper! Did your day yield good fruit? It can when you spend time in God's Word.

Father, thank you for your wonderful Word. Thank you for the joy and life it brings to my spirit. Help me to yield good fruit and prosper as I meditate on your Word.

Delight in God's Word today!

Intimacy with God

God demonstrates His own love toward us, in that while we were still sinners, Christ died for us.

ROMANS 5:8 NKJV

God desires intimacy with you. He fashioned you to be sustained by him, to be holy and pure, faultless and blameless, fully accepted and completely bound up in his love.

You have been chosen to enjoy increasing measures of God's favor and grace. At this moment, take time to step into greater intimacy with him. You have the opportunity now to accept greater measures of his unconditional, limitless love.

God, thank you for your perfect love. Please pour it into every area of my life that is thirsty and dry. I love you.

God demonstrates his own love for us in this: While we were still sinners, Christ died for us.

ROMANS 5:8 NIV

Jesus' blood has washed you clean, and nothing stands between you and his benefits. When you drift, you only need to call upon him and step back into the interaction of love.

Bring everything to God, exchanging stumbling points for stepping-stones. He relentlessly works for your good and desires for you to remain close to him. Draw near tonight as you spend quiet time with him.

Father, it is my goal to please you, not because you need it, but because I need it. I want to overflow with love for you the way you do for me. Thank you for your demonstration of love.

Can you sit with the Father for a while tonight?

Joyful Living Overflows

"I have told you these things so that you will be filled with my joy. Yes, your joy will overflow!"

JOHN 15:11 NLT

Before this verse, what had Jesus told his disciples? He told them that the key to a joy-filled life was love. If you keep God's commands and abide in his love, you will be complete in him, and your joy will be full.

Out of the overflow of being loved, we love God back, and we love others as well. In loving this way, we are filled with joy.

God, I come to you in humbleness. Will you please journey with me into your love? Let me be your servant of love, and let me experience your purest joys firsthand.

"I have told you this so that my joy may be in you and that your joy may be complete."

JOHN 15:11 NIV

Loving others and receiving complete joy is not about racing to do good or act righteously. It does not mean achieving everything on our own. It also doesn't mean that sadness or pain results from failing God's command to love.

We desperately need Christ. Having joy that is complete is about abiding in him and in his love. When we do that, we receive his joy and the ability to love others as he loves us.

Father, I want to abide in you with greater love and a purer commitment of my life to you. I know this will bring me joy and be pleasing to you as well.

Abide in God's love today.

Rich Rewards

Do not throw away your confidence; it will be richly rewarded.
You need to persevere so that when you have done the will of God,
you will receive what he has promised.

HEBREWS 10:35-36 NIV

Remember the early days of your relationship with God?
Perhaps you were a child, full of wonder and excitement.
Maybe you were an adult when you discovered his love, and it
filled you to the brim with joy.

Continue to persevere. Breathe in God's peace today, and
rejoice in it. He will give you the strength you need to
continue in him.

Lord, I pray I'd be restored to the excitement of the early days of
our relationship. Thank you for the promises you've made to be
with me. I know you are faithful.

Do not lose the courage you had in the past, which has a great reward. You must hold on, so you can do what God wants and receive what he has promised.

HEBREWS 10:35-36 NCV

As you walk with Christ, life's ups and downs can get to you. The confidence that you placed in God to save you from yourself may waver.

Don't lose heart! God promises to reward your faith. Place your trust in him, and he will help you persevere through any situation. When you feel like you may falter, turn to him and seek the joy that only he can provide.

God, help me to remember your joy and peace when I feel like I'm going to stumble. I place my continued confidence in you.

Where is your confidence today?

The Eternal Kingdom

Since we are receiving a Kingdom that is unshakable, let us be thankful and please God by worshiping him with holy fear and awe.

HEBREWS 12:28 NLT

Kings and queens hold their throne for a time, but ultimately their reign ends, either through defeat or death. The kingdom of God is not like the kingdom of men. It is undefeatable and unshakeable.

Take heart today that the king you worship will be on the throne forever! Worship him as he deserves.

Lord, you are my king and I honor and adore you. Help me to remember that your kingdom has the authority over all, and that it will not be defeated.

Let us be thankful, because we have a kingdom that cannot be shaken. We should worship God in a way that pleases him with respect and fear.

HEBREWS 12:28 NCV

You belong to God's kingdom, and it will never be defeated. His power will not be surpassed by any other principality or power. Be thankful that you belong to this kingdom.

God is the king of this universe and the king of your heart. This evening as you reflect on his majesty, worship him in awe for all he has created and all he has done.

God, even though you are a great and awesome king, you love me as your child. Teach me to worship you reverently.

What does an unshakeable kingdom look like in your mind?

Mephibosheth

David said, "Is there still anyone left of the house of Saul, that I may show him kindness for Jonathan's sake?" ... And David said to him, "Do not fear, for I will show you kindness for the sake of your father Jonathan, and I will restore to you all the land of Saul your father, and you shall eat at my table always."

2 SAMUEL 9:1, 7 ESV

After becoming king, David wanted to show kindness to the family of the previous king. David's treatment of Mephibosheth, Jonathan's son and Saul's grandson, provides a great picture of Jesus bringing people into his presence.

Jesus combs through your circumstances, identifying the means by which he can bring you into his joy. Be blessed by his selection of you today.

Jesus, I am blessed by the richness of your kindness and grace. Please enliven my heart toward your blessings. I am excited to start this new day with you. Thank you for your kindness!

One day David asked, "Is anyone in Saul's family still alive—anyone to whom I can show kindness for Jonathan's sake?" ... "Don't be afraid!" David said. "I intend to show kindness to you because of my promise to your father, Jonathan. I will give you all the property that once belonged to your grandfather Saul, and you will eat here with me at the king's table!"

2 SAMUEL 9:1, 7 NLT

The kindness of God reaches beyond our understanding and draws us right into his kingdom. We've been invited to dine with the King of the universe! God always blesses us as we step into his presence. He is more joyful, fun, inspiring, and engaging than anyone else. He made each of us unique, and he made us for joy.

Jesus doesn't want you to wait for heaven's blessings only. He wants you to experience joy now too. Take up his invitation to a day of blessing every day.

Show me your kindness, God, that I may recognize it and praise you. Show me where you have filled my life with kindness. It is nectar for my soul, sweet and satisfying.

Pull up a chair to his banquet of kindness today!

Joyfully I Wait

I wait for the LORD, my whole being waits,
and in his word I put my hope.

PSALM 130:5 NIV

We so often think of waiting as being hard, even unpleasant. But sometimes, waiting is wonderful: waiting to deliver great news, waiting for the birth of a child, waiting to give a special gift.

If you are in a season of waiting on the Lord, take heart! When you put your hope in him, you will not be disappointed. Wait in hopeful expectation and expect good things.

Lord, I love waiting for you! Because I know you bring only goodness, I can wait for you forever.

I am counting on the LORD;
yes, I am counting on him.
I have put my hope in his word.

PSALM 130:5 NLT

When the thing we wait for is a good thing, waiting itself is a gift. This is how it is to wait for the Lord. With all our hope in him, the outcome is certain. The outcome is eternity. Let every part of us wait on him in joyful anticipation.

God, your Word is my hope. It promises life and light forever with you. Gratefully, joyfully, I wait and I hope.

Can you wait patiently on the Lord today?

Promoted

"His master said to him, 'Well done, good and faithful slave. You were faithful with a few things, I will put you in charge of many things; enter into the joy of your master.'"

MATTHEW 25:23 NASB

Faithfulness brings exponential rewards in the kingdom of God. Not only do we receive the joy of obedience, but we receive more rewards from the trust God places on us. All of us can look forward to the day we stand before God, by his grace, having used our gifts well.

As we look ahead to the final day, let us use our gifts to further glorify our Lord.

God, thank you for your faithfulness. You have longed to give me certain gifts. Guide me through the opportunities you present.

"The master said, 'Well done, my good and faithful servant. You have been faithful in handling this small amount, so now I will give you many more responsibilities. Let's celebrate together!'"

MATTHEW 25:23 NLT

Here on earth, the application of that increased trust can come into our lives in the forms of greater responsibility and influence. It could look like promotions and prestige, earthly responses to the glory God has placed upon us and we have ably carried.

When earthly blessings come your way, accept them with humbleness and gratitude.

Father, show me where you want your faithfulness to make a difference in me. I choose to accept your challenges; help me see them through to completion.

What gifts do you feel like you use frequently?

Thirsty for Mercy

"Come, all you who are thirsty,
come to the waters;
and you who have no money,
come, buy and eat!
Come, buy wine and milk
without money and without cost."

ISAIAH 55:1 NIV

Money is used for what we want, but mostly for the things that we need—like food and even water. Imagine walking into a grocery store and being offered anything you want without having to pay a cent! This is a picture of the mercy that Jesus has shown all of us through his sacrifice.

Think about God's amazing free gifts as you go through your day. If that doesn't put a smile on your face, what else could?

God, I am so thankful for the free gifts you have so richly blessed me with. Help me not to take them for granted, and to remember to give you glory for everything I have.

"Is anyone thirsty?
Come and drink—
even if you have no money!
Come, take your choice of wine or milk—
it's all free!"

ISAIAH 55:1 NLT

We need God's mercy in the same way that we thirst for water. Wine and milk were expensive items in the time this was written, and to offer these free of charge would have been a great sacrifice.

What Christ did for you on the cross came at a great price, but it was all because of his great love for you. Embrace the free gift of forgiveness and rest in freedom tonight.

Lord Jesus, I come to you as a thirsty child in need of your mercy. You have paid the price for me to receive your forgiveness. I am thankful for the grace that you have freely given me.

Are you thirsty for God's mercy tonight?

He Likes to Be Thanked

Enter his gates with thanksgiving
and his courts with praise;
give thanks to him and praise his name.

PSALM 100:4 NIV

The morning alarms came too soon today. Whether they were in the form of children, an alarm clock, or a heavy heart that is restless even when sleeping, your slumber is over. Your mind immediately starts going over your to-do list for the day as you stumble through your morning routine. You glance at your watch. How can you already be running late?

It is at this moment that you must stop to thank God. That's right, actually stop what you are doing, get down on your knees (to ensure you are stopping), and thank him. Pausing to thank God gives him the honor he's due, but it also kisses your heart with peace and joy in the midst of busy morning routines.

Loving Father, I enter into your presence now on another one of your creations—this day. Thank you for giving me another day on earth. Thank you for life in my body and your love.

Come into his city with songs of thanksgiving
and into his courtyards with songs of praise.
Thank him and praise his name.

PSALM 100:4 NCV

A thankful heart prepares the way for you to connect rightly with God's heart. He isn't someone we use to get what we want. He is a sincere, loving provider for everything we will ever need.

As you close out your day, spend some time singing praise to God. Thank him for your day, no matter how hectic, sad, or boring it was. And if it was a great day, tell him that too! He loves to hear your praise.

God, help me walk in an attitude of thanksgiving every day.
You are worthy of my grateful heart.

Sing a song of thanksgiving to God today.

Receive Wisdom

The wisdom from above is first of all pure. It is also peace loving, gentle at all times, and willing to yield to others. It is full of mercy and the fruit of good deeds. It shows no favoritism and is always sincere.
And those who are peacemakers will plant seeds of peace and reap a harvest of righteousness.

JAMES 3:17–18 NLT

Wise choices bring about peace and righteousness along with a host of other spiritual fruit. These build trust and strength in our relationships. When God's peace is obvious in your life, your seeds of peace will grow in the soil of others' hearts. You will also grow in favor with God and man.

God offers us all we need to create peaceful relationships that are worthy of the high calling God has placed on our lives. Make a point to create peace in a relationship today.

Heavenly Father, there exists no wisdom like yours. My best plans can fall short, but yours never do. Help me live in wisdom, and give me faith to walk in your ways.

The wisdom from above is first pure, then peaceable, gentle, willing to yield, full of mercy and good fruits, without a trace of partiality or hypocrisy. And a harvest of righteousness is sown in peace for those who make peace.

JAMES 3:17–18 NRSV

Spiritual fruit grows when our actions tend to the seeds of wisdom the Holy Spirit plants in our lives. As we listen carefully to God's wisdom and surround ourselves with righteousness, our choices naturally tend toward good decisions.

People enjoy the company of the wise. They bring rest and clear minds to otherwise troubling situations. When considering our relationships, we should remember that wisdom leads to peace, and peaceful friends are the best kind of friends.

God when I listen to your wisdom, your peace seeps into my surroundings. I relinquish my understanding for yours. Let your wisdom be at the front of my mind and deep in my heart.

Can you think of a wise person in your life who carries peace?

Rebirth and Renewal

"I will bring the blind by a way they did not know;
I will lead them in paths they have not known.
I will make darkness light before them,
And crooked places straight.
These things I will do for them,
And not forsake them."

ISAIAH 42:16 NKJV

Spring is a time of rebirth and renewal, a reward for making it through the long, cold, desolate winter. Some parts of the world have enjoyed colorful spring gardens in full fragrant bloom for weeks. In other regions, the cold snow is still melting and the earliest bulbs have yet to reach through the hard soil. Whether above the surface or below, resurrection is happening all around us, rewarding us with new life and vitality.

When this happens around you, let the joy lead you to the empty tomb, where Jesus' miraculous resurrection also brings new life. Resurrection is a revival of hope, of light shining in the darkness, of your glorious reward.

God, I receive the reward of salvation as a gift. Help me to look with hope to the resurrection of Christ Jesus and the new day that rises.

"I will lead the blind along a way they never knew;
I will guide them along paths they have not known.
I will make the darkness become light for them,
and the rough ground smooth.
These are the things I will do;
I will not leave my people."

ISAIAH 42:16 NCV

This verse shares a promise that cannot be taken away from us. He has achieved his glory and we will share in its reward: death cannot conquer or steal our inheritance! Therefore, we can fully trust and believe in Jesus Christ, our hope. There is nothing more magnificent, nothing else worthy of our expectations, for he has made a way for us to share in his glory.

Let the sins that have hindered you melt away like the winter snow, and allow his renewing strength to overwhelm your soul. Breathe in this fresh start. Today is a new day, full of promise and life.

Father, thank you for a fresh start, for new life. You have made rough ground smooth for me, and you will continue to lead me along your path as I submit to you.

Can you let your past melt away and embrace a new day of hope?

From Mountain to Valley

Beloved, if God so loved us, we also ought to love one another.

1 JOHN 4:11 ESV

While we were still sinners, Christ died for us. He lovingly leads us as he cares for our souls over mountains and valleys, in joy and sadness. His love overcomes our foibles. Instead of condemning us in them, he uses them as springboards to call us further into righteousness.

God calls each of us to love others just as we have been loved. We overcome their foibles with love. We call them into righteousness, and we choose to see each person as God's object of affection. Think of others this way today.

God, your love eradicated my sins when you gave me the righteousness of Christ! If my sins and my identity are as far removed from one another as the east is from the west, then I cannot look at one and still see the other. I walk in this truth today.

Beloved, since God loved us so much, we also ought to love one another.

1 JOHN 4:11 NRSV

God unlocks the greatness within each one us as he refuses to see blemishes that the world is quick to point out. He has forgiven and erased those mistakes with his perfect love and mercy.

As God has loved us, we show this same love to others. We refuse to hold them to their past mistakes and old sinful patterns. We believe the best. We endure hardship with them without judgment. Loving others this way is no easy task, but it is what we are called to do.

God, condition my heart as I gaze upon you. Help me to follow your righteous intentions and encourage people toward you. I want to love others the way you love me. I know I need your grace in order to carry out this command.

How can you show unconditional love to someone today?

Relish His Presence

You will teach me how to live a holy life.
Being with you will fill me with joy;
at your right hand I will find pleasure forever.

PSALM 16:11 NCV

Doesn't this verse depict exactly how our relationship with
Jesus works? We spend time with him, and he fills us with
joy. In his presence, we receive what we need: identity,
sustenance, belonging, a way to live.

What a great God we serve! Let us relish his presence and joy.
Take some extra time in his presence today.

God, I think I know you pretty well, but there is always more. Open
my heart to beat with yours today. In our quiet time, unravel the
mysteries of your enveloping joy. I want to understand you more
and be a better friend, child, and servant. Most of all, I just want
to be with you.

You show me the path of life.
In your presence there is fullness of joy;
in your right hand are pleasures forevermore.

PSALM 16:11 NRSV

What can you learn in God's presence? He shows us the path of life—he helps guide us into the calling and promises he desires for us. He brings us joy and delight. Why do we go about our day without spending time in his presence? Why do we try to find joy in other things? It doesn't make sense at all!

Lay your head on his chest and listen to his heartbeat tonight. Let your heart beat in the same cadence and rhythm as God's, skipping for the same pleasures and resting in real joy.

Father, I am so grateful that you love me, and I want to love you deeply in return. I want to relish you. I want to adore you in a way that is fitting of who you are. I want to love you because you love me, and I want to be with you because you fashion my heart in joy.

Can you sense God's pleasure surrounding you today?

Saturated with Goodness

"I will fill the soul of the priests with abundance,
And My people will be satisfied with My goodness,"
declares the LORD.

JEREMIAH 31:14, NASB

Jesus loves us with an everlasting love, continually spilling his goodness upon us. He wants us to overflow with his goodness in every aspect of our lives.

When you actively cooperate with God as he permeates your being and your life, you become increasingly hungry for him, drinking in more and more like a sponge, until you are saturated with his presence. Drink deeply today and be satisfied.

God, satisfy my longing for you, and help me to commune with you in a deep and constant exchange. I believe you for your presence, your goodness, and your abundance. I believe you are my best friend, permeating my life in all aspects.

"The priests will enjoy abundance,
and my people will feast on my good gifts.
I, the LORD, have spoken!"

JEREMIAH 31:14 NLT

Our thirst for his goodness leads us to seek him. When we do, every parched area of our spirits receive the quenching rain of his presence.

We are designed to feast on the continual, daily flow of the Holy Spirit and his blessings in your life. You are designed to be satiated with God's goodness. You were meant to be satisfied. Feast on God's goodness this evening. Drink your fill of his presence and be fully satisfied.

God, in humility, I place myself at your feet. Help me to delve into the intimacy you have prepared for me. May I be completely satisfied with your goodness.

Soak up God's goodness like a sponge today.

Run to the Lord

The humble also shall increase their joy in the LORD,
And the poor among men shall rejoice
In the Holy One of Israel.

ISAIAH 29:19 NKJV

This passage describes Jerusalem's response when God confused the plans of their besiegers. Jerusalem had sinned greatly, and in his love and concern for their welfare and future existence, God authored their rebuke. Although painful, this rebuff ensured preservation and future blessings for Israel. We, too, share in these blessings through Jesus, our King.

Run to Jesus in humility when you are rebuked, and receive your reward. He is a good Father and his desire is to draw you close.

Jesus, I'm running to you! I know that there isn't always good between my ears or in my actions. I want you to be the boss, in charge of every area of my life, and I want your impact there, now.

Once more the humble will rejoice in the LORD;
the needy will rejoice in the Holy One of Israel.

ISAIAH 29:19 NIV

God's rebuke for his people is not a casting away, but evidence of his fatherhood. If you are a child of God, you will endure discipline. You will emerge from it in a better state, even more in love with Jesus, and you will shine his glory as a result.

When God addresses something in your life, throw off whatever it is that has prevented you from fulfilling your destiny, and choose God's perfect way.

I know I need your discipline. As I sit in your presence, ready to listen, share with me what I need to change. I want to be beautifully broken, rejoicing because I came before you and honored you.

Thank God for his lordship and allow him to help you get sorted out.

Standing at the Last

LORD, you are my God;
I will exalt you and praise your name,
for in perfect faithfulness
you have done wonderful things.
things planned long ago.

ISAIAH 25:1 NIV

We serve a God who at the end, after everything has fallen and everything has changed, will still stand. It's easy to become discouraged in this life, but when we adjust our perspective to view everything against the backdrop of a victorious Savior, we can face absolutely anything with great confidence and peace.

Take that confidence with you today and praise God for his promised victory!

Thank you, Lord, that in you I can have the confidence of a victorious outcome—no matter how great the obstacles are that I am facing.

O LORD, I will honor and praise your name,
for you are my God.
You do such wonderful things!
You planned them long ago,
and now you have accomplished them.

ISAIAH 25:1 NLT

In all of our confusion, suffering, and hopelessness, we have the enduring promise of serving the one who will always be greater. We don't have to guess who wins in the end—we already know! God is victorious.

It's fun to be on the winning team. Though it may not feel like you're winning at times, you can know without a doubt that if you stick it out to the end, you will be victorious.

God, help me walk as one who is assured of victory, trusting fully in you who won the battle for me.

Thank God for his uncontested victory!

Completed

Those the Lord has rescued will return.
They will enter Zion with singing;
everlasting joy will crown their heads.
Gladness and joy will overtake them,
and sorrow and sighing will flee away.

ISAIAH 51:11 NIV

Laugh until your stomach hurts! Take a dance around the kitchen! Sing in the shower! As a believer, this promise is for you: everlasting joy will crown your head!

When Jesus is your strength, you can rejoice through his salvation. His strength never wavers, and neither does his righteous cloak over you.

Heavenly Father, help me to understand and appreciate all I have in your salvation. Let me not take for granted what I have received from your sacrifice; instead, let me explore and revel in the joy you have set before me.

Those who have been ransomed by the LORD will return.
They will enter Jerusalem singing,
crowned with everlasting joy.
Sorrow and mourning will disappear,
and they will be filled with joy and gladness.

ISAIAH 51:11 NLT

Because we have been reborn in Christ, we can be the happiest people on the earth. Gladness and joy will overtake us as we realize that we have been rescued by God. He has paid our ransom and we are free.

The Lord is good. He loves you with an everlasting love, and he wants his joy to be complete in you. Through salvation, this is your promise.

God, fill my heart with your joy, so I will partner with you in the eternal completion and celebration of you in me: the resurrected, eternal life.

Celebrate with the one who paid your ransom today!

Jailhouse Rock!

About midnight Paul and Silas were praying and singing hymns to God, and the prisoners were listening to them.

ACTS 16:25 NRSV

Being thrown into prison for your faith is one of the hardest forms of persecution believers can face. It is worth noticing that despite the walls around them, Paul and Silas continued to praise God with praying and singing. It must have been loud for the other prisoners to have heard them.

We are a light to the world and God uses us in many different ways. Perhaps you have had it tough lately, or maybe things are going very well. Either way, people are listening. Use your voice to glorify God today.

Father God, thank you that you are with me in all circumstances. Help me to remember that what I say and do can encourage others around me.

Around midnight Paul and Silas were praying and singing hymns to God, and the other prisoners were listening.

ACTS 16:25 NLT

Paul and Silas were able to be a witness to others in the most severe of circumstances. Praying and singing to God in the middle of a jail cell doesn't seem like a very typical response—especially when your faith in God landed you there in the first place. But a choice to rejoice can be the best witness to those near you.

Who are the prisoners around you that need to be set free by the love of Christ? Who needs to hear your prayers and singing? Can you trust that God is good wherever you are in life right now?

God, give me boldness to praise you as a witness to others. I need your strength to be able to choose praise at all times.

It's your choice to rejoice.

Apples of Gold

A man has joy in an apt answer,
And how delightful is a timely word!

PROVERBS 15:23 NASB

"Apples of gold in settings of silver" is a Biblical metaphor that describes the use of the correct words for the circumstance. In tough circumstances, everyone needs encouragement.

If you have been on the receiving end of a timely word of encouragement, you understand the instant rush of joy, hope, and comfort. Can you be that for someone today?

Heavenly Father, thank you for your timely words that bring hope and joy. Help me be in tune with your Holy Spirit so that my golden words can carry silver hope and joy to others.

Everyone enjoys a fitting reply;
it is wonderful to say the right thing at the right time!

PROVERBS 15:23 NLT

Not all encouragement is created equal; the best comes from God. We can place apples of gold in settings of silver when we ask him for the words to say to encourage others. Sometimes, God wants to say something very special to a person, something you couldn't think of on your own.

When you feel God's prompting to speak, don't hold back. You can be the vehicle for a timely blessing.

Thank you, God, that through your Word and your church your refreshing encouragement blesses me. I need those timely, fitting words in my moments of fear, doubt, anxiety, and despair.

When was the last time you spoke a timely word of encouragement?

Sing, Sing, Sing!

*They celebrate your abundant goodness
and joyfully sing of your righteousness.*

PSALM 145:7 NIV

There are some church services, or Christian celebrations, that are so full of the Holy Spirit it's beautifully overwhelming. Have you experienced that? In a remarkable way, believers come together to celebrate all that God has done in their lives. They dance, sing at the top of their lungs in praise, and cry tears of joy for his abundant grace and sacrifice. How happy that sight must make our Father in heaven!

Today, find a song and joyfully sing out to the God who loves you. He does not care what you sound like—your praise is music to his ears!

Father, thank you for loving me so well. Today I want to spend time praising you in song! I thank you for the gift of your goodness and love.

Everyone will share the story of your wonderful goodness;
they will sing with joy about your righteousness.

PSALM 145:7 NLT

Wonderful goodness. Abundant goodness. These are words used to describe how good God is. It seems over the top, impossible, unbelievable. But it is the truth!

God adores you and cherishes you, no matter what you look like, or what you've done. He is so good that he will never abandon or forsake you. He is proud to call you his child. Let his goodness overflow in your heart this evening.

God, I'm forever thankful for the way you love me. You truly are
good. You are the very definition of good itself. I am blessed to be
called your child.

God's goodness cannot be measured.

Consider the Sparrows

"Look at the birds of the air; they neither sow nor reap nor gather into barns, and yet your heavenly Father feeds them. Are you not of more value than they? And can any of you by worrying add a single hour to your span of life?"

MATTHEW 6:26-27 NRSV

Jesus told us that when we're faced with the worries of this life to consider the sparrows. Jesus and his Father created the sparrows as well as the whole earth that sustains the life of sparrows. When he used them as an example to believers, he didn't just come up with the comparison the night while preparing his sermon.

Jesus created sparrows thousands of years before he taught this truth. With every ounce of intent at the point of creation, he foresaw the day he would make this point through them. He eagerly wants to communicate his care for you today.

God, thank you for sparrows that show me how to live. Help me live in total trust of you today!

"Look at the birds in the air. They don't plant or harvest or store food in barns, but your heavenly Father feeds them. And you know that you are worth much more than the birds. You cannot add any time to your life by worrying about it."

MATTHEW 6:26-27 NCV

Sparrows were designed to make beautiful sounds, to bring joy to those who watch and listen to them, and to show children of God how to live. Sparrows wake up knowing that worms will come to the surface. They fetch what they need for the day, carelessly soar around for no apparent reason, then find some more worms and grubs when they're hungry. They go to sleep with total trust that tomorrow will be no less delightful than today.

When we fully trust God, we can be as carefree and expectant as those sparrows. We don't need to worry about anything because God has everything under control.

Father, thank you for caring so much for your creation. It is clear that you care deeply about me and want what's best for me. Help me to stop worrying and start trusting you.

Have you watched a carefree sparrow recently?

Our Creator

When I look at the night sky and see the work of your fingers—
the moon and the stars you set in place—
what are mere mortals that you should think about them,
human beings that you should care for them?
Yet you made them only a little lower than God
and crowned them with glory and honor.

PSALM 8:3-5 NLT

Skydiving looks absolutely thrilling and completely terrifying. Those who have had the courage to leap from a plane say it is an exhilarating experience that cannot be replicated. A woman shared that as she floated through the air, praise welled up in her soul as she saw God's magnificent creation from a completely new viewpoint.

Are you feeling somewhat insignificant this morning and maybe a bit forgotten? Through the vast splendor of the universe, God sees you, he thinks about you, and he cares for you. Revel in that for a moment.

Oh God, it is amazing that you, the God of the universe, care about me! You have fashioned me in your image for a divine purpose. Help me to live in the wonder of this truth.

When I consider Your heavens, the work of Your fingers,
The moon and the stars, which You have ordained;
What is man that You take thought of him,
And the son of man that You care for him?
Yet You have made him a little lower than God,
And You crown him with glory and majesty!

PSALM 8:3-5 NASB

The psalmist was enthralled with the mighty works of God and in awe of the fact that God could stoop to even notice or care about mere mortals. God created man is his very own image with a coronation of sorts as he crowned him with glory and honor and gave him dominion over the earth.

Consider this: you are fearfully and wonderfully made! Your value cannot be measured and God cares very deeply about you.

God, I am in awe of your work. I cannot fathom your power and splendor—and yet, you think of me. You care for me. Thank you.

Consider carefully the artwork of God.

Praise the Lord!

Let all that I am praise the LORD.
I will praise the LORD as long as I live.
I will sing praises to my God with my dying breath.

PSALM 146:1-2 NLT

God commands us numerous times in his Word to praise him. How can he expect us to fulfill such a directive? On some days, digging through the rubble to find a nugget to be thankful for is flat out formidable. Negative thoughts can float through the mind like a shadowy cloud, and if allowed to remain, can darken the entire day.

When you have one of those days, and maybe today feels like it might be that way, let all that you are praise the Lord. You may be surprised how the cloud passes and the sun shines through.

Lord, you are great and worthy to be praised! I lift my voice in praise and thanksgiving this morning. Blessed be your name.

Praise the Lord!
Praise the Lord, O my soul!
I will praise the Lord while I live;
I will sing praises to my God while I have my being.

Psalm 146:1-2 NASB

The psalmist understood darkness and hardship. Even though his life was in constant danger, he knew that as he centered on the greatness of God, his problems would be divinely solved. He wasn't engrossed in his own stuff. He looked at God and saw him for who he was: a helper, creator, promise keeper, provider, deliverer, healer, protector, and defender.

Make David's words your prayer to the Lord this evening. As you do, your heart will nod "yes" and hope will arise.

I will praise you Lord while I have breath. You are worthy of all my praise. I offer it to you this evening and trust that your peace will flood my heart.

It is good to praise the Lord.

Ransomed

I will shout for joy
and sing your praises,
for you have ransomed me.

A boy whittled a little boat out of a scrap of wood. Proud of himself for his accomplishment, he decided to test it out in a stream that wound through his family's property. He ran alongside the boat on the bank, watching it bob through the water. Soon the current picked up, and away his boat went... faster than he could follow.

What do you think may have happened to the little boy's boat? He had no idea, but he was hopeful that one day he would find it. On this fine morning, remember to thank God for finding you. Shout for joy and sing his praises!

Oh, Lord, you created me, but I was lost in sin until you found me.
Thank you for loving me just as you found me. Thanks for never
giving up on me.

My lips will shout for joy,
when I sing praises to you;
my soul also,
which you have redeemed.

PSALM 71:23 ESV

Weeks passed. The boy and his dad took a trip into town.
While there, they spied the boy's little boat in the window of
a store with a price tag on it! With joy, he ran into the shop
expecting to retrieve his lost boat. But he was told he would
have to pay for it. In the end, the boy earned enough money to
buy back what was already his.

Isn't that what Christ did for us? He made us, lost us, and
then bought us back, paying for us with his life. The psalmist
couldn't contain his joy as he contemplated that wonder! God
has ransomed us.

God, thank you for buying me back! I was lost but you found me
and rescued me. Blessed be your holy name.

When was the last time you shouted for joy… to the Lord?

Real Love

Since ancient times no one has heard,
no ear has perceived,
no eye has seen any God besides you,
who acts on behalf of those who wait for him.

ISAIAH 64:4 NIV

Authenticity. It matters, doesn't it? We wonder if the gem, the handbag, the promise, is real. We've all heard the expression, "If it's too good to be true, it's probably not true," so we scrutinize the people and possessions in our lives, looking for authenticity.

What great comfort we can take in our God: the one, true God! All his promises are true; all his gifts are good. His love is authentic, and it is ours to claim.

Lord, you are the one, the only, the Almighty God. Who am I that you should act on my behalf, that you should speak into my life? And yet you do. May my love for you be authentic, may my words of praise be true.

Since the world began,
no ear has heard
and no eye has seen a God like you,
who works for those who wait for him!

ISAIAH 64:4 NLT

You've probably heard the saying, "True love waits." It can mean so many things, but if we apply that to our relationship with God, it has the very best meaning of all. If we truly love God with all of our hearts, we will eagerly wait for him. We will spend time quietly listening for his voice. We will joyfully anticipate his return.

Waiting for God isn't easy. We become restless quickly. Calm your heart tonight and tell yourself that true love waits.

God, waiting is hard. Trusting and believing that you will return for me doesn't come naturally or easily most days. But I love you. And I choose to wait patiently.

A future forever with God is worth waiting for.

Whole Restoration

My whole being, praise the LORD
and do not forget all his kindnesses.
He forgives all my sins
and heals all my diseases.

PSALM 103:2-3 NCV

Our God is a God of restoration. He shows us his kindness, through his love, in that he cares for our entire being. Not only does God want to restore a right relationship with you, he also wants to restore your body to health.

Are you feeling tired, sick, or weak today? Ask God to bring healing to your body. Praise him with your whole being.

Heavenly Father, I praise you with my whole being. I remember your kindness toward me, and I ask you to show me your mercy. Heal my body and restore my health.

Praise the LORD, my soul,
and forget not all his benefits—
who forgives all your sins
and heals all your diseases.

PSALM 103:2-3 NIV

When we are spiritually or physically weak, we can sometimes forget the promises of God. In these times, think on his character; remember that he is a loving Father who wants the best for you.

Praise God with all of your heart, soul, and mind, and watch him bring restoration to the areas of your life that need it the most.

God, I need your healing touch tonight. Forgive my sins and renew my heart. Bring restoration and wholeness to my body.

Experience the healing touch of the Father today.

Supreme Judge

"I, the LORD, love justice,
I hate robbery in the burnt offering;
And I will faithfully give them their recompense
And make an everlasting covenant with them."

ISAIAH 61:8 NASB

One of the areas often ignored or softened when describing the loving God we serve is that he is a God of justice. The God who will put all things right someday is not a God who is easily accepted. We enjoy our freedom and sometimes want to do what we want without any consequences.

We walk in thankfulness for Jesus Christ coming to take the place for our sin and dying for us. All things will be made right one day. Let's make sure we keep short accounts with God so we benefit from his justice.

God, thank you for being a loving and just God. Help me keep my eyes on you today when I make decisions, and confess and repent when I need to!

I, the LORD, love justice;
I hate robbery and wrongdoing.
In my faithfulness I will reward my people
and make an everlasting covenant with them.

ISAIAH 61:8 NIV

God loves justice. He will be faithful in his promises to us.
There will come a day when he returns and a new world will
be established. Everything that is wrong will be made right.
This is a wonderful covenant!

Let's be faithful in our pursuit and relationship with Jesus,
deepening our understanding of right and wrong in the world
we live in. Thank him tonight for his justice and mercy.

Father, thank you that you are just. You know everything, and
you will make all things good and right. I am so grateful for your
mercy which is shown to me each day. I rely on that mercy like the
air I breathe.

Praise God for his mercy.

Glory

All of God's promises have been fulfilled in Christ with a resounding "Yes!" And through Christ, our "Amen" (which means "Yes") ascends to God for his glory.

2 CORINTHIANS 1:20 NLT

All throughout the Old Testament we are given hints about a Messiah, a Savior who would come to redeem us. Reading the Gospels sheds light on who this Savior is—Jesus Christ. He came as a baby and experienced many of the same things we do in our flesh. He never sinned, but he paid the ultimate price for our sins—dying on a cross after suffering immensely.

Give God the glory and praise for your freedom today! His wonderful promises are yours through Christ his Son.

Jesus, thank you for the price you paid for me, a sinner, so I might fully live. You are good, Father, and I praise and give you glory!

No matter how many promises God has made, they are "Yes" in Christ. And so through him the "Amen" is spoken by us to the glory of God.

2 Corinthians 1:20 NIV

What a joy it must be for our amens, shouts of praise, and singing to be heard above. What a warm sound it must be to hear our desperate prayers whispered in the middle of the night. What a smile it must bring to see us witness to a friend or serve someone in need.

What a glorious task we are left with as believers: doing God's work for his kingdom. As we spread his love and amazing promises with hope, we can shout, "Amen!"

God, I want to spend my days praising and thanking you. I am grateful for the gift of eternity and freedom that you have given me.

God's promises will all be fulfilled. We can count on that!

Legacy

"Only the living can praise you as I do today.
Each generation tells of your faithfulness to the next."

ISAIAH 38:19 NLT

Family trees can be really interesting: where people came from, what their heritage is, and how they ended up where they did. Sometimes they contain mystery and questions. At other times they might shed light on an unexplained hair color of a grandchild. When you're staring at a family tree, you're staring at a long lineage of a beginning and ending.

Is your family telling God's faithfulness from generation to generation, or are you the beginning of God's story? Either way, you can choose a heritage of faith for those who come after you. Pray for strength to root your family tree in God's love.

I praise you for the family and friends you've given me, Father. Help me to remember my calling here—to preach your name and share the gospel. I want to leave a legacy of other believers in my family.

"The living, the living—they praise you,
as I am doing today;
parents tell their children about your faithfulness."

ISAIAH 38:19 NIV

Our hope is always that our loved ones will be with us in eternity, together forever. What we do each day matters. From children, to spouses, to parents and siblings, we have an important legacy to leave.

Tell your family about the faithfulness of God in your life. It will bring encouragement to those who share your faith, and a witness to those who don't.

Lord, show my family your love through me. Help me to stay focused on the prize that is eternity with you!

What family member can you share God's faithfulness with today?

Love of a Father

"He arose and came to his father. But while he was still a long way off, his father saw him and felt compassion, and ran and embraced him and kissed him."

LUKE 15:20 ESV

The picture this verse paints is a beautiful one: a son, returning to his father in repentance, and the father running to embrace him as soon as he sees him. The father wanted to reach his son first. He didn't want him to feel shame and regret; he showered him with the finest, forgiving and forgetting all the trouble the son had caused.

Today as you spend time with your loving Father, picture him running to you and extending his grace over all of your weakness and sin. He wants you to walk in freedom from shame and guilt.

How grateful I am that you don't give up on me, Father God! Thank you for loving me in the best way, for knowing my heart and loving me despite my faults. I'm thankful to be called your child!

"He returned home to his father. And while he was still a long way off, his father saw him coming. Filled with love and compassion, he ran to his son, embraced him, and kissed him."

LUKE 15:20 NLT

This parable parallels the love of God. God created us with the finest in mind. He is a Father who loves without limits, forgiving and forgetting all when he sent his Son to die for our sins. We can walk in freedom, knowing when we repent, we are truly forgiven.

God runs toward us when we come with repentant hearts. He doesn't stand with his back turned and arms folded, waiting for us to grovel. He pursues us with compassion. He desires an intimate relationship with us.

Thank you, God, for your compassion and kindness. You run toward me when I come to you with a repentant heart. Help me to remain humble and come to you often for forgiveness and mercy.

Take a step toward the Father today, and watch him run to meet you.

Blessings

*"May the Lord bless you
and protect you.
May the Lord smile on you
and be gracious to you.
May the Lord show you his favor
and give you his peace."*

NUMBERS 6:24–26 NLT

Imagine every day someone laying their hand on your forehead and blessing you before you start your day. You wake up, roll over, and before you've even poured your coffee for the day, you've got someone whispering this prayer over you. What a gift it would be to start your day that way!

The good news is that you can. Every day you can start in communion with the Lord. Speak this prayer over yourself and your family today. Ask for God's favor and peace to go with you.

God, I need your blessing today. Thank you for being a loving Father who walks with me in my everyday routine. Grant me your favor and peace, your protection and grace as I move through my day.

"The LORD bless you, and keep you;
The LORD make His face shine on you,
And be gracious to you;
The LORD lift up His countenance on you,
And give you peace."

NUMBERS 6:24–26 NASB

Before anything else each day, invite God's Spirit into your life. Ask him to guide your day and steer you in the right direction. Invite his holy presence to uphold you and sustain you in your trials. Ask him to walk with you as you encounter various people in conversation.

What a loving God we serve, one who says he will be there with us through everything! Let his smile bring you peace as you lay down to rest this evening.

Father, I invite your presence into my life and into everything I do this evening. I ask your Spirit to guide me and uphold me. Help me pursue your joy and peace.

Feel the smile of the Lord resting on you today.

Hope in God

"Lord, where do I put my hope?
My only hope is in you."

PSALM 39:7 NLT

It was a day like every other. The lame man arrived with the help of his family to spend his waking hours begging at the temple gate. Crippled from birth, it was about the only thing he could do to survive. It was the last formal prayer time of the day when the Jews would make their sacrifices and give alms to the poor. As Peter and John arrived at the gate, the lame man asked for money, hoping for a coin or two. Imagine his utter amazement when he was healed instead.

Are you sitting at that gate this morning, hoping you will receive a bit of joy or encouragement from someone passing by? Remember this. No human can meet your needs—only God can. The lame man "looked up" and received much more than he ever dreamed. This day, put your hope in God.

Lord, today I choose to put my hope in you. You are the source of everything I need. Forgive me for looking elsewhere and help me to keep my eyes on you.

"Now, Lord, what do I look for?
My hope is in you."

PSALM 39:7 NIV

When we look for hope on the earth—whether in people or things—we will be disappointed. Even if we get what we hope for, it won't be long before we have to place our hope in something else. We got the new job, now we want a new house. We found a spouse, now we want a family. We made the team, now we want to win the championship.

Though none of these "hopes" are wrong, they are only temporary. Fulfilment of this hope doesn't necessarily bring contentment. Are you placing your hope horizontally rather than vertically? Hope in God is the only hope that will never disappoint.

God, help me to place my hope in you. I know you are the source of hope, and you fill me with contentment. When I hope in the things of this world, help me to remember that they will not bring the joy and peace that you do. Turn my face toward you instead.

God holds the only hope that does not disappoint.

The God of All Comfort

Praise be to the God and Father of our Lord Jesus Christ, the Father of compassion and the God of all comfort.

2 CORINTHIANS 1:3 NIV

Comfort is what our hearts cry out for in times of trouble or sorrow. We need someone to sit beside us, listen to our story, put a comforting arm around our shoulders, and just be there.

Our friends and families, though they love us, are limited by time and resources. They cannot always meet our needs. Turn to God today and ask him to comfort you like only he can. He is the source of all comfort—not just a little comfort… all!

Father, you are my God—full of compassion and eager to comfort my soul. I give you my distress and ask that you would bind up my heart. I begin this day with your strength.

All praise to God, the Father of our Lord Jesus Christ. God is our merciful Father and the source of all comfort.

2 CORINTHIANS 1:3 NLT

When you feel alone in your sorrow, it's the perfect moment to look to God—the source of compassion and comfort. Read the Psalms and hang on to the promises found there. God does not grow tired or weary of us; he is always near.

You can be joyful this evening because you have a God who loves you. He is full of peace and joy. Run to him tonight and let him soothe your troubled soul.

God, I ask you to take away my sorrow and replace it with joy. You are merciful and compassionate, and you care about what I'm going through. Be my source of comfort tonight.

Sense God wrapping you in a big hug and holding you close for a while.

Wholly Devoted

He alone is your God, the only one who is worthy of your praise,
the one who has done these mighty miracles that you have seen
with your own eyes.

DEUTERONOMY 10:21 NLT

At the unveiling of the city's newest skyscraper, crowds
gather to celebrate the feat of architecture and engineering,
commerce and creativity. Sunlight pours onto the observation
deck as a city official cuts the yellow dedication ribbon.
Behind him are some of the many construction workers,
designers, and engineers whose imagination, insight, and
expertise contributed to making mere drawings a reality.
Everyone wants a piece of the praise, but not everyone is
worthy of it.

Have you heralded to God a song of thanksgiving? The mighty
miracles of your life are his careful design, plain for all to see.
He alone is worthy of your praise.

God, thank you for your hand of blessing. I give you the glory and
honor for all you have done in my life. Only you deserve the glory
for the goodness in my life.

*He is the one you praise; he is your God, who performed for you
those great and awesome wonders you saw with your own eyes.*

DEUTERONOMY 10:21 NIV

Only one expert can truly take credit for a building's
inception—the architect. He intimately knows it. Everyone
around him may reach for the spotlight, and he may be lost in
the noise and clamor for glory, but the reality is that he is the
one worthy of praise.

You know the architect of your life. He is your designer: the
one responsible for your soaring heights and multitude of
blessings. *He alone is your God.* Have you singled him out for
glory? Give God praise tonight for his carefully planned design.

*God, I want to be wholly devoted to you, the architect of my life.
You know me inside and out. You made me who I am and gave me
specific purpose. Thank you.*

What does full devotion look like to you?

Glad

"Then young women will dance and be glad,
young men and old as well.
I will turn their mourning into gladness;
I will give them comfort and joy instead of sorrow."

JEREMIAH 31:13 NIV

You've probably heard stories of unexplainable hope on the news, or experienced it yourself firsthand. Stories that are filled with despair and tragedy, and yet, in the midst of it, those who should be suffering are filled with joy. Filled with hope and renewal: the opposite of what one would expect.

You can be filled with hope as you look to God to turn your mourning into dancing and your sorrow into joy. He wants us to sing and be glad in all circumstances.

Father, thank you that you can take an impossible situation and turn it to good. Thank you for turning my mourning into dancing and my sadness into joy.

"The young women will dance for joy,
and the men—old and young—will join in the celebration.
I will turn their mourning into joy.
I will comfort them and exchange their sorrow for rejoicing."

JEREMIAH 31:13 NLT

There is no reason for a joy-filled response to a tough situation. There is no understanding of why that would happen. You might look at your own life, or the life of someone else, in total disbelief because of the reaction to tragedy.

The only explanation is Jesus and his grace. Jesus, in his immense love for us, takes something so difficult and uses it for good. He is the only one capable of such a glorious feat, and let's be thankful he is.

God, help me be full of joy especially when that seems like the
opposite of how I should be feeling. You know me, and you know
my emotions. I want to be glad even in tough times.

Do you have an opportunity to dance and be glad today?

Encouragement in God's Word

I long for Your salvation, O LORD,
And Your law is my delight.
Let my soul live that it may praise You,
And let Your ordinances help me.

PSALM 119:174-175 NASB

There is wonder to be found in snowflakes, raindrops, and even strange bugs. Though we often don't love the idea of encountering too many of those things, if we stop and look, if we allow ourselves to really *see* what is there, it's pretty amazing.

The same can be true of God's Word. It may be displayed in various forms and places throughout our homes, schools, work places, or church buildings, but if we don't stop to really drink in the words that are there, we can miss the rich blessing behind them. Don't miss that today.

God, help me not to gloss over the beauty and depth of your
Word. Only your Word carries the richness of eternity and the
encouragement I need for each new day.

I long for your salvation, O LORD,
and your law is my delight.
Let my soul live and praise you,
and let your rules help me.

PSALM 119:174–175 ESV

When we believe that God wants to encourage us through his Word, we will no doubt find encouragement in it—because God intended it to be used for that purpose. His words are a delight to our spirits.

Don't gloss over the beauty and depth of God's Word. It's the only Word that carries the richness of eternity. Drink it in deeply tonight.

God, your Word fills me with delight. Help me to spend time in it more often so I can carry it with me and be encouraged by truth.

Let God's Word be a delight to you tonight.

Garment of Praise

Enter his gates with thanksgiving,
and his courts with praise.
Give thanks to him, bless his name.
For the LORD is good;
his steadfast love endures forever,
and his faithfulness to all generations.

PSALM 100:4-5 NRSV

Have you ever looked into a child's grumpy face and demanded that they don't smile? Even the most stubborn child can often be coaxed out of their funk by a few tickles or funny faces. Unfortunately, the same can't be said for adults. Imagine trying to change the attitude of a crotchety older woman with the same method. The picture is somewhat ridiculous.

Sometimes the only thing that can coax us out of our bad attitudes is thanksgiving. When we choose to be grateful to God for all that's around us, we will naturally be happier people.

God, you don't only deserve my praise when life is going well. You are worthy of my adoration every second of every day—no matter what the situation. Today I choose to put on a garment of praise.

Enter his gates with thanksgiving,
and his courts with praise!
Give thanks to him; bless his name!
For the LORD is good;
his steadfast love endures forever,
and his faithfulness to all generations.

PSALM 100:4-5 ESV

When life's situations get us down, and all around us is darkness and depression, it takes a great deal of faith to choose praise. But often that's the only thing that can really pull us out of those dark moments.

When we choose to thank God for his goodness and grace, we can't help but see life in a more positive light. As we praise God, our focus shifts from ourselves to him.

God, let my focus be on you tonight. Thank you for your love that endures forever. Thank you for your faithfulness. I am so grateful for your mercy.

What song of thanksgiving is on your lips tonight?

Eternal Mindset

"You too have grief now; but I will see you again, and your heart will rejoice, and no one will take your joy away from you."

JOHN 16:22 NASB

This life is not going to be void of hardships; of trials and grief, of tragedy and deep sorrow. That pain is like nothing else, and it's often hard to keep peace at the forefront of your mind.

When you follow Jesus, and read his Word, however, you can find peace. You are reminded of his promise: to one day come back and make all things right. He will be with us forever and that means our joy will not be taken away.

Jesus, when you return, I want to be ready! I want to be in eternity with you where my joy can't be shaken. I know that, for now, this life is what I have and I'm grateful.

"So also you have sorrow now, but I will see you again, and your hearts will rejoice, and no one will take your joy from you."

JOHN 16:22 ESV

Jesus knew that we would have pain and sorrow in this life. He knew everything wouldn't be easy. He gave us this wonderful promise that we can always look forward to. One day he will come back and wipe every tear from our eyes, heal every broken bone, and cure every disease.

God's promises are rich with goodness. We get to spend an eternity with him, where joy cannot be destroyed.

God, help me to live with an eternal perspective, so that everything I encounter can be seen through your eyes. Remind me that you are the rock that I stand on and you are always with me.

How can you ensure you are viewing life with an eternal perspective?

A Sweet, Sweet Sound

Our mouths were filled with laughter,
our tongues with songs of joy.
Then it was said among the nations,
"The LORD has done great things for them."

PSALM 126:2 NIV

Laughter is one of the greatest sounds in the world. An old married couple dancing and flirting. A toddler being tickled, giggling until she cries. A pair of best friends, rolling with laughter on the floor. When you hear laughter, you can't help but crack a smile yourself.

Raise your voice to God in worship today—laugh with him! All of your honor and praise glorifies him and he delights in it. He loves to hear you laugh.

Oh, how I love you and worship your name, Father! I want to start my day in praise and laughter. May my voice be pleasing to you.

We were filled with laughter,
and we sang for joy.
And the other nations said,
"What amazing things the Lord has done for them."

Psalm 126:2 NLT

Can you imagine what God must feel when he hears his children laughing, singing, and praising him together? Can you imagine what happiness sounds like to him? Picture a room full of believers singing in harmony, showing their love for their God. What a joyous, beautiful sound that must be!

God doesn't require certain types of worship. He created us all uniquely to praise him in our individual way. Use whatever talents he's given you to honor him. What a proud Father he must be when his children worship him from their hearts.

Father, you have made us all unique in our worship styles. I want to honor you in my daily praise, in my creative style. If that means laughing with you, I want to laugh freely. Thank you for giving me the opportunity to express my praise in my own way.

Can you laugh with God today?

Promises of God

As they were talking about these things, Jesus himself stood among them, and said to them, "Peace to you! … And behold, I am sending the promise of my Father upon you. But stay in the city until you are clothed with power from on high."

LUKE 24:36, 49 ESV

Our God does not mess around. He doesn't make promises and then not fulfill them. He doesn't tell us life is going to be all rainbows, ponies, and happy times. No, he tells us the areas we need to work on, gives us commandments to follow, and promises *big* things like sending a Savior to rescue us all from our sin.

God sent his one and only Son to come to earth as a tiny, helpless babe. He suffered horrifically and died on a cross. But Jesus promised that he would rise again. And he did! And because of that, we are free from our sin and shame today.

Father, thank you for your sovereignty! Thank you that I don't need to worry about tomorrow because I walk with you. Thank you for keeping your promises and for saving me. I love you.

While the two followers were telling this, Jesus himself stood right in the middle of them and said, "Peace be with you." ... I will send you what my Father has promised, but you must stay in Jerusalem until you have received that power from heaven."

LUKE 24:36, 49 NCV

Jesus will come again, as God says in Revelation, to make the world right. He will come again to judge the living and the dead, and his kingdom will reign forever. This is both a terrifying and glorious thought!

Let's praise God for giving us his Spirit: our helper on our journey to eternity with God. Seek his wisdom and let him breathe life into your soul.

Thank you for giving me an eternal perspective, so I can focus on my relationship with you. Thank you for the gift of your Holy Spirit who guides and encourages me along the way.

Thank God for being a keeper of promises.

Vengeful Hearts

Those who plan evil are full of lies,
but those who plan peace are happy.

PROVERBS 12:20 NCV

Have you ever planned to do something not-so-nice? Thought out the steps, or the thing you wanted to say to whomever betrayed you or wronged you? This plotting is *revenge* and it almost always ends up doing more harm than good.

We serve a God who tell us that when we plan for peace, we are filled with joy. If we give up whatever is ailing us, and instead ask for God's peace, he will shower joy on us! It sounds so much better than plotting revenge, doesn't it?

God, thank you for being a God who gives me peace and joy in place of deception! Thank you for taking difficult situations and turning them to good.

Deceit fills hearts that are plotting evil;
joy fills hearts that are planning peace!

PROVERBS 12:20 NLT

Revenge can take up a lot of heart space that could be used for good things, for amazing things. It pushes out the space that could be filled with love, joy, and peace. It turns smiles to glares, and peace to unsettledness. It fills our minds with chaos and darkness.

Don't waste your heart space, your thoughts, or your time plotting evil. Instead, trust God to defend you. Let go of all the junk invading your peaceful space tonight.

Father, help me to let go of any ill will I harbor in my heart, any space that is being taken up for revenge, and instead focus on your goodness! I want your peace to flood my heart.

Don't be a hoarder of evil thoughts! Throw them out before they take up any space in your heart.

Tender Love

Brothers and sisters, we urge you to warn those who are lazy.
Encourage those who are timid. Take tender care of those who are
weak. Be patient with everyone.

1 THESSALONIANS 5:14 NLT

As our creator, God knew exactly what he was doing and
where we would struggle! He also gave us tools to help one
another on the journey. We are to encourage each other in our
gifts, sharpen each other when necessary, and be accountable
to one another as brothers and sisters.

Take a look inside today and see where you may need to lend
an encouraging hand to someone. Be tender, child of God, for
we are all weak.

Father God, I thank you that you're all-knowing and you created
us each with a purpose. Use me where my gifting is and help me to
encourage and be tenderhearted to those who need it most today.

We urge you, brothers, admonish the idle, encourage the fainthearted, help the weak, be patient with them all.

1 THESSALONIANS 5:14 ESV

God was so creative when he made us. He created us in his image, but no two of us are exactly the same. We all have strengths, differences, varying gifts, and personality traits. We're a giant melting pot of individualism and it's glorious.

Differences aren't always easy to accept, but God asks us to be patient with each other. To encourage each other. To love each other. Ask God for grace to love those who are different than you.

God, I'm thankful to be in this melting pot of your children. Help me to be patient with everyone. Help me to love like you love. Help me to see people the way you do.

God's unique creativity is displayed in his children. Embrace it!

Joy

"Do not grieve,
for the joy of the LORD is your strength."

NEHEMIAH 8:10 NIV

Joy is not necessarily happiness. Happiness is dependent on circumstances; joy is not. Happiness is fleeting; joy is constant. Happiness disappears when trials come; joy grows through troubles. Good times bring happiness and laughter; difficulties bring sorrow and grief, but joy resides beneath.

Let the joy of the Lord be your strength today. No matter what you face, his joy can be yours.

Thank you, Jesus, for the joy that gives me strength. I choose today to fill my mind with truth, to think about those things that are praiseworthy, and to trust you fully.

*"Don't be dejected and sad,
for the joy of the LORD is your strength!"*

NEHEMIAH 8:10 NLT

Joy is not an emotion that can be fabricated or faked. It is a deep-seated sense that all things are good because God is in charge. Joy is expressed in praise, song, laughter, a peaceful countenance, light in the eyes, or a serenity that belies adversity.

God is our substance. We can trust that he does all things well. Let him be your strength tonight.

Father, with a thankful heart I choose your joy to be my strength.

Trust God's joy to be your strength.

Acting in Your Gift

Every good gift and every perfect gift is from above, coming down from the Father of lights with whom there is no variation or shadow due to change.

JAMES 1:17 ESV

When you do something really, really well, it makes you feel good. You feel as if you're accomplishing something important and you know, in your hearts of hearts, that you were truly made to do it. You feel a sense of worth and purpose.

To feel that way is a beautiful gift! Knowing you're doing exactly what you were created to do feels wonderful. Act in your gifts today!

God, thank you for the gifts you've given me! Help me to continue to discover what those are and use them well.

Whatever is good and perfect comes down to us from God our Father, who created all the lights in the heavens. He never changes or casts a shifting shadow.

JAMES 1:17 NLT

It is easy to give yourself credit in the moments you do really well. Don't forget that God has showered his gifts on you, with intention, and he deserves the glory. When you're walking in your God-designed purpose, there is nothing you'd rather be doing. When you're acting in your gifting, you know it, and God rewards you for it.

Just be sure to give him credit where credit is due. There is nothing purposeful in this life without him.

Father, I praise your name and give you the glory for the areas in my life where I act in my gifting. Thank you for giving me purpose.

What is your favorite God-given gift?

It Was Good

Then God looked over all he had made,
and he saw that it was very good!
And evening passed and morning came,
marking the sixth day.

GENESIS 1:31 NLT

God created the heavens and the earth in six days. As he created, formed, and molded, he said the same thing: "It is good." Think of the creator of the universe looking out at you, saying, "You are *good*," because this is how he first designed everything. For good. For good purpose, for good reason, for good cause.

Everything worked together for good. And then we fell. And sin entered. And the enemy prowls around searching for victims to be deceived by his scheming. Don't fall in his trap today! Remember the good that you were created to do and be.

Father, thank you for planning everything with purpose. You created everything for good, knowing we would fail, and then you gave us Jesus so we could still walk in goodness and freedom!

God saw all that he had made, and it was very good. And there was evening, and there was morning--the sixth day.

GENESIS 1:31 NIV

There is such power in the name of God; this is the good news of today! The living, active Word of God is available to us, to direct our lives and breathe freshness into our souls. The same Spirit that created everything good can live inside of us when we invite him in.

There is nothing about this that isn't good, friends! Embrace the goodness this evening and be thankful for your specific purpose.

God, I am thankful for your goodness, mercy, and justice. You have created me for a specific good purpose. Help me to think about that this evening.

What good purpose were you created for?

A Beautiful Gift

No matter what happens, always be thankful, for this is God's will for you who belong to Christ Jesus.

1 THESSALONIANS 5:18 TLB

It is easy to be thankful when everything in life is going well. But it's a whole other story to be thankful when life is difficult. We always have a choice.

We can be disgruntled with everything that is going wrong around us, allowing bitterness and discontentment to rob us of our joy and blessings. Or we can quiet our worried spirit, and choose gratitude.

Thank you, Jesus, that gratitude is a gift. Help me count all the blessings around me. Thank you that even in times of trouble, my heart is still able to rejoice in your goodness.

Give thanks in all circumstances; for this is the will of God in Christ Jesus for you.

1 Thessalonians 5:18 esv

Gratitude is a beautiful gift. It opens our eyes and hearts to all of the blessings that remain even in dire circumstances. Our bills may be mounting, but we can still be thankful for our healthy bodies. Our relationships may be hurting, but we can still be thankful to serve a God who heals and redeems. Our health may be failing, but we can still be thankful for God's unending mercy, compassion, and grace.

We may feel overwhelmed and stressed, but we still have a God who is in control. Give thanks to him for that this evening.

I choose to thank you tonight, God, because you deserve my gratitude. Your blessings are plentiful and I am so grateful.

Name ten things you are grateful for right now.

Sweet Relief

When you pass through the waters, I will be with you;
and through the rivers, they shall not overwhelm you;
when you walk through fire you shall not be burned,
and the flame shall not consume you.

ISAIAH 43:2 ESV

There is nothing worse in life than going through a hard time and feeling like you are all alone in it. Facing difficulties alone can be heart wrenching, confusing, and, well, lonely. If we are able to take a trusted friend into our hard times, the journey becomes easier. Having a support system, an ally, someone to whisper encouragement and love to our spirits, takes the edge off. It lightens our burdens.

God promises to be with us through our difficult seasons and situations. Take him up on that promise today.

Jesus, your presence is such a sweet relief. Thank you that I don't have to journey alone; rather, I can always journey with you, my faithful and trusted friend.

When you go through deep waters, I will be with you.
When you go through rivers of difficulty, you will not drown.
When you walk through the fire of oppression, you will not be
burned up; the flames will not consume you.

ISAIAH 43:2 NLT

Thankfully, it doesn't matter what we are enduring; we are never alone. Jesus is our faithful and trusted friend, and he is present. He is present in the good times and in the bad.

Take a deep breath tonight and know that even though this season in your life is difficult, you can lean into him and gather strength from his presence.

Thank you, Father, for your promise to stay with me. Thank you for your hand that holds me and guides me through the difficult times. Stay with me tonight as I lay down to sleep.

You are never alone.

Faithful Friend

A real friend sticks closer than a brother.

PROVERBS 18:24 NLT

At the end of a long day, sometimes all we want is to sit with a good friend and talk—not for the purpose of speaking alone, but simply from a deep longing to be heard. We want to share our joys, our worries, our frustrations, and our hopes with someone who will listen, someone who will focus on what we are saying. Someone who really cares. Everyone needs a friend like that.

You have a friend in God. Ask him to stick close to you today. Talk to him about how you feel. Share what's on your mind. He loves spending time with you.

God, I am thankful that you are my faithful friend. You know me by name, and you are always willing to sit and listen to what is on my heart.

There is a friend who sticks closer than a brother.

PROVERBS 18:24 NIV

It feels good to be heard. If we feel like we aren't, it is easy to fall into the trap of thinking we don't matter. We believe the lie that no one cares. God *does* care, and he *is* listening.

When no one else is available, God is. He sees you. He wants to fill that lonely place inside you with his presence. Let him be close to you tonight.

God, thank you for your nearness. Be with me this evening as I sit in quietness for a while. You are the best friend I could possibly have. You always know what's best for me and you love me in spite of my shortcomings. Thank you.

Pour out your heart to God today.

Joy in the Shadow

Because you are my helper,
I sing for joy in the shadow of your wings.

PSALM 63:7 NLT

God is our greatest cheerleader. He watches as we take flight in a calling he has put before us and he gently encourages us, urging us forward and cheering us on. The God of the universe, the creator of everything, the one living on the throne of righteousness, knows us and cheers us on.

Today, cheer right back at him! Let him hear your shouts of praise and joy for who he is!

Father God, thank you that you help me in times of trouble and times of joy. Thank you for being my constant cheerleader and encourager.

You are my help.
Because of your protection, I sing.

PSALM 63:7 NCV

What a privilege and an honor to know that once God sets us on a path, he will not let us stray. He urges us forward for his mission, putting stepping-stones down for us to walk on.

What confidence we can have when we know he is our helper. What joy we can proclaim when we know we are in his shadow. He leads the charge! There is no one else we should want to follow.

Thank you, Father, that I walk safely in the shadow of your wings, every day, and that you are my shield and protector. I follow you with my whole being tonight.

What is God calling you to follow him in today?

Temporary Struggles

"God blesses you who are hungry now,
for you will be satisfied.
God blesses you who weep now,
for in due time you will laugh."

LUKE 6:21 NLT

Sometimes it seems as if life will never get easier. We wake up with the same struggles and trials day after day. Trials that we grow weary of battling. We wonder when we will find rest and relief.

In our suffering it can be difficult to see God's goodness, and we feel as if we will never experience joy or happiness again. Today, place your trust in God's promise that you will laugh again.

Jesus, I am thankful that my struggles are only temporary. I am thankful that you promise to lift my pain and fill my heart with joy and peace.

You people who are now hungry are blessed,
because you will be satisfied.
You people who are now crying are blessed,
because you will laugh with joy.

LUKE 6:21 NCV

It's not pleasant to feel constantly hungry, nor is it wonderful to collapse in a puddle of tears at any given moment. Life is just plain hard sometimes.

God promises that our trials and struggles are only temporary. He assures us that he will replace our aches and pains with happiness and laughter. It's in that promise that we can find comfort.

Thank you for comforting me when I need your presence. I need to be able to laugh tonight. I want to be satisfied. I trust you, God, to fulfill your purpose in me and to help me through my struggles.

Are you struggling today? Turn to God's promises and be comforted.

All Joy

Indeed, you are our glory and joy.

1 THESSALONIANS 2:20 NIV

How beautiful it would be to live every day in the assurance of one thing: Jesus is our glory and our joy. Come what may, that is the truth we cling to in every circumstance. That our joy is not found in the things of this world—our home, our children, our job, or social status. Those things will vanish and be left here when we die. None of that truly matters.

Our joy is made complete in only one thing—Jesus Christ. Be joyful in him today!

Jesus, I know my joy can only come from you. There is nothing else here that can fill me the way you do. I've tried and failed and always come back to the truth: you are my constant source of joy.

Truly you are our glory and our joy.

1 THESSALONIANS 2:20 NCV

When you've experienced extreme difficulty, tragedy, or sadness in your life, this concept is made apparent: God is our glory and joy.

Can we rise above our circumstances, in the name of Jesus, and still find joy in him? Can we wake up every day and choose him? Choose joy? Think on this the next time you are tested in various ways. Where does your joy truly live?

Especially in times of trial, God, may I look to you as the perfecter of my peace and joy. I know you are the only one who can bring joy from sadness and peace from anxiety. Thank you for your dedication to me.

Find true joy in God today!

Eternal Joy

The kingdom of God is not a matter of eating and drinking but of righteousness and peace and joy in the Holy Spirit.

ROMANS 14:17 ESV

We live in a society that constantly desires more. More means more of everything, including happiness that comes from attaining it. But acquiring more stuff does not bring lasting happiness. It may provide a brief moment of joy at first, but that vanishes, leaving an empty hole that needs to be filled with something else.

Don't get caught in the trap of wanting more—unless it's righteousness, peace, and joy that you want. More of God in your life today will give you all of those in full measure.

God, help me remember that living with you is the only thing that will bring true, lasting happiness and joy in my life. I want more of you.

The Kingdom of God is not a matter of what we eat or drink, but of living a life of goodness and peace and joy in the Holy Spirit.

ROMANS 14:17 NLT

When we believe in eternity, in a life beyond what is right in front of us, our perspective shifts and we see the truth in desiring more. No earthly possessions will be taken with us. Our joy doesn't come from more stuff, or more recognition. No, our kingdom with the Father is about the state of our hearts.

Joy comes in the form of living in unity with God—of listening to his voice and obeying his commands. Find joy in wise decisions tonight.

God, my heart can only be completely satisfied with your Spirit. Help me get rid of the clutter and focus you. I want to live in unity with you so I can experience eternal joy.

How can you live in unity with God?

A Peaceful Tomorrow

"Do not worry about tomorrow, for tomorrow will worry about its own things. Sufficient for the day is its own trouble."

MATTHEW 6:34 NKJV

Many people today are overwhelmed and overbooked. Life is fast and it doesn't want to slow down for anyone. There are multiple assignments to complete, schedules to keep up with, meals to cook, chores to do, and relationships to foster. And if that's not enough, you may feel it all needs to be done with excellence.

Time out! When you are feeling stress creep into your life, it is important to get back to where God wants you to be—right next to him. He wants to gently walk with you and teach you how to overcome stress.

Father, you know all the things that stress me out. Help me to run to you before everything is overwhelming. Thank you for the peace you give me in place of my anxiety.

"Don't worry about tomorrow, for tomorrow will bring its own worries. Today's trouble is enough for today."

MATTHEW 6:34 NLT

All you can do is try your best and that is enough. Did you get that? Trying your best is enough! Nobody expects you to have super powers.

Often we put an unnecessary pressure on ourselves because we only see things through our own eyes. When we begin to spend more time with Jesus and ask him to help us see things as he sees them, we can begin to accept that trying our best is enough. Accept it tonight!

God, give me confidence to stand through the stress, knowing that doing my best is all that matters. I can have peace now knowing you will continue to take care of me through all my tomorrows.

What areas of your life are most stressful right now?

No Temptation

No temptation has overtaken you that is not common to man. God is faithful, and he will not let you be tempted beyond your ability, but with the temptation he will also provide the way of escape, that you may be able to endure it.

1 CORINTHIANS 10:13 ESV

Wouldn't life be so much easier without temptation? Temptation has this sneaky way of pressing in on every angle of our lives. It surrounds us. It can be relentless, and it is always unwelcome. Often it feels like we can't look left or right without it presenting itself.

A general misconception is that if we are tempted, then we must be weak in our faith. This is not true. No one is immune to temptation—even Jesus was tempted. The struggle was as real for him as it is for you. Go to him today with your struggle. He knows just what you need to do.

God, I need your help today. It's hard to share my temptation with you because I know you are perfect and you have never sinned. But you are full of grace. Help me bring my temptation into the light so it can't fester in the darkness.

The temptations in your life are no different from what others experience. And God is faithful. He will not allow the temptation to be more than you can stand. When you are tempted, he will show you a way out so that you can endure.

1 CORINTHIANS 10:13 NLT

We don't have to give into our temptation because in every moment of every day we are given choices. God's grace lies in those choices. We can bend a knee to our temptress and give up, or we can take up the shield of faith and fight.

When our temptation becomes too much for us to bear alone, we can go to the church, loved ones, or trusted family members and friends to help us. Shedding light on dark areas is a great way of escape. Those who really love us won't judge us; they will offer grace, compassion, and understanding. We don't have to battle temptation alone. God gives us others to battle with—we just have to be bold enough to ask them for help.

God help me to show humility by asking my trusted friends and family members for help in my area of weakness. I need your mercies that are new every morning. Thank you for your forgiveness and grace.

What temptation are you fighting? Don't attempt to battle it alone.

A God in Control

We ourselves boast of you among the churches of God for your patience and faith in all your persecutions and tribulations that you endure.

2 THESSALONIANS 1:4, NKJV

When life is going well, it's much easier to have faith, patience with the unknown, and trust in God's plan. There is nothing much to worry about, nothing really to fear, nothing to get caught up on. You can float through the day-to-day, loving the way God has made your life turn out.

It is a good thing to be thankful for what God has given you. What gives you credibility, though, is being thankful in hardship. Be someone who others boast about when it comes to faithful endurance.

God, I thank you that you are a God who gives me so much but also requires much. Help me endure through hardship and trial. I need you in every moment.

We proudly tell God's other churches about your endurance and faithfulness in all the persecutions and hardships you are suffering.

2 Thessalonians 1:4 nlt

When your life feels out of control, when tragedy has struck, when fear sets in, this is when you are truly tested. This is when your dependence on God is most evident. Do you handle it on your own or rely on God? Do you act out in anger or trust his next step for you? Do you seek him first before you leap?

Endurance is not built by a quick fix. Endurance is built when you keep coming back, time and time again, putting more and more trust in God's hands.

Father, I don't want the quick fix. I want to take my time and learn how to endure with you. All of this testing will be worth it in the end.

Can you see how testing causes endurance?

Serving for Everyone

Your love must be real. Hate what is evil, and hold on to what is good…. Do not be lazy but work hard, serving the Lord with all your heart. Be joyful because you have hope. Be patient when trouble comes, and pray at all times. Share with God's people who need help.

ROMANS 12:9, 11-13 NCV

How many times a day do we see our hands but fail to recognize their potential, their power, their ability? Our hands can be used to bless many people around us. They can wipe away tears. They can work. They can comfort. They can serve!

There are many practical ways to serve those around us. We could give our time to a lonely friend, buy a meal for someone in need, spend an afternoon cleaning our elderly neighbor's home, or visit someone who is in the hospital. Think of how you can serve someone else today.

God, thank you that you made us to love each other and to give ourselves to each other. I know this might mean helping with jobs that don't seem rewarding or pleasant. But there is both joy and eternal blessing to be found in serving. I want to choose that today.

Don't just pretend to love others. Really love them. Hate what is wrong. Hold tightly to what is good. Never be lazy, but work hard and serve the Lord enthusiastically. Rejoice in our confident hope. Be patient in trouble, and keep on praying. When God's people are in need, be ready to help them. Always be eager to practice hospitality.

ROMANS 12:9, 11-13 NLT

We often think of serving others as a job for those in ministry: pastors serve, missionaries serve, humanitarians serve. But serving is something we can all do.

Think back to the last time you were served. Maybe someone finished a task that you were dreading or unknowingly provided for a great need. In an act of service, we not only receive a tangible gift, we also catch a glimpse of God's love for us. When we serve others, we are being used by God to show his love. Were you able to serve someone today? Could you serve again tomorrow, or tonight?

God, please show me who is in need of my time or resources. I want to love and serve the way you want me to. Give me clear instructions so I can be a blessing to those around me.

How can you serve someone today?

Praise Always

Let everything alive give praises to the Lord! You praise him!
Hallelujah!

PSALM 150:6 TLB

We can praise God and weep at the same time. It sounds
impossible, but with God it is not. Our hearts can feel heavy;
yet, we can still praise God in our trials because he is good.
He is good when things are hard. He is good when the future
seems bleak. He is good when the rest of the world isn't. He is
good all the time.

Praise God for his goodness today. Let everything praise him
today!

Jesus, may I always glorify and praise you regardless of how my
days are going. May my reaction to hard times be to speak of your
goodness and your faithfulness. Let me never forget how worthy
you are.

Let everything that breathes sing praises to the LORD!
Praise the LORD!

PSALM 150:6 NLT

Sometimes praising God when it's the last thing we want to do is actually the best thing we can do. When we praise God, we draw nearer to him. We can praise God with our actions, with our voices, and with our attitudes. Our praise confirms in our spirits that he is worthy, that he is holy, and that he is sovereign.

Praising God declares that he is the center of our lives, and that he has overcome every struggle we face.

God, I declare your faithfulness this evening. Everything in my life exists because of you. I want you to be at the center of my heart and my mind every day. You are so worthy of my praise.

Is God at the center of your life?

Priceless Love

Though you have not seen him, you love him. Though you do not now see him, you believe in him and rejoice with joy that is inexpressible and filled with glory, obtaining the outcome of your faith, the salvation of your souls.

1 PETER 1:8—9 ESV

It's kind of a strange thing, loving someone you have never seen. And yet, when you experience the love of your almighty Father, there is no doubting his existence. There's a joy that comes from knowing his love and from seeing it play out in your life.

Though words don't do it justice, once you've felt it, there can be no denying God's love is something absolutely breathtaking. Be encouraged by the love of God today.

Lord, thank you for your incredible love. You have filled my very soul with a joy that is truly inexpressible, and I am no longer the same because of it. I praise you for saving me with your beautiful love.

You love him even though you have never seen him. Though you do not see him now, you trust him; and you rejoice with a glorious, inexpressible joy. The reward for trusting him will be the salvation of your souls.

1 PETER 1:8–9 NLT

While others may think it's a little weird to love someone you can see only through spiritual eyes, you can rejoice in the knowledge that you have a love that surpasses everything else. It's one that floats your spirits and makes you want to sing with joy that bubbles up from the inside and spills out into all areas of your life.

Let God's love fill you to overflowing tonight. Look forward to the reward waiting for you because you have trusted in the God you cannot see.

Father, even though I can't see you, I know you are with me. Your love and your joy surround me. They are undeniable!

Love without sight is a strange but wonderful thing.

A Beautiful Song

Sing praises to God, sing praises!
Sing praises to our King, sing praises!
For God is the King of all the earth;
Sing praises with understanding.

PSALM 47:6-7 NKJV

We may not all have the voice of an angel, but we can all sing, no matter how good or bad it sounds. God created you with a voice and with lips that can praise him for all the good things he has done.

Sing to the king of the earth and the king of your heart. He will delight in your song of praise, even if he is the only one that appreciates it. Sing because you understand his goodness. Sing because you understand his grace. Sing because he is worthy!

God, you are the king of all the earth. You have been good to me.
You have shown your grace to me. Teach me to delight in singing
your praises. I know you delight in me when I praise you.

Sing praises to God. Sing praises.
Sing praises to our King. Sing praises.
God is King of all the earth,
so sing a song of praise to him.

Have you ever thought about what happens in church on a Sunday morning? We gather together in a building with a bunch of people we may or may not know, and we… sing? That must seem pretty strange to people who have no concept of praise and adoration.

No matter how weird it seems, singing praise to God by yourself or with others is an amazing act of worship that God loves. Hearts united in praise singing to our creator—that's a pretty big deal to God. Sing to him this evening! Sing, sing, sing!

God I am full of adoration and praise. I sing to you tonight because you are worthy of my praise and worship. You are the King of all the earth. I bless your name.

Sing your own beautiful song to your Creator tonight.

Beauty Itself

You are altogether beautiful, my darling;
there is no flaw in you.

SONG OF SONGS 4:7 NIV

Do you ever hear voices in your head that tell you you're not good enough? Do you need others' approval and opinions to give you confidence in a particular area? There is good news: you are enough! God made you just the way he wants you. Those voices in your head that say you're not good enough are lies.

You can do anything God calls you to. When the voice of discouragement comes, silence it. What God thinks of you matters the most.

God, I don't feel flawless at all. Thank you that you see me that way. You speak the truth to me. Help me to be confident of the beauty that you see in me.

My darling, everything about you is beautiful,
and there is nothing at all wrong with you.

SONG OF SONGS 4:7 NCV

The more you practice dwelling on the truth, the more you will see how valuable you are in your Maker's eyes. Allow him to define you and be proud of who that is. Who God has created you to be is much better than anyone you could even try to become on your own.

When you find yourself desiring approval, shift your thinking and seek God for confidence. He will speak the truth over you. He says everything about you is beautiful—and he knows you better than anyone else does.

It's hard to believe that you think I am beautiful, God. But I choose to believe those words. I let your truth wash over me now, scrubbing off the lies and opinions of others. I find my confidence in you and you alone.

In which areas of life do you feel most insecure?

Clothed in Beauty

Above all, clothe yourselves with love, which binds us all together in perfect harmony.

COLOSSIANS 3:14 NLT

Women, in general, were created with a gift for appreciating beauty. We have an eye for lovely things. For many of us, this includes clothing. Adding to our wardrobe can be such fun! But what's the best thing we could ever put on? It's a cloak of love.

When we are wrapped in love, and covered with it from head to toe, it changes everything.

Lord, I pray that I'd cover myself in love, each and every day. I praise you for giving me the gift of love, and I pray that I'd pass it along to everyone I meet.

Over all these virtues put on love, which binds them all together in perfect unity.

COLOSSIANS 3:14, NIV

A love cloak always fits, and the bigger it is the better it is. It's something that looks good on everyone, and it never goes out of style. When you wear your love for all to see, you can't help but feel peace and harmony with those around you.

When you're dressing yourself tomorrow, don't forget to take a moment and put the love of God on first. You'll never look better!

God, I want others to see your love in me before they see anything else. Help me to wear your cloak of love proudly. Bring unity in all my relationships as I continue to wear your love.

Are you still wearing God's cloak of love?

Accepted

Long ago, even before he made the world, God chose us to be his very own through what Christ would do for us; he decided then to make us holy in his eyes, without a single fault—we who stand before him covered with his love.

EPHESIANS 1:4-5 TLB

Applications are essential for gleaning the promising applicants from the inadequate. Fill out this form, and find out if you're approved for a home loan, for college admittance, for a credit card. We put our best qualities on paper, tweak our weaknesses, and hope for approval. But rejection is always a possibility.

With God, however, our acceptance has already been promised. We must only appeal to his son Jesus, who steps in on our behalf and petitions for our approval. Feel his acceptance of you today!

Father, I stand on the promise that there is nothing in my history— no past or present sin—that can separate me from your love.

He chose us in him before the creation of the world to be holy and blameless in his sight. In love he predestined us for adoption to sonship through Jesus Christ, in accordance with his pleasure and will.

EPHESIANS 1:4 -5 NIV

There is no credit flaw, no failing grade, and no past default that Jesus' death on the cross doesn't redeem completely. Because we are covered with his loving forgiveness, there is no flaw in us. We are accepted by God as part of his family and redeemed by his grace for his eternal kingdom.

Cast everything upon God and have faith; you are wholly accepted and abundantly loved!

God, this is too great to fathom. You have wholly accepted me into your family and I will spend an eternity with you. Thank you for choosing me. I choose you tonight too.

Can you believe your acceptance in God's family?

Courtyard or Castle?

When the right time came, God sent his Son, born of a woman, subject to the law. God sent him to buy freedom for us who were slaves to the law, so that he could adopt us as his very own children.

GALATIANS 4:4-5 NLT

Once upon a time, a courtyard in a faraway land overflowed with lost children. They were all very dirty, dressed in threadbare garments, and deeply hungry. Some children had gaping wounds, others were bruised or limping. A man walked among them, gently tending to their needs.

Next to the courtyard was a majestic castle with bright flags and high winding turrets. The doors of the castle were wide open, and inside was a banquet with delicious food, warm fires, and robes of velvet. A king sat inside, surrounded by his children who were clean, fed, and smiling. He looked out over the courtyard with longing… to be continued tonight!

God, this courtyard sounds intriguing, and the majestic castle even more so. Give me a picture of you caring for your children as I go about my day.

When the set time had fully come, God sent his Son, born of a woman, born under the law, to redeem those under the law, that we might receive adoption to sonship.

GALATIANS 4:4-5 NIV

Two children approached the doorway, smelling the food and feeling the warmth from the castle. The man in the courtyard took their hands and asked if they would like to join the king as his children. One leaped for joy, and, not waiting another second, ran into the castle. The other held back, looked down at her filthy rags, and shook her head. She wandered back amongst the other children.

Daughter, are you wandering in the courtyard? Why do you believe that your sins make you unworthy of God's banquet? You have been bought at a high price and are adopted into the family of God. He is your Father, and he offers the only cleansing redemption you need.

Oh Father, I want to come into your castle. I want to accept all you have to offer me without hesitation or shame. Thank you for your loving grace that has set me free.

Will you accept the invitation into the castle?

Blessed Assurance

"I know that my Redeemer lives,
and he will stand upon the earth at last.
And after my body has decayed,
yet in my body I will see God! I will see him for myself.
Yes, I will see him with my own eyes.
I am overwhelmed at the thought!"

JOB 19:25-27 NLT

In a matter of days, everything was destroyed. First his 11,000 livestock and servants were stolen, burned, or killed. Then his ten children died at once. To make matters worse, this unfortunate man's skin was plagued with painful sores, which he scraped with a piece of broken pottery.

How could anyone endure such tragedy? To be fair, Job mourns, and laments, and weeps. He is confused, hopeless, and weak. On top of feeling cursed and desperate, he is taunted by his friends and wife: "Give up on God; he has given up on you! Stop waiting on God to redeem you; he has obviously forgotten you!" But Job refuses to curse God, as God knew he would, and despite the tragedies he endured, Job is assured that God will not fail when it matters most.

God, thank you that with you by my side I can endure testing and trials. You have always been faithful. My hope is in you.

"I know that my Redeemer lives,
and that at the last he will stand upon the earth;
and after my skin has been thus destroyed,
then in my flesh I shall see God,
whom I shall see on my side,
and my eyes shall behold, and not another.
My heart faints within me!"

JOB 19:25-27 NRSV

Job's faith had been weakened by testing, but he clutched desperately to the one promise that could sustain him: no matter what happened to Job in his earth-bound life, nothing could take away the joy he would share with God in his eternal life.

Everything on earth is a fleeting treasure, a momentary comfort that can be lost in a flash. But the assurance of your eternal place in his kingdom, if you have submitted your life to Jesus Christ, is indestructible.

Father, assurance of a better life with you is all the hope I need.
You are on my side, and you will be standing when all else falls.
Help me to keep my gaze fixed on you.

How does Job's story bring you comfort today?

He Is Real

He has given us his very great and precious promises, so that through them you may participate in the divine nature, having escaped the corruption in the world caused by evil desires.

2 PETER 1:4, NIV

The test for authenticity is often measured by applying some kind of force or foreign substance to that which is being tested. Determining whether something is made of real gold can be accomplished in a number of ways. Perhaps the most simple is by rubbing the gold on an unglazed ceramic plate. The color of the mark left on the plate determines the authenticity of the gold. Real gold will leave a gold mark. Fake gold will leave a black mark. You can see the analogy, can't you?

God is real, and he is good. He has given us an example of how to remain authentic in a world full of fraud and deception. If you have been hurt by someone you thought was being real with you, you are not alone.

God, I remember your great and precious promises today. I press on in your strength. Help me to be real with you and with others.

Thus he has given us, through these things, his precious and very great promises, so that through them you may escape from the corruption that is in the world because of lust, and may become participants of the divine nature.

2 PETER 1:4 NRSV

At some time in our lives, we will undergo an authenticity test. We might be put through several—daily. What mark will we leave when we encounter those tests? When we brush up against difficulty? If we are authentic Christians, the mark we leave will be gold—the true mark of Christ.

Unfortunately, black marks and scars cover many people who have been hurt by fakes. Be authentic about who you are and share the true love of God with others.

Father, I want to be full of your real, authentic love. Help me to have grace for others' mistakes. I want to leave a mark that is golden—a mark that reflects your good character.

How can you continue to leave an authentic mark of gold when you brush up against difficult situations?

A Joyous Time

"My heart rejoices in the LORD!
The LORD has made me strong.
Now I have an answer for my enemies;
I rejoice because you rescued me."

1 SAMUEL 2:1 NLT

Consider for a moment the most joyous time of your walk
with Christ. Imagine the delight of that season, the lightness
and pleasure in your heart. Rest in the memory for a minute,
and let the emotions come back to you. Is the joy returning?
Do you feel it? Now, hear this truth: The way you felt about
God at the highest, most joyful, amazing, glorious moment is
how he feels about you all the time!

What a glorious blessing! Our joy is an overflow of his
heart's joy toward us; it is just one of the many blessings God
showers over us. When we realize how good he is, and that
he has granted us everything we need for salvation through
Jesus, we can rejoice!

God, today seems so far away from when I first found you. Help
me to remember the delight of the season when I was so close to
you. You delight in me all the time! That truth is amazing.

"My heart exults in the LORD;
my strength is exalted in my God.
My mouth derides my enemies,
because I rejoice in my victory."

1 SAMUEL 2:1 NRSV

The season of your greatest rejoicing can be now, when you consider the strength God provides, the suffering from which you have been rescued, and the rock that you can stand on. His blessings don't depend on our feeling joyous; we experience joy because we realize his gracious blessings.

Lift your praises to him and let your song be never-ending. Relive the season of blessing each and every day!

Father, thank you that I can always find joy when I consider your blessings. You have rescued me, stood me upon your rock, and given me strength. I honor you today.

Do you remember the most joyous time of your walk with Christ? Relive it today!

Stronger than You Know

Do you not know? Have you not heard?
The LORD is the everlasting God, the Creator of the ends of the earth.
He will not grow tired or weary,
and his understanding no one can fathom.
He gives strength to the weary and increases the power of the weak.
Even youths grow tired and weary, and young men stumble and fall;
but those who hope in the LORD will renew their strength.
They will soar on wings like eagles; they will run and not grow
weary, they will walk and not be faint.

ISAIAH 40:28-31 NIV

No matter how puny your muscles may seem to you, you
are stronger than you know. You can do anything you set
your mind to. And you'll do it because God gives you a
supernatural strength to power through and endure.

God never wearies. He never gets too tired to make it
through the worst the world can throw at you. Put your hope
in him, and he will give you strength beyond your wildest
imagination.

God, I simply put my hope in you today and ask for you to give me
strength to run and not grow tired.

Surely you know. Surely you have heard.
The Lord is the God who lives forever, who created all the world.
He does not become tired or need to rest. No one can understand
how great his wisdom is.
He gives strength to those who are tired and more power to those
who are weak.
Even children become tired and need to rest,
and young people trip and fall.
But the people who trust the Lord will become strong again.
They will rise up as an eagle in the sky;
they will run and not need rest;
they will walk and not become tired.

ISAIAH 40:28-31 NCV

Others around you may stumble and fall, but not you! God gives you the tenacity to make it through your toughest of times when you just ask him. He wants to run with you until the very end.

Ask God for strength in each area where you feel weak. He loves it when you admit your need for him. It's when he gets to show off his strength the most!

God, I need your help tonight. There are many areas of weakness in my life and I want you to be shown strong through my weakness. Help me to glorify you as you give me strength.

In what areas do you feel weak right now?

My Comfort

To all who mourn… he will give: beauty for ashes; joy instead of mourning; praise instead of heaviness. For God has planted them like strong and graceful oaks for his own glory.

ISAIAH 61:3 TLB

How many thoughts does the human brain conceive in an hour? In a day? In a lifetime? How many of those thoughts are about God: who he is and what he has done for his children? Imagine your own thoughts about life—grocery lists, dentist appointments, song lyrics, lost keys—and your thoughts about God—his majesty, holiness, comfort, creativity—weighed against each other on a scale. Likely, it would tip in favor of the many details of human existence.

These temporary details overshadow the one comfort and promise we can rely on: the gospel of Jesus' birth, death, resurrection, and ascension for our eternal salvation. Wipe every other thought away. For those burdened by their sin it is of great comfort: Jesus came to give us new life!

Father, help me not to let the details of life overshadow the promise of comfort you bring me. You are my salvation and my peace.

Provide for those who grieve in Zion—
to bestow on them a crown of beauty
instead of ashes, the oil of joy instead of mourning,
and a garment of praise instead of a spirit of despair.
They will be called oaks of righteousness, a planting of the LORD
for the display of his splendor.

ISAIAH 61:3 NIV

You are not a weak sapling limited by inadequate light and meager nourishment. You are a strong and graceful oak, soaring and resilient for the glory of God. Ashes and mourning and heavy burdens are relieved. The scales tip to this one weighty thought: you are his.

Let your thoughts stretch above the canopy of everyday human details to bask in this joy: he has given you everything you need in Jesus. Think on that for a while to tonight and declare it as truth over your life.

God, you have given me everything I need. Sometimes I don't see it,
but I choose to ponder that tonight. You are my comfort and my joy.

How does the thought of having everything you need in Jesus bring you relief today?

The Source of Compassion

The LORD is compassionate and gracious,
Slow to anger and abounding in lovingkindness.

PSALM 103:8 NASB

Consider the Israelites wandering in the desert: God had rescued them out of bondage and went before them in a pillar of fire, providing for their every need and protecting them. What did they offer him? Complaints. Listen to the psalms of David—the man after God's own heart—as he lays his burdens at the feet of God, praising his majesty and might. But what does David do when he wants what he cannot have? Steals, murders, and lies.

God loves his children regardless of their sin, their past, and their failings. This love is poured out on us with consideration and patience. We aren't dealt with as we deserve; rather, according to his great love for us. Can we say the same about how we treat those around us?

Father, help me to show compassion to others as you have shown it to me. You see everything I don't and I trust that you know what is best in each situation.

The LORD is compassionate and gracious,
slow to anger, abounding in love.

PSALM 103:8 NIV

Paul, who gave his life to preach the gospel to people near and far, shared the astounding gift of God's grace to Jews and Gentiles alike. But who was he before his conversion? A hateful, persecuting murderer of Christians.

God sees the great potential in each of us. Are we compassionate, slow to anger, and full of love like he is? Or are we offended, impatient, and aggravated? Repent, and then rejoice! God has compassion for you. You are forgiven and he loves you abundantly!

God, thank you for forgiving me over and over again. Thank you for seeing something beautiful and special in me and not giving up on me when I sinned, and sinned again. Help me to show this compassion and grace to others.

How does God's compassion change the way you face each day?

Calm My Heart

When you go through deep waters and great trouble, I will be with you. When you go through rivers of difficulty, you will not drown! When you walk through the fire of oppression, you will not be burned up—the flames will not consume you.

ISAIAH 43:2 TLB

When the hospital doors slide open and we aren't sure what news will greet us, God is compassionate. When the boss calls us for a meeting and dismissal is a real possibility, God is gentle. When we return home late at night to find our personal treasures stolen or destroyed, God is comforting. He cares so deeply for us.

Some see God as distant, vengeful, or condemning. Others see God as kind, affectionate, and attentive. Make sure you are one who sees his kindness. He is faithful and he can calm your heart today.

God, I need your calm in my storms. I need to know that you are right beside me in the rivers of difficulty. You will not let me drown or be consumed by the circumstances around me. I take this promise with me today.

When you pass through the waters,
I will be with you;
and when you pass through the rivers,
they will not sweep over you.
When you walk through the fire,
you will not be burned; the flames will not set you ablaze.

ISAIAH 43:2 NIV

Sometimes circumstances become too overwhelming.
Mountains of anxiety rise up and we feel isolated and alone.
Let no doubt take root; God cares deeply, loves fully, and
remains faithful, ever at our side in times of trouble. Though
our sorrows overwhelm us, he is the comfort that we need.

Will you take his hand, offered in love, and receive his
comforting touch? Will you remember his faithfulness and
let it calm your heart? He is with you! You will not drown! The
flames will not consume you! Cling to his promises, and the
mountains, as high as they may seem, will crumble at your feet.

Father I hold on to this sweet promise today—you are with me
always.

Which mountains of difficulty do you need to see crumble in
your life today?

Sober and Alert

Think clearly and exercise self-control. Look forward to the gracious salvation that will come to you when Jesus Christ is revealed to the world.

1 PETER 1:13 NLT

Every day we face situations where we need to exercise self-control: in our attitudes toward others, especially when we disagree with them; with our friends when faced with conviction differences; with social media and maintaining healthy boundaries and time limits; with work commitments and making sure we try our best.

The wonderful news is that we don't have to be controlled by our own desires, whims, or strongholds. We are not weak; in fact, God has made us strong. We can be patient with our family, hold to our convictions, and develop healthy habits and boundaries. God's power lives within us!

God, thank you that your power lives in me, and that power gives me the ability to do what is right. Help me to remain sober and alert.

With minds that are alert and fully sober, set your hope on the grace to be brought to you when Jesus Christ is revealed at his coming.

1 PETER 1:13 NIV

Sometimes the pressure or expectation to have self-control can be overwhelming—especially when we are struggling with habits that are proving difficult to break free from. We might feel like we are at the mercy of our temptation.

There is no need to become frustrated with our sin. Instead, we can hold our heads high and defeat whatever habit enslaves us or temptation that entices us because God has given us self-control. There is hope to be free from old patterns. We don't have to let our sin patterns control our lives. We can take charge, make changes, and break bad habits.

Father, I don't want to forget that self-control isn't something I have to muster up; it is already in me! I want to take hold of it, and take back control today. Thank you for giving me the strength to do so.

In what areas of your life do you need to exercise more self-control?

Lifted Up

You, O LORD, are a shield about me,
My glory, and the One who lifts my head.

PSALM 3:3 NASB

Picture a young girl running a race. She leaps off to a great start when the gun sounds. She pushes her way to the front of the pack in no time and sets a pace that is tough to compete with. As she rounds the final corner with the finish line in sight, she stumbles. She tries desperately to regain her balance, but it's too late. She crashes to the ground. Trying to be brave, she jumps up and sprints the final yards to complete the race—in fourth place.

Head hung low, skinned knees burning, and vision blurry, she walks over to her coach. He gently lifts her chin to the sun, and brushes away the tears that have spilled over. As her bottom lip begins to quiver, he reassures her that everything is going to be ok. That life is full of painful moments that creep up unexpectedly, but it's also full of second chances. "Don't give up on yourself," he says, "I haven't given up on you."

Father, you don't give up on me. Thank you for your tender voice that encourages me to keep going when I stumble.

You, LORD, are a shield around me,
my glory, the One who lifts my head high.

PSALM 3:3 NIV

When we've given up, run away, lost the plot, or stumbled and fallen, God doesn't give up on us. When we come to him with our heads hung low, he lifts our chins, looks deep into our eyes, and whispers tender words of compassion that reach the deepest places in our hearts.

Do you feel like you can't look up? Let your face be tipped to the Son. Allow the words of Jesus to wash over your wounds and bring healing to your heart, soul, and mind this evening.

God, so many times I trip and fall. It's embarrassing and I feel ashamed. Thank you for your love that washes over me and removes my shame. I look to you tonight for healing and renewal.

How do you think God feels about you in this moment?

All I Need

I know what it is to be in need, and I know what it is to have plenty. I have learned the secret of being content in any and every situation, whether well fed or hungry, whether living in plenty or in want. I can do all this through him who gives me strength.

PHILIPPIANS 4:12-13 NIV

It happens on occasion, when the heavy spring rains come, that some homeowners find themselves on hands and knees trying to staunch the flow of water into their basement. The water rushes in, not down from the walls or windows, but up from the rising water table and through the foundation. And they bow low, soaking up all that they can.

It's a trying time, to be sure, as patience wears thin and towels pile high. But remember the living water, which springs up and gives life to the full! We can remind ourselves that it is only on our knees as servants that we draw abundantly from these waters, because they rush quickly to the lowest places— places that only a humble servant can access.

God, I know the best place for me to be in trying circumstances is on my knees. Help me to be patient and humble so I can access your rivers of strength.

I know how to live when I am poor, and I know how to live when I have plenty. I have learned the secret of being happy at any time in everything that happens, when I have enough to eat and when I go hungry, when I have more than I need and when I do not have enough. I can do all things through Christ, because he gives me strength.

PHILIPPIANS 4:12-13 NCV

It's painful at times, hard on the back and knees, to be brought low. But the heart soars, and all your thirsts are satisfied when you are content with what you have been blessed with and you choose to serve others instead of yourself.

Jesus came not to be served, but to serve. Can you think of any better place for you to be than serving others? Let his living water fill you up to overflowing with gratitude and praise.

Father, I see how good it is to be content with what I have and to serve others who have less. Fill me with your living water as I choose to give of myself not expecting something in return.

What areas of your life do you struggle to be content in?

Supernatural Courage

I eagerly expect and hope that I will in no way be ashamed, but will have sufficient courage so that now as always Christ will be exalted in my body, whether by life or by death.

PHILIPPIANS 1:20 NIV

That's a pretty strong declaration: one exemplified in the life of Vibia Perpetua, a married noblewoman and Christian martyr who died at twenty-two years of age in Third Century Rome. There is a record of her diary entries detailing her life in prison and final hours. Perpetua was arrested for her profession of faith in Christ and threatened with a harrowing execution if she did not renounce her faith. She had many compelling reasons to do just that—a nursing infant for one!

Early martyrdom wasn't only about dying for the profession of faith. It was about humiliation and torture carried out in a kind of sporting arena—with fans celebrating the demise of the victims. Yet, Perpetua displayed incredible fortitude in her final hour. Read her account and you'd have to agree that her courage could not possibly have been attributed to a human characteristic. Her courage came from God.

God, I know my story is very different than Perpetua's, but I want that kind of courage to show in my everyday decisions. I ask for your courage to be in me today.

I expect and hope that I will not fail Christ in anything but that I will have the courage now, as always, to show the greatness of Christ in my life here on earth, whether I live or die.

Having courage, being brave, remaining firm—we can only hold on for so long. Sometimes we need to recognize that it's time to call on the supernatural strength of our Father. He gives us enough courage to walk through any trying circumstance.

When you find yourself at the end of your courage supply, boldly ask God to replenish the stock. What are you going through today that needs a touch of supernatural courage to get through?

Father, you know how very weak I am. Thank you that I don't have to muster up enough courage to get through every situation. You have more than enough courage for me. I ask you for a measure of that courage this evening. I want to live a pure and holy life for you.

Can you be honest with God about your need for him?

Delighted in Me

My beloved speaks and says to me:
"Arise, my love, my beautiful one,
and come away,
for behold, the winter is past;
the rain is over and gone.
The flowers appear on the earth,
the time of singing has come."

SONG OF SOLOMON 2:10-12 ESV

When we read this verse in Song of Solomon, we may feel like looking behind us for the person God is really talking to. It can be a little uncomfortable to have his gaze so intently upon us. We're nothing special, after all! Not beauty queens, academic scholars, or athletic prodigies of any kind. We might not be musical, or crafty, or organized. Our house might be a mess, and we could probably use a manicure.

Some say that romance is dead. It's not for God: the lover of our souls. He desires nothing more than time with his creation! Spend some time with him this morning before life gets hectic.

God, I want to spend time with you this morning. I need your touch. I need your reassurance that I am yours and that you desire to be with me. I need to know that you are bringing a time of singing into my life.

My lover spoke and said to me,
"Get up, my darling;
let's go away, my beautiful one.
Look, the winter is past;
the rains are over and gone.
Blossoms appear through all the land.
The time has come to sing;
the cooing of doves is heard in our land."

Song of Solomon 2:10-12 NCV

Do you feel a bit squeamish under an adoring gaze? There is good news for you! You are, in fact, God's beautiful one! And he does, indeed, want to bring you out of the cold winter. He's finished the watering season and it is finally—FINALLY—time to rejoice in the season of renewal.

Why do you feel uncomfortable under the gaze of the one who loves you more than anyone else ever could? The time has come. He is calling you, regardless of how unworthy you may think you are. Arise! He is waiting for you.

Father, thank you for waiting for me. Thank you for calling me into your arms. Thank you for continuing to pursue me.

Will you arise and come away with your beloved?

My Deliverer

I waited patiently for the LORD;
he turned to me and heard my cry.
He lifted me out of the slimy pit,
out of the mud and mire;
he set my feet on a rock
and gave me a firm place to stand.
He put a new song in my mouth,
a hymn of praise to our God.
Many will see and fear the LORD
and put their trust in him.

PSALM 40:1-3 NIV

God loves us with a sacrificial love that escapes our human understanding, overwhelms our human selfishness, and humbles our human pride. Through the sacrifice of his only Son, Jesus Christ, mankind is delivered from the fate of eternal separation from God.

When we are separated, bowed low and desperate, he hears our cry. When we are forgotten and despairing, he comforts our loneliness. And when, because of our own sin, we are wicked and depraved, he cleanses us of our offensiveness and makes us suitable for glory.

Father God, thank you for delivering me out of my sin and
wickedness. I wait for you this morning. Hear my cry, I pray.

I waited patiently for the LORD.
He turned to me and heard my cry.
He lifted me out of the pit of destruction,
out of the sticky mud.
He stood me on a rock
and made my feet steady.
He put a new song in my mouth,
a song of praise to our God.
Many people will see this and worship him.
Then they will trust the LORD.

PSALM 40:1-3 NCV

God has done the impossible task of making us into something worthy of his name; he takes us from instability to security, gives us a song of praise, and makes our conversion a testimony for all creation to see. Our deliverance is an opportunity for many more to hear of his love and trust him to deliver them as well.

He has delivered you, perhaps from a pit whose depth is beyond your understanding. Be assured today that your deliverance is a miracle; it is steady and safe, and the song in your heart will be a message for many.

God, let my testimony of your love and grace be shown to those around me as I share your wonderful story of deliverance.

How can you sing God's promises loud and clear today?

Devotion

I will sing of the LORD's great love forever;
with my mouth I will make your faithfulness known
through all generations.
I will declare that your love stands firm forever,
that you have established your faithfulness in heaven itself.

PSALM 89:1-2 NIV

God in his great power and faithfulness never fails us, never gives up on us, and will never leave us alone, out on a limb, to fend for ourselves. His love for us remains—regardless of our circumstances or our weaknesses—strong and immovable. His devotion to his children exceeds that of all parents, whose love for their children seems unmatched, but is only human.

Not only does God match our love, he surpasses it. He is without limits, and nothing can ever change God's devotion for you. Think on that today.

God, thank you for a love that is without limits. Even just the thought of that sounds impossible. But you are the God of the impossible! You are forever faithful.

I will always sing about the LORD's love;
I will tell of his loyalty from now on.
I will say, "Your love continues forever;
your loyalty goes on and on like the sky."

PSALM 89:1-2 NCV

This truth is overwhelmingly satisfying; when such devotion has been proven, what else could attract our gaze? Where else could our eyes find such beauty and purity as they do upon the face of Jesus? In awe, we recognize that his gaze is fixed right back at us, seeing us as a lovely and worthy prize. We can neither deserve this gaze nor escape it. We are flawed, but he is unwavering in his love for us.

Do you know that the Father is wholly devoted to you? Do you know that he longs to be with you—to comfort the deepest part of you that aches and burns? His great love for you is yours to enjoy forever. Do you doubt it, or can you accept that it is true?

Father, help me truly see your devotion toward me. When doubts creep in and thoughts overwhelm my mind, give me reassurance that your love for me is beyond measure.

How do you feel about God's devotion toward you?

He Encourages Me

The humble will see their God at work and be glad.
Let all who seek God's help be encouraged.

PSALM 69:32 NLT

"Come on!" "You can do it!" "You're almost there!" Strings
of praise and faces filled with expectant wonder look on. If
you were standing outside the door, you'd think someone was
about to accomplish something extremely difficult. You might
rush into the room to examine for yourself what momentous
occasion was taking place. And you'd perhaps be perplexed at
the scene in front of you. The adults in the room are crouched
down on the floor looking intently at… an infant rocking
back and forth on hands and knees. It's an amusing picture,
but one we can learn from.

Even when you feel your daunting milestone is somewhat
pathetic—like moving and arm and a leg—God wants to be
your constant source of encouragement. Ask for his help, and
acknowledge his work in your life as you move from stalling
to crawling.

God, sometimes I need encouragement just to move from one
place to another. Thank you for your patience and constant
encouragement.

The poor will see and be glad—
you who seek God, may your hearts live!

PSALM 69:32 NIV

Obstacles in life come our way, and sometimes we feel like we have to figure them out all on our own. We rock forward in faith and then back as doubt creeps in. Forward again as emotions propel us, and back once more as they overwhelm.

What we fail to recognize is that our Father delights in seeing us make that first move forward. He looks on in excitement as we lift an arm and then a leg. Ever encouraging, our God beckons us: *Come to me. You can make it. You're almost there.*

Father, this evening I choose to move toward you. I want to be closer. I want to be with you. Thank you for helping me to press on even when you could have given up long ago. You are a wonderful Father.

What do you need encouragement for today?

Royalty

Listen, daughter, and pay careful attention:
Forget your people and your father's house.
Let the king be enthralled by your beauty;
honor him, for he is your lord.

PSALM 45:10-11 NIV

Beautiful princess adorned with grace, you were created for greatness. You are royalty. Your Creator, the King of kings, is your heavenly Father. This is not just a name that we use loosely as another way to describe God. He is both your Father, and the King of all kings. Your Father is the King, and he adores you.

As a princess, are there areas in your life that you need to refine? Rest in the knowledge that your Father loves you just because you are his daughter.

Heavenly Father, I am so blown away that I am your princess. It's what most girls dream of and so many of us miss. You are the King and you are enthralled by me, your daughter. What could be better than that?

Listen, O daughter,
Consider and incline your ear;
Forget your own people also, and your father's house;
So the King will greatly desire your beauty;
Because He is your Lord, worship Him.

PSALM 45:10-11 NKJV

We need to fully understand what it means to be God's princess. We have a very special calling. Representing what a young woman should be, in the eyes of the Lord, is very important. The music we listen to, the clothes we wear, and the shows we watch all reflect on our position as princess.

If we take pride in being royalty and want to represent our Father's kingdom well, we are more likely to make decisions that will bring him honor. Think about those things tonight as you get ready for your beauty sleep.

My King, I want to represent your kingdom well. I know I have a lot of work to do, but I also know that your grace and your love wash over my flaws. I worship you this evening and ask you to work on me so I can better represent you.

With which areas of your life do you best honor your Father, the King?

A Future

"He will wipe away every tear from their eyes, and death shall be no more, neither shall there be mourning, nor crying, nor pain anymore, for the former things have passed away."

REVELATION 21:4 ESV

The sin and sadness of life can make it seem like an endless night, where we are continually waiting for the dawn of Christ's return. In the darkest of nights, it doesn't always help to know that he will return someday, because this day is full of despair.

We live for the promise of his return. This promise overcomes our pain, our longing, our desperation, and our limits. All things become bearable and light under the assurance of seeing Jesus, embracing him, and gazing on his beauty!

Oh Jesus, a bright future with you, full of hope and joy and void of pain, suffering, and tears, sounds so good. Help me to patiently wait for you.

"God will wipe away every tear from their eyes; there shall be no more death, nor sorrow, nor crying. There shall be no more pain, for the former things have passed away."

REVELATION 21:4 NKJV

Beloved, God is your comforter. Don't lose heart. He is coming for you! It can be hard because he seems to be taking a long time, but he is preparing a place for you. You are not forgotten in this long night; your pain is familiar to him.

Keep your eyes fixed on him, and soon you will hear his voice! He is also longing for that moment when we will be made into a pure and spotless bride. There is nothing more for us in that moment but to marvel at him. Glorify him. Love him. Thank him.

God, I believe you desire to see all sorrow wiped away. I know eternity is not so far away; yet it sometimes feels like it is. Help me tonight to see the promise of eternity anew.

How does the promise of eternity help you through your current situation?

Trusting the Rock

Through Christ you have come to trust in God. And you have placed your faith and hope in God because he raised Christ from the dead and gave him great glory.

1 PETER 1:21 NLT

Balancing at the edge of the cliff, a climber clutches the ropes. Far below, waves crash against the rocks, the spray reaching up toward her toes. She looks up at the guide, firmly gripping the rope, and then beyond his firm stance to the anchor hammered into the cliff side. With a firm push, her legs propel her beyond the ledge and out into space, dropping toward the sea.

Of course she trusts the guide. His strong grip, years of experience, skill, and familiarity with the landscape go a long way in convincing her that she will belay safely to the bottom of the cliff. But it's the rock, pierced by the anchor, which gains her deepest faith. The rock will not fail, will not crumble, and will never falter under her weight. Sound familiar?

God, you are my rock. I depend on you for strength today.

Through Him believe in God, who raised Him from the dead and gave Him glory, so that your faith and hope are in God.

1 PETER 1:21 NKJV

As we leap, sometimes stumbling, along the cliffs of life, who can we trust? God our Father offers us an anchor in Jesus Christ, who overcame death and is the only hope we have. We can jump with ease from any height, knowing that his strong arms of love will surround us and that our destiny is sure.

Our faith grows stronger in this truth: we share in the glory of Jesus through his death and resurrection. Have you had to really trust God lately? How did you place your faith and hope in him?

Father God, thank you for being so trustworthy. Thank you that I never have to doubt you. You have anchored me in your Son, and your strong arms of love surround me tonight.

Are you willing to jump, knowing that God is your anchoring rock?

He Is Faithful

Your lovingkindness, O LORD, extends to the heavens,
Your faithfulness reaches to the skies.

PSALM 36:5 NASB

Few love stories demonstrate a higher level of faithfulness than that depicted by the life of Hosea the prophet. He was given what seemed to be a very unfair task—to take a prostitute as a wife and commit to loving her. He would watch as his wife and the mother of his children chose to leave the family and return to her life of prostitution. But it didn't end there. Hosea went in search of his wife, and finding her in her debauchery, he paid to bring her back home with him— guilty, broken, and dirty.

It would seem a romantic tale of undying love had it happened naturally. However, this story is even more inconceivable when considering that Hosea walked into it with his eyes wide open. Hosea's choice to obey God in spite of what he would suffer is beyond admirable.

God, I want to display my faithfulness to you like Hosea demonstrated. Help me not to chase after things of the world, but to remain faithful to you and your purpose for me instead.

Lord, your love reaches to the heavens,
your loyalty to the skies.

PSALM 36:5 NCV

The loyal story of Hosea sounds oddly familiar, doesn't it? Jesus, commissioned by the Father, pursued us until we decided to become his. But we just can't seem to keep ourselves out of the mess of this world.

Jesus doesn't quit. He comes for us again. The price he paid to restore our relationship was his life. He gave up everything to bring us home. That is faithfulness in its fullest measure. Do you know how precious you are to the Father? His faithfulness toward you cannot be exhausted. Let yourself believe it this evening.

Jesus, thank you for coming to rescue me time and time again. You have paid for me and yet still I struggle. Thank you for your grace and patience. You are my wonderful, merciful God.

How does your unfaithfulness cause you to doubt the faithfulness of God?

Make Me Brave

When you lie down, you will not be afraid;
Yes, you will lie down and your sleep will be sweet.
Do not be afraid of sudden terror,
Nor of trouble from the wicked when it comes;
For the LORD will be your confidence,
And will keep your foot from being caught.

PROVERBS 3:24-26 NKJV

A pilot watches the flashing red light. A mother searches frantically for her child between the aisles. A driver glances in the rearview mirror at an oncoming truck. Certain fears have a gripping embrace, paralyzing to the body. The heart pounds, pupils dilate, palms sweat.

Other fears overwhelm the mind, causing anxious thoughts and sleepless nights. How will the bills get paid this month? Will the doctor have bad news? Family members need help, friends are overwhelmed with suffering, and we can't make it all okay. That's when we need to trust God for the right kind of help at the exact right time.

God, I trust you with my fear and worry. You tell me not to be afraid. I need your help to make that a possibility.

When you lie down, you won't be afraid;
when you lie down, you will sleep in peace.
You won't be afraid of sudden trouble;
you won't fear the ruin that comes to the wicked,
because the LORD will keep you safe.
He will keep you from being trapped.

PROVERBS 3:24-26 NCV

When fearful thoughts flood our minds, God's words of wisdom and comfort can get washed away. If we can learn to fully trust him, he will calm our fears and still our quickened hearts. We can be fearless because our confidence is in God and his promises.

Let the flood of terror subside and be assured that God is your refuge. He lovingly attends to your every need. Do not be afraid!

Father, I admit, it's not easy to just stop being afraid. I need you to help me re-train my mind. Help me to take thoughts captive. Help me to lie down tonight to a sweet sleep full of peace.

What fears are holding you captive today?

A Temper Tantrum

What is causing the quarrels and fights among you? Don't they come from the evil desires at war within you? You want what you don't have, so you scheme and kill to get it. You are jealous of what others have, but you can't get it, so you fight and wage war to take it away from them.

JAMES 4:1–2 NLT

Temper tantrums are as common for adults as they are for children; they just look different in action. Children haven't learned to curb the screaming and stomping vent of frustration or anger, while adults have more restrained behavior. But the heart is the same, and the reactions stem from the same provocation.

Let us submit to God's forgiveness and draw near to him for his cleansing and purifying grace. It washes over us, and our tantrums are forgiven. When we humble ourselves, he promises to exalt us. What more could we want?

God, as I go about my day, help me to trust you fully and not try to get my own way. I don't want to be selfish and pushy with others. I want to love. I want to be happy for other people when they have things I want.

Do you know where your fights and arguments come from? They come from the selfish desires that war within you. You want things, but you do not have them. So you are ready to kill and are jealous of other people, but you still cannot get what you want. So you argue and fight. You do not get what you want, because you do not ask God.

JAMES 4:1-2 NCV

James cuts right to the heart of sin. We want what we want but we don't have it, so we throw a tantrum. It's amazing how simple it is! Watch a child and this truth will play out soon enough. Watch an adult, and it may be more difficult to discern, but unfortunately it is there in all of us.

Praise God for his amazing grace, which is extended to us for this very reason. God's forgiveness is bigger than all of that. Thank him tonight for his mercy and grace. He loves it when you dwell on that.

Father, I know I am selfish and sometimes very childish in my behavior. Help me to mature in this area. I want to be kind and forgiving toward others. I want to be generous and helpful. Help me to put myself in the position of a servant instead of arguing and fighting to get my own way.

Do you see responses in yourself that remind you of a child throwing a tantrum?

When I Am Weak

"My grace is sufficient for you, for my power is made perfect in weakness." Therefore I will boast all the more gladly of my weaknesses, so that the power of Christ may rest upon me.

2 CORINTHIANS 12:9 ESV

Do you ever find yourself suddenly aware of your own glaring weaknesses? Aware that, if left up to your own good works, you wouldn't stand a chance of attaining salvation? We should find great comfort in the fact that we are nothing without salvation in Christ Jesus.

Thankfully, God made a way for us to be united with him, despite impatience, selfishness, anger, and pride. God deeply cares for us and patiently sustains us with steady, faithful, and adoring love.

God, I prayerfully submit my weaknesses to you, so through you I can be strong. Your transformative love is waiting to graciously restore me.

"My grace is enough for you. When you are weak, my power is made perfect in you." So I am very happy to brag about my weaknesses. Then Christ's power can live in me.

2 CORINTHIANS 12:9 NCV

Amazingly, God's love embraces and transforms our weakness when we yield it to him. Weakness isn't something to be feared or hidden; weakness submitted to God allows the power of Christ to work in and through us.

When we know our weakness, we are more aware of our need for his strength. And we know that he hears our cry for help before we even utter it. When we put ourselves in a position of humility and ask him to be strong where we are weak, he is delighted to help. You don't have to ask a knight in shining armor twice to rescue his princess.

God, rescue me from myself. I know I am weak, and I know I need you. I humble myself before you tonight and ask that my weakness would be a place for you to show off your strength.

What does it look like to boast in your weaknesses?

My Freedom

Creation itself will be set free from its bondage to corruption and obtain the freedom of the glory of the children of God.

ROMANS 8:21 ESV

Some days begin with praises on our lips and a song to God in our hearts. Humility covers us like a velvet cloth, soothing and delicate and gentle. The truth of God plays on repeat: "God is good! God is good! I am free!" and the entire world's darkness cannot interrupt the chorus.

But other days begin by fumbling with the snooze button and forfeiting the chance to meet him in the quiet stillness. Pride, then, is a sneaky companion, pushing and bitter and ugly, and we wonder if we will ever delight with God again. How did you wake up this morning?

God, regardless of how I feel this morning, you are good and I am free! Help me to make this day the best day by dwelling on your incredible gift of freedom and grace.

That everything God made would be set free from ruin to have the freedom and glory that belong to God's children.

ROMANS 8:21 NCV

The ups and downs should be familiar by now, perhaps, but can we ever become accustomed to the holy living side-by-side with our flesh? One glorious day, flesh will give way to freedom, and there will be no side-by-side. Only the holy will remain. This leaves praise on our lips and a song in our hearts, the unending chorus of his goodness, the velvet covering as we sit before his heavenly throne.

Do you know how much God wants you to rest in his presence? He is waiting and faithful and tender. When you spend time with him, there is no need to hide. You can be exactly who you are. You can say everything you want to say. There is freedom in his presence.

God, I want to share my heart with you this evening. Thank you that you have allowed me the freedom to do just that.

How does freedom sound to you right now?

Dine with Me

"Here I am! I stand at the door and knock. If anyone hears my voice and opens the door, I will come in and eat with that person, and they with me."

God created you for relationship with him just as he created Adam and Eve. He delights in your voice, your laughter, and your ideas. He longs to fellowship with you just as he did with his first son and daughter.

When life gets difficult, do you run to him with your frustrations? When you're overwhelmed with sadness or grief, do you carry your pain to him? In the heat of anger or frustration, do you call on him for freedom? He is a friend that offers all of this to you—and more—in mercy and love. He is worthy of your friendship.

God, you are my best friend. You care about me more than anyone in the world, and you know me better than I know myself. Thank you for your friendship.

"Here I am! I stand at the door and knock. If you hear my voice and open the door, I will come in and eat with you, and you will eat with me."

REVELATION 3:20 NCV

The friendship God offers to us is a gift of immeasurable worth. There is no one like him; indeed, there is none as worthy of our fellowship than God Almighty, our Maker and Redeemer. Train your heart to run first to God with your pain, joy, frustration, and excitement. His friendship will never let you down!

Write down your criteria for great friend, and then look no further. God's friendship surpasses all expectation.

Lord, sometimes I can't get over the fact that you want to be with me all the time. You never get sick of me and my annoying habits. You love spending time with me. I am so grateful for a friend who sees everything there is to see about me, and still wants to hang out.

What are you looking for in a "perfect friend"?

More Grace

He gives more grace. Therefore He says:
"God resists the proud,
But gives grace to the humble."

JAMES 4:6 NKJV

Maybe you've heard stories of people suffering tragedy, or maybe you're living through a tragedy yourself. Either way, if you had been told you would encounter tragedy, you'd probably have thought, "There's no possible way I could go through that." And you would be right. You couldn't. You couldn't watch a loved one suffer, couldn't handle losing someone close to you, couldn't continue on if your family turned against you. Why? Because you hadn't yet been given the grace to walk through that situation.

There's enough of God's grace for every situation. Admit your weakness and ask for grace. The moment you ask, his grace is yours in the precise measure you need it.

God, I need your grace in perfect measure today. Help me through this situation I find myself in today.

He gives more grace. Therefore He says:
"God resists the proud,
But gives grace to the humble."

JAMES 4:6 NKJV

Do we really believe that people who go through tragedy and come out stronger on the other side are any different than ourselves? That they are superhuman somehow? They aren't. They just got to a place where they recognized their desperate need for God's grace in their circumstance—and they asked him for it.

God doesn't call us to walk through seasons of difficulty on our own. He desires to pour out his grace on us. When we need more, he'll pour out some more. And still more. His grace is limitless. His only requirement for ample grace is humility.

Father, help me to stop thinking I can get through life just fine on my own. I can't. I need your grace.

Have you found yourself in a situation that seems far beyond your scope?

Irrational Path?

Lord, teach me your ways,
and guide me to do what is right.

PSALM 27:11 NCV

There is a Family Circus cartoon where the son is asked to
take out the garbage. The drawing then traces the tangled and
erratic pathway between the boy and his final destination.
He bounces over couches, through windows, under
wheelbarrows, around trees, between siblings, all on the way
to the curbside trash can.

Our lives can feel like this at times: unpredictable, illogical,
and inconsistent. Changes in work, marriage, family, or
church can make the road seem irrational, uneven, and
confusing. But God makes us the promise of a steadfast path
when we keep his covenant.

God, teach me your paths. I know they are different than the ones
I think are best. Your paths really do make the most sense because
you know the full picture.

Teach me how to live, O Lord.
Lead me along the right path.

PSALM 27:11 NLT

When we consider our lives through our limited human perspective, the path seems wavering. But the guidance of Jesus Christ is, in fact, steadfast! Your path has been chosen and your feet have been set upon it. Truly, it is a path of love and faithfulness.

God has made a covenant with you and you keep it when you trust him—even in the refinement of your path. It will be uncomfortable at times and you might ask yourself why his guidance is winding you around in the craziest of directions, but trust him! His paths are perfect.

Father, I admit at times I feel like your path takes unnecessary turns, and there are never any shortcuts. But I know that you are perfect and you desire to make me more like you. I trust you with the path for my life.

How do you recognize God's faithful leading even when your path feels a little uncertain?

My Healer

"Daughter, your faith has made you well; go in peace and be healed of your affliction."

MARK 5:34 NASB

The woman in the crowd had suffered for more than a decade. All of her money had been spent on doctors, but instead of finding healing she was worse than ever. She had one hope, and she reached for it as Jesus passed by her in the crowd. She believed that just a touch, not even from his holy hand but from his garment alone, would bring the healing she desired.

In his brief but blessed response, we hear Jesus' heart for his ailing child: "Daughter, I love your faith! You came to the right place for healing; I know everything about you and the pain you have suffered. Because you have believed in my love for you, you are healed! Be at peace."

Healing Father, I believe these words for myself today. You know what I have suffered and you desire to see me healed. Thank you.

"Daughter, your faith has healed you. Go in peace and be freed from your suffering."

MARK 5:34 NIV

Often, we become fixated on doctoring our own wounds so we can make it through the day. They may be physical, emotional, mental, or spiritual and we may have tried every possible means to treat them. Why not turn instead to the one who can fully repair us? To the one who knows the temperature of our faith in him, rather than just diagnosing our present and burdensome afflictions? Only faith will give us the peace we need to go forward.

He calls you his daughter. He knows your burdens, and he wants your faith to be in him. Put your faith in his goodness and be made whole.

God, make me whole. I ask for your healing touch tonight. You know everything I need healing for and I believe you can do it. Speak wholeness and life into my body this evening.

What are you seeking healing for today?

Do I Dare Hope?

There is surely a future hope for you,
and your hope will not be cut off.

PROVERBS 23:18 NIV

Abraham took God at his word. Everything about his present circumstance made the idea that he would have a son ridiculous. His body was as good as dead. His own wife laughed at the thought that she, a woman of ninety, body worn out and barren, would nurse a child of her own.

And yet, God had said it—this God that could give life even to the dead and who could call into existence things that didn't yet exist. Abraham would have a son. More than that, his descendants would one day be as numerous as the stars in the sky. Abraham was fully convinced that God was able to do what he promised even when it looked impossible.

God, help me to have faith like Abraham had. He believed you could do what seemed to be impossible. Your promises are always fulfilled, in your perfect time. Help me to trust in your timing.

You will be rewarded for this;
your hope will not be disappointed.

PROVERBS 23:18 NLT

Hope starts with the promises of God. When doubt, discouragement, or despair threatens your soul, take heart. We have a God that has already spoken words of life and certainty that will prove to both revive and carry us.

Hope is taking God at his Word, believing that all he has said is sure. We have this hope as a trustworthy anchor for the soul (see Hebrews 6:19), allowing us to confidently expect that God will do all he has said he will do.

Father, you say that those who hope in you will not be put to shame. I thank you for that promise this evening. I do place my hope in you.

Which promise from God's Word will you choose to believe this week?

Beauty Imagined

The precepts of the LORD are right,
giving joy to the heart.
The commands of the LORD are radiant,
giving light to the eyes.

PSALM 19:8 NIV

Children often wonder about the face of God, imagining what he looks like and how his voice might sound. "I want to see God! Where is he?" Where, indeed, beloved? God is in the beauty, showing off for you. When you see something lovely, you are seeing your Daddy's handiwork. When you hold a newborn baby, and look up and marvel, "I see God!" truly, God is there.

Yes, he has created something miraculous, and the miracle inspires his creation. Let him be your inspiration and see him in the beauty all around you today. Don't let his handiwork go unnoticed!

Creator God, you have created so many beautiful things. How can I possibly stop and marvel at all of them today? I am so appreciative of your creativity and inspiration.

The commandments of the LORD are right,
bringing joy to the heart.
The commands of the LORD are clear,
giving insight for living.

PSALM 19:8 NLT

It's an amazing circle, God's inspiration. He gives us many good gifts—vibrant colors, bursting flavors, comforting warmth, moving melodies, and unimaginable beauty—that our hearts cannot help but respond. And our inspirations pour out in a beautiful offering of worship back to our Creator.

Even his commands, his laws, and his guidance are inspiring! Described as right and radiant, his acts of loving and devoted instructions keep us safe. They also draw us nearer to our Father and give joy and light.

Father, I am inspired by your creation and your Word tonight.
There is so much beauty to be imagined in this life and the next.
I am in awe of your creativity.

Can you prayerfully submit to God's leadership and the creative gifts he has planned for you?

Known By Name

Lord, you have examined me
and know all about me.
You know when I sit down and when I get up.
You know my thoughts before I think them.
You know where I go and where I lie down.
You know everything I do.
Lord, even before I say a word,
you already know it.

PSALM 139:1-4 NCV

There are people who are terrible with names. And then there are parents. They address you by every name in the household—quite possibly including the dog—all while looking you in the eye… and they gave you the name in the first place!

Chances are, if your name is Mary, Elizabeth, Sara, or Rachel, you've met someone with the same name. There may be thousands of people with your name, or there might just be a handful. Either way, it makes no difference to God. He knows you fully. Listen to God as he calls out, "My daughter, beloved one, I know you."

Father, you know me completely. Thank you for loving me and wanting a relationship with me. Thank you for investing so heavily in my life to know me so well.

O Lord, You have searched me and known me.
You know my sitting down and my rising up;
You understand my thought afar off.
You comprehend my path and my lying down,
And are acquainted with all my ways.
For there is not a word on my tongue,
But behold, O Lord, You know it altogether.

PSALM 139:1-4 NKJV

God doesn't take a stab in the dark when you are approaching him, guessing a name and hoping he gets it right. He knows exactly who you are and why you are coming to him. He knows why you've stayed away for so long.

God knows the way your mind works, what you find funny, your favorite place to go and thing to do—and he loves you. He knows your deepest need, your most painful wound, and your darkest thoughts. And still he loves you. Bask in his intimate love tonight.

God, there is so much you know about me that I don't even know about myself. Teach me why you do the things you do, and why I respond the way I do. I want to be fully known by you, and I want to know you too!

How does hearing that you are intimately known by God bring you comfort?

He Is My Joy

Be truly glad. There is wonderful joy ahead.
You love him even though you have never seen him. Though you do
not see him now, you trust him; and you rejoice with a glorious,
inexpressible joy.

1 PETER 1:6, 8 NLT

Life is full of pain and sorrow. Jesus, described as a man
of sorrows and acquainted with grief, was no stranger to
mourning, weeping, and at one point even declared in agony
that he was sorrowful unto death. Jeremiah cried out that
his heart was sick within him and his sadness could not be
healed. Paul carried burdens so far beyond his strength that
he despaired of life. David's pain groans off the pages of the
psalms, and Job went so far as to say he wished he had died at
birth.

Can joy be found within the piercing anguish of loss? The
purest form of joy is often experienced in the arms of sorrow.
Joy flows in the middle of the darkness as we trust in God's
perfect ways, whispering through our tears, "Not my will, but
yours be done."

Father God, in my sorrow, help me to find your joy.

In all this you greatly rejoice, though now for a little while you may have had to suffer grief in all kinds of trials. Though you have not seen him, you love him; and even though you do not see him now, you believe in him and are filled with an inexpressible and glorious joy.

1 Peter 1:6, 8 NIV

Joy is clinging to our Savior with the knowledge that Jesus is still who he says he is, even when our pain feels overwhelming. Joy is going to the cross of Christ to sustain us, to give us hope, and to receive his grace and mercy for the days ahead.

Delighting in the Lord in the midst of heartache doesn't only produce joy. It is joy. Find God's joy in your heartache and difficulty tonight.

Finding joy in my difficulty isn't usually the first place I think of finding joy, Lord. But I want to start making this a habit. I can experience your joy this evening.

Which circumstance in your life is giving you the opportunity to experience joy in the Lord even as you walk through difficulty?

Life's Not Fair

He did not retaliate when he was insulted,
nor threaten revenge when he suffered.
He left his case in the hands of God,
who always judges fairly.

1 PETER 2:23 NLT

Our parents were right: life's not fair. We probably learned that first when we didn't get the larger half of the cookie, or when one of our siblings got to go somewhere special while we were at school. As we got older, we might have learned about the lack of fairness a little more harshly: perhaps through wrongful accusations, denied promotions, or unmet expectations.

It's easy to be disappointed with the unfairness of life. When wrongfully accused or misunderstood, it's hard not to take it to heart. We either want to defend our reputation until the bitter end, or disappear. When faced with these situations, we can rest in the knowledge that God is just. He will judge everyone fairly.

God, you see everything and you know the truth. Help me to be able to leave what I think is unfair in your hands. You are more than capable of sorting it all out.

When they hurled their insults at him, he did not retaliate;
when he suffered, he made no threats.
Instead, he entrusted himself to him who judges justly.

1 PETER 2:23 NIV

We hear about big trials, read about complicated court cases,
and watch movies dedicated to the theme of justice. But many
times even after a verdict is reached, the truth is uncertain.
It's all about how the case was fought—who had the best
lawyers and the most money. Has justice truly been served?

We don't have to worry about our accusers fighting their case
more convincingly. We don't leave our judgment in the hands
of a jury. Even the most expensive defense attorney can't
make a case against us that will last into eternity. God knows
what happened, and, more importantly, he knows our hearts.

Thank you, Father, that you know my heart and my intentions.
Help me to forgive others when they wrongly accuse me, and help
me not to quickly judge others so I won't wrongly accuse them.
I need your wisdom and your grace.

How does knowing that God is a fair judge help you let go of
your need to defend yourself?

Which Reward?

Remember that you will receive your reward from the Lord, which he promised to his people. You are serving the Lord Christ.

COLOSSIANS 3:24 NCV

It feels pretty good when we do something that goes above-and-beyond expectation and then we receive recognition through praise or a reward. It's ok that it feels good. If someone recognizes us for doing a good job, great! However, there are some people that can't wait to tell others about their achievements or acts of service so they can receive instant gratification and praise. This isn't the type of reward God wants us to have.

Take a moment to ask God to help you in seek his reward only. He will give you the grace you need to keep your good works between the two of you. God's reward is so much better than what anyone can give you here on earth.

Father, I know your reward is worth waiting for. Help me to be patient and wait for your inheritance.

You know that you will receive an inheritance from the Lord as a reward. It is the Lord Christ you are serving.

COLOSSIANS 3:24 NIV

It is God's heart for you to do things not for the reward and praise here on earth, but to keep the good things that you do between you and him. When you choose to do this, you are building up treasure in heaven.

If you show goodness to others and then choose to keep it quiet, you will be greatly rewarded. Don't worry. Your Father in heaven always sees. He doesn't miss a thing. Someday your reward will be of great worth!

God, you are always watching. You see everything I do—all the effort I put into my relationships, work, and home. Thank you that you will reward the work I do for you in full.

Are there areas in your life where you have been seeking an instant reward?

True Life

"I am the resurrection and the life. He who believes in me, though he may die, he shall live."

JOHN 11:25 NKJV

Do you want to know a secret? The world has been lying to us. It says, "Seize the day for pleasure; it might be the only one you have left!" But this is only a half-truth, a deception of God's Word that gives birth to flesh and sin instead of life and hope.

The truth is that we will live forever. Whether in heaven or hell, we will exist for all eternity. It is because of this truth that we must seize the day. Not because we fear our own death, which leads to light, but because we fear the death of those walking in darkness. Death has been sold as being the end of everything, but it is only the end of opportunities to put our trust in Jesus Christ.

God, I want to seize today for the right reasons. I want to make this day worth something because I spend it with you, doing your will. I don't want to be led by the world's definition of truth. Only you are truth and only through you do I have life.

"I am the resurrection and the life. The one who believes in me will live, even though they die."

JOHN 11:25 NIV

It's said that for those who don't have salvation in Jesus Christ, this side of life has the greatest happiness they will ever experience; for followers of Jesus, it has the least. It will only get better when we are face to face with our Savior, through whom we have hope, joy, peace, and the comfort of eternal light.

Find people to share the truth with. Be the light in the darkness, that they too might receive eternal life in Jesus!

Father, this life doesn't have the happiness I seek. Only you can truly fill every fiber of my being with joy and peace. Thank you for the abundant life you have promised after this life for those who believe in you. Help me to share this truth with others.

How can you embrace the truth that the best is yet to come?

He Is Love

We love because he first loved us. If anyone says, "I love God," and hates his brother, he is a liar; for he who does not love his brother whom he has seen cannot love God whom he has not seen.

1 JOHN 4:19-20 ESV

God's greatest commandments are to love him and to love one another. Loving him may come easy; after all, he is patient and loving himself. But the second part of his command can be difficult because it means loving intrusive neighbors at the backyard barbecue, offensive cousins at Christmas dinner, rude cashiers at the grocery store check-out, and insufferable guests who have stayed one night too many in the guestroom.

Loving one another is only possible when we love like Jesus. When we love out of our humanity, sin gets in the way. Obeying the command to love begins with God's love. When we realize how great his love is for us—how undeserved, unending, and unconditional—we are humbled because we didn't earn it. But he gives it anyway, freely and abundantly, and this spurs us on to love others.

Father, because you loved me I can love others.
I choose to do that today.

We love because he first loved us. If anyone says, "I love God," and hates his brother, he is a liar; for he who does not love his brother whom he has seen cannot love God whom he has not seen.

1 John 4:19-20 ESV

We represent Jesus Christ to the world through love, and we love to the degree that we understand his love for us. If we know how high and wide and deep and long his love is for us, then we have no choice but to pour out that love on others.

When we emanate God's love, the intrusive becomes welcome, the offensive becomes peaceful, rudeness gives way to grace, and the insufferable is overshadowed by the cross and all that Jesus suffered there. He did it for all of us; he did it for love.

God, help me to love others like you love me—like you love them. I know I need to understand your love for me so I can better understand how to love others. Teach me, God. I want to learn.

How can you show love to the unlovely?

All Things Possible

It is God who makes us able to do all that we do.

2 CORINTHIANS 3:5 NCV

In the midst of trying situations, there are days when we're so exhausted we feel like we can barely put one foot in front of the other. The thought of creating some semblance of a meal, or even getting out of bed for that matter, seems near impossible. Forget about responding gracefully when people say or do ridiculous things. Forget about the project that was supposed to be finished two weeks ago. Forget about going to that event we thought we wanted to attend. We just can't keep up.

What tasks seem impossible to you today? Let God rest on you in your weakness. Ask him to give you the strength you need to either do the things that have to get done, or to say no to the things that can wait.

God, you are the one who helps me do everything I do. I need to know what I should say "no" to. And I think I need to say "no" more often. Give me wisdom in this, I pray.

Not that we are competent in ourselves to claim anything for ourselves, but our competence comes from God.

2 CORINTHIANS 3:5 NIV

The good news is God doesn't expect us to keep up with the crazy life we currently live. In fact, he doesn't even want us to. His power is made perfect in our weakness. He is the one who makes us able. We can't make ourselves able.

When we allow ourselves to be weak in our busy moments, we give God the opportunity to show his ability—and he'll take that opportunity every time we give it to him. We don't have to be "willing and able"; we can just be "willing" because God is able.

God, help me not to boast in my competence or my ability to get things done. I can only do what I do because you have given me the ability to do it. I want to remember that and make sure I honor you for the gifts you have blessed me with.

God will make you able if you are willing.

My Peace

"The Advocate, the Holy Spirit, whom the Father will send in my name, will teach you all things and will remind you of everything I have said to you. Peace I leave with you; my peace I give you. I do not give to you as the world gives. Do not let your hearts be troubled and do not be afraid."

JOHN 14:26-27 NIV

Peace is much desired but often elusive. Just when we seem to be getting life under control, a new disaster strikes. Just when we find enough calm to settle our minds, a bigger calamity arises. Or worse, the waves of difficulty come one after another with no end in sight.

Because he knew our weak flesh, Jesus promised us a path to his peace even in this world of struggle—our Advocate, the Holy Spirit. Is your heart troubled or afraid?

God, please give me your promised peace. I believe that you will accomplish in me what this conflicted world cannot. Help me not to have a troubled heart today.

"The Helper will teach you everything and will cause you to remember all that I told you. This Helper is the Holy Spirit whom the Father will send in my name. I leave you peace; my peace I give you. I do not give it to you as the world does. So don't let your hearts be troubled or afraid."

JOHN 14:26-27 NCV

Those in the armed forces know what it's like to feel one barrage after another and then experience a silence that cannot be trusted. It leads to another onslaught, persistent fighting, and ongoing upheaval. Will there ever be an end to our conflicts? Why does peace elude us?

We find everything we need when we look to God's Word. The peace begged for on bumper stickers will always elude the world; the peace of Jesus Christ is the only lasting peace, the only true peace that we can attain while walking this earth.

Father, you hold the only peace that lasts through everything. I ask for that peace as I lay down tonight. Give me a restful sleep as I dwell on your peace.

Do you trust in the peace of God?

No Retirement

Let us run with perseverance the race marked out for us, fixing our eyes on Jesus.

HEBREWS 12:2 NIV

There is no such thing as retirement for those who serve God. There won't be a spiritual pension waiting for us so that we can finally relax and let others finish God's work. We might have travel ideas, plans to focus on a hobby, or dreams of unwinding and living easy while everyone else labors away, but God doesn't stop using us!

You can't retire yet. He will remain at your side every step of the way, until you bask in the full glory of the only paradise worth persevering for!

God, sometimes retiring sounds like the best idea. I get tired of running, tired of fighting. Give me strength to persevere as I keep my eyes glued to you.

*Let us look only to Jesus, the One who began our faith and who
makes it perfect.*

HEBREWS 12:2 NCV

Our prayers, testimonies, encouragement, wisdom, and faith
must never retire from use. Bringing glory to the kingdom
of God is a full-time effort requiring long-term endurance.
While we wait to enjoy that glory, God has plans that aren't
put off by our aging bodies. We are encouraged to continue
without interruption. We are promised those beautiful words
of approval, "Well done, good and faithful servant!" upon the
completion of our earthly journey.

In case you have doubts, know this: it will be worth it! Keep
your eyes fixed on his. You might run. You might crawl. You
might move mere inches per day. But if you remove the
tangles of sin and keep your eyes fixed on him, you won't
grow weary and lose heart. This is his promise.

*Father, I know at times I falter. Sometimes I need to slow down
and refuel. Other times I need to take a rest because I am fatigued.
Help me to know when you want me to run faster and when I
should slow down. I trust you.*

How does this help you endure through the struggles of life?

Unintelligible Prayers

Why am I praying like this?
Because I know you will answer me, O God!
Yes, listen as I pray.

PSALM 17:6 TLB

There are those days when words fail us. We can barely string a coherent sentence together, let alone articulate exactly what we need. Grief has found us and it seems to have taken over our ability to think, or speak, or pray. Tears roll silently down our cheeks, our hearts ache, and still no words come.

Be encouraged. Not only does God hear your prayers when they tumble clumsily from your lips, he knows what you need prior to you asking (Matthew 6:8). He's aware of what you require to get through today long before you can put it into words.

God, listen to my heart this morning.

I call to you, God,
and you answer me.
Listen to me now,
and hear what I say.

PSALM 17:6 NCV

Your prayers, no matter how unintelligible they seem to you or others, are heard and understood by God. Let your heart be filled with peace as you silently acknowledge your need for him. Your message to God is not lost in translation. He interprets it perfectly every time.

When you finally put words to your thoughts that seem completely inadequate, it doesn't matter. God hears your heart.

Father, thank you for being patient with me and for listening to my heart this evening.

How are you encouraged to pray today?

Delighting in the Storm

Let everyone who trusts you be happy;
let them sing glad songs forever.
Protect those who love you
and who are happy because of you.

PSALM 5:11 NCV

Huddled in the basement of the museum, visitors waited for the hurricane to pass. Children cried or slept, parents' expressions were tight and anxious. Museum staff held walkie-talkies and flashlights, beams bouncing nervously. Sirens wailed, winds howled, and the depths of the shelter shook as the mighty storm raged outside.

Imagine delighting through the storm, singing while the structures come crashing down, knowing all the while that you are standing under the mighty hand of God. When we truly trust God, we can be happy in situations that would typically be scary.

God, thank you for being so trustworthy. I know I don't need to be afraid because you are always near me.

Let all who take refuge in you rejoice;
let them ever sing for joy,
and spread your protection over them,
that those who love your name may exult in you.

PSALM 5:11 ESV

Even with modern engineering advancements implemented, those sheltered from the storm were worried. There was no guarantee of safety. Could we expect the huddled crowds to be singing for joy? Rejoicing in their place of refuge? If they were aware of the one who has promised to always protect, then their praises would echo off the shelter walls!

In the shadow of God's protection, we can be glad. He is the only one able to guarantee our safety! His protection spreads over us, stronger than any bomb shelter or apocalyptic bunker we could engineer.

Father thank you for protecting me. Thank you for showing me how to sing for joy when circumstances are difficult.

Can you relate to the need for protection today?

Substantial Provision

*Because of our faith, Christ has brought us into this place of
undeserved privilege where we now stand, and we confidently and
joyfully look forward to sharing God's glory.*

ROMANS 5:2 NLT

Pull up to the drive-through, place an order for the coffee
that will help start the day, and hear the cashier's words,
"Your order was paid for by the car in front of you." This
unexpected generosity gives birth to humbling gratitude,
and the day is now overcome with God's presence. A stranger
may have been the instrument of kind provision, but the
inspiration is unmistakable.

God is the author of generosity, providing us with all we need.
Some things, like free coffee at the drive-through, are small
provisions. Others are subtle or unseen altogether. But he is
working his love out in generous portions for you, his beloved!

*Father, you surprise me with blessings great and small. You give
me everything I need and so much more. I am truly thankful for
your generosity.*

Through him we have also obtained access by faith into this grace in which we stand, and we rejoice in hope of the glory of God.

ROMANS 5:2 ESV

Look at all God gave to Adam and Eve, and how little he asked for in return. They walked in his presence daily, enjoying authentic relationship with their Father. "Just don't eat the fruit from that tree or you will die." And then, even when they ate it, God provided atonement.

We, like Adam and Eve, have sinned and deserve death. But Christ is our substantial provision! As if eternity in his kingdom weren't enough, he blesses us each and every day, whether we acknowledge it or not.

God, I acknowledge your provision this evening and I thank you for it. There is nothing I have in this life without you having given it to me. I am so blessed.

In what ways have you seen God generously provide for you lately?

Sitting Still

Teach me your ways, O LORD,
that I may live according to your truth!
Grant me purity of heart,
so that I may honor you.

PSALM 86:11 NLT

If you've ever tried to clean a white dog who had decided
to run around in the mud, you'll know it seems like an
impossible task to get rid of every speck of dirt—especially
if said puppy isn't too keen on the bathing procedure. If
it could just sit and allow its owner to work carefully and
methodically, all traces of dirt could likely be eliminated. But
often neither the dog nor its owner has that kind of patience.

Does the thought of being thoroughly cleaned appeal to you,
or does it make you nervous? Maybe the answer is a little of
both. You can trust your Master to gently wash all the filth
away and cause you to be pure again.

God, I know I need to be washed clean by your loving forgiveness.
Do your cleansing work in me today.

Teach me Your way, O Lord;
I will walk in Your truth;
Unite my heart to fear Your name.

PSALM 86:11 NASB

Cleaning up the sin in our lives can feel similar to cleaning a dirty white dog. Finding and ridding ourselves of all impurity can be a slow and painful process. It might seem downright impossible at times. Maybe we don't want to be examined, or perhaps sitting still is the problem.

The good news is we don't have to try to purify ourselves. We allow God to do it for us. Fortunately, he is patient, and he has the perfect solution. He uses the sacrifice of his Son to wash away all of our dirt. Every last speck.

Father help me to submit to your cleaning process. I know I need to be patient while you work on my heart. Thank you for the sacrifice of your Son that makes me completely clean.

Can you sit still for long enough to let God cleanse you?

Promised Purpose

The LORD will fulfill his purpose for me;
your steadfast love, O LORD, endures forever.
Do not forsake the work of your hands.

PSALM 138:8 ESV

Life often doesn't turn out the way we think it should. When we're stuck in the middle of circumstances we never wanted—dreams lost and hope buried—it's difficult to find meaning in it all, and it can seem impossible to keep going. But God gives purpose to our pain and hope to carry on.

Hardships provide a distinct opportunity for the Lord to mold us more into his image. Hardships compel the God-loving souls to hold on to their God because of who he is, not because of what he can give.

Father, thank you for your promise to fulfill your purpose for me. I know you love me and you desire to help me be more like you.

The LORD will accomplish what concerns me;
Your lovingkindness, O LORD, is everlasting;
Do not forsake the works of Your hands.

PSALM 138:8 NASB

God promises that he will complete the work he began in us, making all things beautiful in his time. We have the blessing of embracing all that is going on in our lives as part of his trustworthy plan to glorify himself and to accomplish his loving intentions for us.

Have you seen God mold you more into the image of Jesus through painful circumstances? Allow him to show you his purpose this evening. He has a reason for everything he does.

God, I trust you with everything that concerns me. I know you have a purpose for my life and everything you allow to come at me will help me achieve that purpose somehow. Teach me to rely on you and allow hope to fill my spirit as I wait for you to do your work in me.

What hope does the promise of a fulfilled purpose bring you?

Relationship Reconciliation

Draw near to God, and he will draw near to you. Cleanse your hands, you sinners, and purify your hearts, you double-minded. Do not speak evil against one another, brothers. The one who speaks against a brother or judges his brother, speaks evil against the law and judges the law.

JAMES 4:8, 11 ESV

We were created for relationship. Since Adam expressed the need for a companion, people have sought fellowship together. But no matter how strong our desire to have healthy, loving relationships, it can be hard to move past the pain of a broken one. It may be a divorce, an estranged relative, or a longtime friend who has somehow become a bitter rival.

In order for reconciliation to take place, we must look to God for direction. Ask God to reveal what you can do to move forward in a relationship today.

God, if there's something I need to do in a broken relationship, please reveal it to me today. I want to be at peace with those in my family and with my friends.

Come close to God, and God will come close to you. Wash your hands, you sinners; purify your hearts, for your loyalty is divided between God and the world. Don't speak evil against each other, dear brothers and sisters. If you criticize and judge each other, then you are criticizing and judging God's law. But your job is to obey the law, not to judge whether it applies to you.

JAMES 4:8, 11 NLT

In order to reconcile a relationship, first you have to pray. Submit yourself to God and refuse to allow the enemy any further destruction. Next, ask God what sin, if any, you have committed to contribute to the dissent. Confess it, repent, and let it go. Now comes the hard part: don't speak out against the one you are at odds with. Don't slander, gossip, or share your grievance; it won't make things better. In fact, it only makes things worse.

Let the love of God flow through you and onto those you are at odds with. Begin to pray daily for reconciliation and restoration. God is your healer and he wants this relationship to be restored more than you do!

Father, I trust you to help me mend my broken relationships. Help me to forgive.

Can you extend forgiveness instead of judgment?

My Redeemer

The Spirit of the Lord is upon me,
because he has anointed me
to proclaim good news to the poor.
He has sent me to proclaim liberty to the captives
and recovering of sight to the blind,
to set at liberty those who are oppressed,
to proclaim the year of the Lord's favor.

ISAIAH 61:1-2 ESV

When Jesus, the long awaited Messiah, revealed his deity to his family, his disciples, and the crowds, they were expecting a mighty king who would deliver them from their oppressors and establish his everlasting kingdom. What they got was a humble servant who dined with tax collectors and whose feet were cleansed by the tears of a prostitute. Jesus wasn't exactly what they thought he would be. He was better!

Jesus delivers you from the bonds of sin and oppression through his death and resurrection and through your repentance from sin by faith. Proclaim this good news today; you have been set free!

Jesus, thank you for being so much more than anything I can imagine. Thank you for your Spirit that dwells in me and gives me confidence to share my faith with others.

The Spirit of the Sovereign LORD is upon me,
for the LORD has anointed me
to bring good news to the poor.
He has sent me to comfort the brokenhearted
and to proclaim that captives will be released
and prisoners will be freed.
He has sent me to tell those who mourn
that the time of the LORD's favor has come,
and with it, the day of God's anger against their enemies.

ISAIAH 61:1-2 NLT

Jesus came to bring salvation to those who were drowning in a sea of sin and sickness; those who were cast out and in need of holy redemption; those whom the religious leaders had deemed unworthy but whose hearts longed for true restoration. He came to redeem his people, but not in the way they expected.

It's hard to accept things a certain way when you were expecting them to happen a different way. But when God is the one in charge, you can trust that his way is so much better than yours. Believe that today and receive his wonderful favor.

God, you know all things. Thank you for giving me the opportunity to share your good news and see people saved, healed, and set free!

The Spirit of the Lord is upon you, and he has anointed you!

Perpetual Spring

"The water I give them," he said, "becomes a perpetual spring within them, watering them forever with eternal life."

JOHN 4:13–14 TLB

Have you ever been so thirsty you thought you'd never be able to take in enough water to quench your thirst? Maybe you've been somewhere so hot you were sure you would jump in a dirty puddle just to cool off. Imagine stumbling upon an oasis in the middle of the desert or a crystal clear swimming hole at the bottom of a waterfall in the jungle. How refreshing that would be!

God's Word will never run dry. His water is life-giving and eternal—refreshing! That perpetual spring is in you ready to be drawn upon at any moment of the day or night. What an encouragement that is when we are tired, frustrated, sad, or confused.

Father, thank you for the gift of your Word. You bring refreshment right when I'm feeling dry. You fill me up to overflowing with your spring of living water. I want to take your living water with me throughout my day.

"Everyone who drinks this water will be thirsty again, but whoever drinks the water I give them will never thirst. Indeed, the water I give them will become in them a spring of water welling up to eternal life."

JOHN 4:13–14 NIV

The word refreshment itself sounds like a cool drink for the weary soul. The Bible says, "The law of the Lord is perfect, refreshing the soul" (Psalm 19:7 NIV). God's Word is our source of life and energy. It gives us what we so desperately need, and it's available all the time! If you spend time in the Scriptures, you'll find his Word is in you, waiting to revitalize and invigorate you.

Spend time in the Word of God tonight and find that long, cool drink you are looking for.

God, I need your refreshing Word tonight. I want to be completely satisfied, my thirst totally quenched, by your life-giving Word.

In what areas of your life do you sense a need for refreshment?

Accepting Help

"Come to me, all of you who are weary and carry heavy burdens, and I will give you rest. Take my yoke upon you. Let me teach you, because I am humble and gentle at heart, and you will find rest for your souls. For my yoke is easy to bear, and the burden I give you is light."

MATTHEW 11:28-30 NLT

There are times when grief leaves you bone tired. The thought of doing even the most simple task seems overwhelming. Getting out of bed, getting dressed, cooking dinner, or taking kids to practice become insurmountable chores. The world continues to spin, and you can think of nothing you'd like better than to stop and get off for a while. Trying to keep up with life's demands feels impossible.

So don't try. Tell God how you feel. Bring your burdens to him and let him take care of it from there.

God, I surrender all of my burdens to you this morning. You care for me and you want to give me rest. Thank you for your easy yoke and light burden. I trade them for my worries and concerns today.

"Come to me, all of you who are tired and have heavy loads, and I will give you rest. Accept my teachings and learn from me, because I am gentle and humble in spirit, and you will find rest for your lives. The burden that I ask you to accept is easy; the load I give you to carry is light."

MATTHEW 11:28-30 NCV

Admit your weakness and ask God for his strength. You will find that he is very resourceful when you allow him to be. Someone shows up on your doorstep with dinner? Accept it. That was a gift of rest from God. A friend swings by to pick up your kids for practice? Say thank you. That was God, too.

Accepting that we need help can sometimes be the hardest part. Once we let go of the need to appear as if everything is ok, we are in a better position to receive help. How do you feel knowing that God is gentle, humble, and easy to please?

Jesus, you told me to come to you with my heavy burdens and you will give me rest. I ask for peaceful rest tonight as I sleep. I hand over my cares and concerns and let you create peace where there is chaos.

Can you find your rest in God today?

The Majestic King

Since you are God's children, God sent the Spirit of his Son into your hearts, and the Spirit cries out, "Father." So now you are not a slave; you are God's child, and God will give you the blessing he promised, because you are his child.

GALATIANS 4:6-7 NCV

Picture a beautiful white castle perched on a mountain top overlooking a crystal-clear lake surrounded by trees. Decadent turrets and towers reach high into the sky, affording a breathtaking view to all who are privileged enough to enter. High walls, a watchtower, and open parapets ensure maximum protection from enemy forces. Inside, vaulted ceilings and crystal chandeliers tower above sprawling staircases. Ornate sculptures and paintings grace the walls, and the grand hall echoes with laughter.

The King appears. For a moment, you tremble, unsure of how to respond. Then, as he advances toward you with arms wide open, you remember—this is your Daddy. And this is your home. You run as fast as you can into those arms, and lose yourself in his warm embrace.

Father, today, I revel in the eternity that awaits me.

Because you are sons, God has sent forth the Spirit of His Son into our hearts, crying, "Abba! Father! Therefore you are no longer a slave, but a son; and if a son, then an heir through God.

GALATIANS 4:6-7 NASB

The story from this morning sounds like a fairytale, but that picture doesn't even do justice to the home or the Father awaiting us. Gold, silver, sparkling jewels, decadence, opulence, splendor, immeasurable love, joy, peace, and unbroken relationship—it's our inheritance! The King of all kings calls us his children. That means we are royalty, and everything he has he wants to share with us.

In this life we will have trouble. We will suffer; we will hurt. But the promise of eternity with our majestic King and all he has created is more than worth it.

My King, I am humbled by your acceptance of me. Thank you for the beauty of eternal life and all you are preparing for me to enjoy.

How does eternity give you hope in the middle of your present circumstances?

Soul Restorer

"Stop wailing," Jesus said. "She is not dead but asleep." They laughed at him, knowing that she was dead. But he took her by the hand and said, "My child, get up!" Her spirit returned, and at once she stood up. Then Jesus told them to give her something to eat.

LUKE 8:52-55 NIV

Do you know who you belong to? Your father and mother rightly claim you as their child, but do you recognize Jesus as the one who restores you as his? He knows your coming and going, your every inner working; you are his.

God is faithful to the deepest needs of your heart; he knows you full well! Are you in need of healing? Of hope? Hear his voice and let your spirit be renewed!

God, I belong to you. Even though I have earthly parents, you are the one who claims me as your own. You love me deeply and you bring me refreshment and renewal. Thank you for bringing me into your family.

All the people were crying and feeling sad because the girl was dead, but Jesus said, "Stop crying. She is not dead, only asleep." The people laughed at Jesus because they knew the girl was dead. But Jesus took hold of her hand and called to her, "My child, stand up!" Her spirit came back into her, and she stood up at once. Then Jesus ordered that she be given something to eat.

LUKE 8:52-55 NCV

How difficult it is to put our needs into the hands of the Father! Do we dare hope? Imagine watching your child die and feeling the despair of her absence, only to have Jesus claim that she is asleep. Both the girl's father and Jesus loved the child; both claimed her as their daughter. But only Jesus commanded her spirit and her life. His child hears his voice and obeys his command; she gets up and is restored!

Listen to the voice of the Father today. He is calling you to hope and restoration.

Father, I gladly come to you asking for healing and hope. You are my soul restorer and I need you so much this evening.

Where is God directing you today?

Not Home Yet

"There are many rooms in my Father's house; I would not tell you this if it were not true. I am going there to prepare a place for you."

JOHN 14:2 NCV

Our homes on earth are significant. They are where we lay our heads, where we display our style, and where we commune with family and friends. But, truth be told, they are imperfect. Try as you might, you can never get that paint color right on your wall. Or when you buy the bedding that you love, you notice it has begun to fray. None of it lasts forever.

That is part of the reason that Jesus told us about our eternal homes. He wants us to look forward to them. He is preparing a place for us. Think about the place Jesus is preparing for you now.

Jesus, thank you that you are preparing a place for me. Thank you that my greatest joy in heaven won't be the place you prepared for me, but it will be dwelling in your very presence.

"In my Father's house there are many dwelling places. If it were not so, would I have told you that I go to prepare a place for you?"

JOHN 14:2 NRSV

We all have different tastes. Walk into the home of ten different friends and not one will be the same. How incredible then, that Jesus is preparing dwelling places for each one of us. Places that are designed for us to enjoy. How can he possibly know what each person will love?

We may not know exactly what our new homes will be like, but we can know that the one who is preparing them is the same one who knows our tastes better than anyone else. He sees your heart—and that's exactly how he knows where you will love to dwell.

Lord, you know everything there is to know about me. You know me even better than I know myself. Thank you that you carefully prepare a dwelling place for me that I will love. More importantly though, thank you that I will get to dwell with you!

Think of all the things you love about your home. Will it even compare to the dwelling place Jesus is preparing?

A Good Friend

A friend loves you all the time,
and a brother helps in time of trouble.

PROVERBS 17:17 NCV

God does not want us to see him as an ominous dictator but as a friend. He longs to talk to us and share in our joy and pain. In the same way, he wants us to have close, healthy friendships with others.

When we are purposeful about surrounding ourselves with people who encourage us, challenge us, and love us, we are better because of it. Think of one of those friends in your life and make sure you reach out to them today.

God, thank you for being my friend. Help me to be a good friend to others, encouraging, challenging, and loving them well.

A friend is always loyal,
and a brother is born to help in time of need.

PROVERBS 17:17 NLT

A true friend is one who loves and supports you through all of life's ups and downs. Friends lovingly tell you when you are making unwise choices, they congratulate you in your achievements, and they always encourage you in your relationship with God.

A good friend is one that will pray with you and for you. Their intention toward you is always good. Does this sound like another friend you know? Thank God for his friendship with you tonight.

Lord, I am so blessed to have you as my friend. Thank you for being with me through all of life's ups and downs, congratulating me and challenging me as I need along the way.

How does God show himself to be a good friend to you?

A Hiding Place

Wherever I am, though far away at the ends of the earth, I will cry to you for help. When my heart is faint and overwhelmed, lead me to the mighty, towering Rock of safety. For you are my refuge, a high tower where my enemies can never reach me.

PSALM 61:2-3 TLB

When emotional injuries—insecurities, anxieties, memories of abuse, conflict, or pain—that were buried long ago come to the surface of life, they transform from past scars to raw, gaping wounds, brand new and scorching.

Earthly bandages cannot completely heal the pain. We need God's touch, the balm of his tenderness, upon us. It aches, but he is a safe hiding place—a refuge when we are afraid to walk through the pain.

Do you believe that you are precious to him? That he loves you with a fiercely protective, eternally faithful, inescapable love? Well, he does.

God, I submit my wounds to your careful attention. Thank you for being my hiding place today.

From the end of the earth I call to you
when my heart is faint.
Lead me to the rock
that is higher than I,
for you have been my refuge,
a strong tower against the enemy.

PSALM 61:2-3 ESV

Abiding in his safety and leaving a wound open is hard. We have to see it, feel it, and let God walk us through the healing process. And that might take time. But he is a loving, worthy, compassionate Father, whose treatment roots out all infection and disease so that the scars can remain healed. We are safe when we are in his care, and he promises to protect us.

He is true and worthy and invites you to bring him all of your hurts, pains, regrets, and brokenness so he can put it back together.

Father, thank you for being a safe place for me to rest in. I come to you tonight ready to walk through the healing process.

Will you take refuge in God's arms tonight?

Sweet and Lovely

O my dove, in the clefts of the rock,
in the crannies of the cliff,
let me see your face,
let me hear your voice,
for your voice is sweet,
and your face is lovely.

SONG OF SOLOMON 2:14, ESV

Stress threatens to get the better of us, and sometimes we just want to hide. Remembering that secret bar of chocolate in the pantry, we may scurry off to do just that: bury ourselves away with the temporary but sweet comfort that helps the world slow down, if only for a moment.

We cannot outrun God's love for us, nor should we try. Instead, let's leave the false safety of the clefts and crannies and pantries with hidden chocolate and feel the pleasure of his friendship.

God, how can it be that you see me as beautiful and lovely? I am in awe of your gentle and perfect love. Help me to remember this throughout my day.

My beloved is like a dove hiding in the cracks of the rock,
in the secret places of the cliff.
Show me your face,
and let me hear your voice.
Your voice is sweet,
and your face is lovely.

SONG OF SOLOMON 2:14, NCV

Sometimes we want to scurry away from God. We get overwhelmed by his ministry, overdue for his forgiveness, or out of touch with his Word and we lose track of who he is. Instead of running toward him, we hide from him and look for other ways to meet our needs. We cannot hide from him, and in love he calls out to us.

God wants to hear your voice and see your face because he finds them sweet and lovely. Give him that pleasure this evening.

Father, I turn my face to you tonight. Thank you for looking at me with eyes of love and mercy. Thank you for finding me sweet and lovely. It is beyond what I can fathom.

Is there anyone else who can satisfy you so perfectly?

False Security

In peace I will lie down and sleep,
for you alone, Lord,
make me dwell in safety.

PSALM 4:8 NIV

Have you ever spent hours—or minutes that seemed like hours—searching frantically for Blankie, Paci, or Lambie in an attempt to quiet the inconsolable child sprawled on the floor? Ah, that wonderful security item. The magic silencer. The instant peace maker. The middle-of-the-night sanity that we are willing to fumble around in the dark for.

Think of all the times you've walked through trials and found yourself at a loss. Where do you go to feel secure? The best place you can go is to God. He is your security, and he gives you the strength you need to press on.

God, I don't want to look anywhere else for my security. I want to find it in you only.

I go to bed and sleep in peace,
Because, LORD, only you keep me safe.

PSALM 4:8 NCV

As kids grow older, we try to wean them off security items: the blankets that are torn to shreds, the teddy bears with missing eyes, or the pacifiers that are chewed beyond recognition. Most children don't agree that they could do without the security of those things—and they have a point.

We should feel lost when we don't have God—our ultimate security—nearby. When he's right beside us sharing our pillow in the dark of night, riding beside us in the car, or sitting next to us at our desk, we sense that everything is going to be ok. What do you need to trust God with tonight?

You are the best source of security, God. You give me peace in the darkness and you keep me safe. Thank you for always being near me.

How does it look to have God as your security?

A Great Counselor

Do not be anxious about anything, but in every situation, by prayer and petition, with thanksgiving, present your requests to God. And the peace of God, which transcends all understanding, will guard your hearts and your minds in Christ Jesus.

PHILIPPIANS 4:6-7 NIV

The counselor's suggestion box overflowed with ideas from the school's young students, varying from inventive and reasonable (replacing fluorescent lights with tons of twinkling Christmas lights) to imaginative but impractical (covering the hallways with giant slip n' slides). But each one was read aloud during weekly staff meetings. The children's ideas never decreased in volume or zeal; they believed that their school could be greater than any other, and that their school counselor not only respected but valued their input.

God bends his ear to our anxieties, our longings, our frustrations, and our worship. And we trust him because we want to be better than ever, to be more and more like him. We trust that our Counselor values our petitions. Bring him your requests this morning.

God, you are always in control. You don't worry about my fears or anxieties because you know what you have planned for me. Thank you for listening to my requests and always wanting the best for me.

Do not worry about anything, but pray and ask God for everything you need, always giving thanks. And God's peace, which is so great we cannot understand it, will keep your hearts and minds in Christ Jesus.

PHILIPPIANS 4:6-7 NCV

Students approached their favorite counselor with their personal troubles; he heard about failures on the soccer field, fights with best friends, botched geometry quizzes, and sibling rivalries. His door was always open, and the seats weren't empty for long. What did he offer the young hearts and minds? What was the secret to giving them serenity in the midst of those tumultuous years? He mimicked the example set by God, our great Counselor, who hears our worries and protects us with his peace.

It may seem difficult to give thanks in the midst of trouble and fear, but when we do, God replaces our worries with peace. He listens to our petitions and answers with what he knows is best for us. That is someone you can trust to share your heart with.

Good Counselor, thank you for your listening ear, your loving heart, your kind words of encouragement, and your arms of comfort. I am blessed to be able to seek advice from you.

Will you fill the suggestion box of your wonderful Counselor?

Finding Motivation

"I will sing to the LORD, for he has triumphed gloriously;
the horse and his rider he has thrown into the sea.
The LORD is my strength and my song,
and he has become my salvation;
this is my God, and I will praise him,
my father's God, and I will exalt him."

EXODUS 15:1-2 ESV

Have you ever watched the Olympics and marveled at the incredible strength, discipline, and God-given talent of the athletes? Watching interviews, we commonly hear the question, "Where do you get the strength—the motivation?"

Daily life, while not an Olympic sport, requires its own motivation if we are to push through the blood, sweat, and tears to the gold medal that awaits us. Moses, after the victorious escape from Pharaoh's army, praises the source of their strength in the Scripture above. You can praise the same source today!

God, I praise you for your strength. I sing to you and honor you for all you have accomplished in the world and in my life. Thank you for giving me the motivation I need to press on!

"I will sing to the LORD, because he is worthy of great honor.
He has thrown the horse and its rider into the sea.
The LORD gives me strength and makes me sing; he has saved me.
He is my God, and I will praise him.
He is the God of my ancestors, and I will honor him."

EXODUS 15:1-2 NCV

Are you facing an Olympic-sized trial? Are you wondering where your strength to endure will come from? Does it seem absolutely crazy that God can and will lift you up to overcome?

Remember that God is your strength and your song; trust his power to be yours and praise him because he is worthy. He alone has the strength you need, and he supports you time and time again. Trust him, thank him, exalt him, and the gold medal will be yours!

You are the greatest motivator, Lord. Thank you for supporting
me in this training field. I need your encouragement and your
strength each day, and your peaceful rest at night.

Is God your source of motivation?

A Firm Foundation

Let your roots grow down into him,
and let your lives be built on him.

COLOSSIANS 2:7 NLT

His brothers laughed at his heavy laboring, day in and day out, while they lounged around. Their homes had taken no time at all to complete, and they liked them just fine. Until the wolf came, with his gusting huffs and puffs and then… The story is as familiar as its lesson: take the time to do things right so when trouble comes you will be safe. Build with worthy materials, and you'll have something that lasts through the fiercest of storms.

The third brother must've been a God-fearing little pig, as he took the advice that Jesus gave to his followers. Build on the rock and your house will not fall. Build on something shifting, like sand, grass, or sticks, and watch it fall when the rains, floods, and winds come. God is the rock on which we can build with confidence.

God, I am so grateful for your wisdom. You prepare me for the storms of life and you give me a place to seek refuge. Thank you for being my steady rock.

Keep your roots deep in him and have your lives built on him. Be strong in the faith, just as you were taught, and always be thankful.

COLOSSIANS 2:7 NCV

Not only can we have assurance in God's firm foundation, but he promises to bless us as we dwell with him. Rains, flooding, gusting wind will come, but he will see us through every storm with truth which will strengthen our faith. We will see him triumph over sin and darkness and we will overflow with thankfulness!

In the midst of the storms, you can rejoice! As the winds howl around you, your faith will grow strong. Nothing will come against you that can blow your house down when you build it on the strong foundation of Jesus.

Father, your foundation is secure. I want to build my life on you. Thank you for sheltering me from the storm, for being a steady place to rest when the storms come.

How have you seen Jesus as your stronghold recently?

Support Beams

Whom have I in heaven but you?
And earth has nothing I desire besides you.
My flesh and my heart may fail,
but God is the strength of my heart
and my portion forever.

PSALM 73:25-26 NIV

When considering a home remodeling project, it's important to determine where the support beams are. If we just knock a wall down here and there to create more space, it could have a detrimental effect on the rest of the structure. In fact, it could even lead to irreparable damage. Whether a building topples because of faulty construction, a bad foundation, or extraordinary loads, you can bet the support beams were compromised.

What support beams have you experienced tumbling down around you? Do you know how much the Lord desires to hold you up while everything else crumbles? Ask him to be your support beam today. He is more than enough for your every need.

God, there is no one like you. You are my strength and my portion.
You are my support beam that is never compromised. I lean heavily
on you today.

Whom have I in heaven but you?
I desire you more than anything on earth.
My health may fail, and my spirit may grow weak,
but God remains the strength of my heart;
he is mine forever.

PSALM 73:25-26 NLT

Support beams can be like those people in our lives that we look up to. People we love. People we respect. People we depend on. Sometimes they fall—and we might not realize we were leaning on them until they do. When they go down, it can be hard to recover. They might leave a wake of destruction in their collapse.

The only support beam you can lean on and guarantee it will never shake, bend, or crumble under pressure is God. When the world around you seems to have collapsed, and you find yourself floundering around looking for something firm to take hold of, grab God's hand. He is steady and sure, and his love is safe.

Father, thank you for holding my hand firmly and keeping me from falling. I am confident in your steady hand guiding me through life's obstacles.

Trust God to be your support beam.

All in All

I fall to my knees and pray to the Father, the Creator of everything in heaven and on earth. I pray that from his glorious, unlimited resources he will empower you with inner strength through his Spirit. Then Christ will make his home in your hearts as you trust in him. Your roots will grow down into God's love and keep you strong. And may you have the power to understand, as all God's people should, how wide, how long, how high, and how deep his love is. May you experience the love of Christ, though it is too great to understand fully. Then you will be made complete with all the fullness of life and power that comes from God.

EPHESIANS 3:14–19 NLT

Gloomy days happen. In the midst of the dreariness it helps to hear the voice of a friend, especially one who points us so perfectly to the sustenance we need.

The prayer of Paul, addressed to those in desperate need of hearing the promises of life in Jesus Christ, is a prayer for you.

Creator God, strengthen and empower me. Make your home in my heart. Give me power to understand how very much you love me. Help me to experience that love even though I cannot understand it. I want to be made complete with the fullness of life that comes from you.

For this reason I kneel before the Father, from whom every family in heaven and on earth derives its name. I pray that out of his glorious riches he may strengthen you with power through his Spirit in your inner being, so that Christ may dwell in your hearts through faith. And I pray that you, being rooted and established in love, may have power, together with all the LORD's holy people, to grasp how wide and long and high and deep is the love of Christ, and to know this love that surpasses knowledge—that you may be filled to the measure of all the fullness of God.

EPHESIANS 3:14-19 NIV

Pray this prayer for yourself, your friend, your neighbor, your coworker. Pray until you feel the roots deepening and strengthening in love. Pray it again and again until the power to understand overwhelms you—he is all you need!

Pray until the fullness of God's love for you overcomes your gloom. Pray until the life and power of God break through the clouds and shine brightly upon your face.

God, you are all I need. I trust you for everything.

Be strengthened out of his unlimited resources!

The Solid Rock

He is a shield for all who look to him for protection.
For who is God except the LORD?
Who but our God is a solid rock?

PSALM 18:30-31 NLT

From famous songs to television commercials to close friends, there's a promise that is often made and rarely kept. "I'm here for you; you can always count on me." Most of us have promised or been promised this sometime in our life, and most, if not all, have felt that sting of rejection or disappointment when things didn't quite turn out that way.

There really is someone you can always count on. You can tell him everything. He listens. He hears you. He'll wrap his arms around you, stroke your hair, and tell you everything is going to be all right. God is perfect—the perfect Father, the perfect friend. He is completely trustworthy.

God, I run to you for protection today. You are my solid rock.
I depend on you for my strength.

He shields all who take refuge in him.
For who is God besides the LORD?
And who is the Rock except our God?

PSALM 18:30-31 NIV

We say nobody's perfect, but somehow we expect that everyone should be. In the midst of our trying circumstances, we call out to the people who promised to always be there, but they don't answer. They don't even call us back. Loved ones will hurt us because they are human. Even the best friend, the closest sister, the doting parent will fail in their ability to be there for you. There's no escaping it.

Have you been disappointed or hurt by someone you love? Trust in the one who is dependable. God is willing and able to be your solid rock. He is the one you can always turn to.

Thank you, Father, that you never disappoint me. You are solid and reliable. I know you are always near me, ready to help me as soon as I call out to you.

How can you extend grace to someone who has disappointed you?

He Is Truth

Send out your light and your truth;
let them lead me;
let them bring me to your holy hill
and to your dwelling.

PSALM 43:3 NRSV

When we are weak, the enemy may just try to sneak in and pepper us with lies—to kick us while we're down. It's an incredibly effective tactic. Our best line of defense is to surround ourselves with the truth. Read it. Think it. Pray it. Declare it.

In John 1:1, we read that the Word was with God in the beginning, and the Word was God. In Psalm 119:160, it says, "The very essence of your words is truth." Using simple logic, we put these Scriptures together and derive the following: If the Word is God and the Word is truth, then God is truth.

God, you are the truth. I can believe everything you say.
Lead me with your truth today.

Send me your light and your faithful care,
let them lead me;
let them bring me to your holy mountain,
to the place where you dwell.

PSALM 43:3 NIV

When you find yourself believing the lies of the enemy, turn to God's Word. Find your encouragement, joy, peace, and strength in his never-changing truth.

No matter how many lies you have believed in the past, or how many you are believing right now, you can shut that deceptive voice down by saturating yourself in the truth of God's Word.

Father, thank you for your Word that declares truth. I seek you out this evening to dispel the lies that are surrounding me. I know you are good, and you will show me what is right.

What lies do you need to expose to God's truth today?

Good Shepherd

*"My sheep hear my voice, and I know them, and they follow me.
I give them eternal life, and they will never perish, and no one will
snatch them out of my hand."*

JOHN 10:27-28 ESV

An international festival is held each year and the most
popular event showcases the talents of Irish sheep dogs.
The shepherd uses whistles and quiet voice commands to
direct the dog, who in turn herds the sheep through various
obstacles and dangers. Audiences marvel at the speed of the
dogs and the swift changes in the herd's direction, all due to
the effective communication between man, dog, and sheep.

When you listen to God, moving in unison with speed and
accuracy, you are an example to a lost world. Trust and obey,
knowing that God understands you and leads you to glory.
Let audiences marvel at your Good Shepherd.

*Lord, thank you that you understand me on a much deeper level
than I know. I want to know your voice and follow it all my days.*

*"My sheep listen to my voice; I know them, and they follow me.
I give them eternal life, and they shall never perish; no one will
snatch them out of my hand."*

JOHN 10:27-28 NIV

Jesus often spoke about shepherds, calling himself our Good
Shepherd. His followers understood that sheep need help
through many obstacles and dangers, just as we do. And we
need Jesus to communicate with us in a quiet, familiar voice
so we will know which way to turn for safety.

Our shepherd has one goal: keep his lambs safe. He hems
us in, depending on our destination, with gentle calls and
prodding where necessary. He understands our limits, our
tendency to wander, our nature to rebel. In his goodness,
he nudges our sides, reminding us to trust him and obey his
commands. We must follow him to safety, to eternal life.

*Good Shepherd, I listen for your voice tonight. I am open to your
gentle guidance and nudges. Thank you that you care enough to
keep me safe. I trust you completely.*

Take some time to listen for the Shepherd's voice today.

Not that Easy

Can anything ever separate us from Christ's love? Does it mean he no longer loves us if we have trouble or calamity, or are persecuted, or hungry, or destitute, or in danger, or threatened with death? No, despite all these things, overwhelming victory is ours through Christ, who loved us.

ROMANS 8:35, 37 NLT

The Miracle Mop promised to be the solution for every mopping mess. No more stubborn stains, stuck-on grime, or back-breaking scrubbing and scouring. The solution was simple! Only $49.95 and pesky housework is defeated! It's a tempting promise, certainly, but could housekeeping victory really be achieved with a credit card? Such assurances tug at our pocketbooks because…well…life is messy and sometimes a short-cut is downright tantalizing! But we know it's never that easy. The mop doesn't push itself, after all!

Don't ever fear that you will be overcome; his love, even in times of despair, is victorious over all. What other promises of victory do you need to shut out? Anything other than Jesus Christ, whose death and resurrection are your great and glorious victory, is a waste of your precious time!

God, I know life isn't always perfect. I mess up. Other people mess up. Thank you for your victory on the cross that allows me to overcome the difficulties and move on.

Who shall separate us from the love of Christ? Shall trouble or hardship or persecution or famine or nakedness or danger or sword? No, in all these things we are more than conquerors through him who loved us.

ROMANS 8:35, 37 NIV

It's tempting to take short-cuts, but a life of victory isn't a life without disappointment or hard work. Jesus promised us trials and difficulties as we follow him. This world is a fallen one, full of people using their free-will for sin and destruction. Jesus' promise was meant to prepare us for the rejection, bitterness, and hatred we would encounter.

Jesus also promised us grace, strength, hope, and victory. Don't be deceived to think that good works, prayers, or even faith will produce a life of ease and earthly blessing, showered down from above. We have one promise of victory and that is the saving love of Jesus Christ.

Father, I don't want to take short cuts in my relationship with you. I know I need you desperately, and I know I'm a mess. Help me to put in the work necessary to create an intimate relationship with you.

Are you willing to put in the time and effort required for intimacy?

Scars of Brokenness

*He will take our weak mortal bodies and change them into
glorious bodies like his own, using the same power with which
he will bring everything under his control.*

PHILIPPIANS 3:21 NLT

When a flower pot crashes to the pavement or a vase shatters
to the floor, we consider the damage in hopes that it can be
repaired. What is left? Dangerously tiny shards of glass, too
small to piece back together? Or simple, bulky pieces, like
those of a puzzle, needing only glue and patience? One thing
is certain: we will work harder to fix something that has great
value to us.

Hold everything up to God, who fully covers everything and in
the process makes you whole.

*Father, thank you for picking me up and putting me back together
again. You will make me glorious as I continue to submit to your
work in my life.*

Who, by the power that enables him to bring everything under his control, will transform our lowly bodies so that they will be like his glorious body.

PHILIPPIANS 3:21 NIV

Just like broken pottery, we are broken vessels in need of extensive repair. No elaborate doctoring is required, however, just the humblest of procedures. We hold out our hands and give our broken, desperate, painful, sinful, prideful selves over to the one who mends us into wholeness without a single remaining scar or crack.

How can God do this? Because he is both holy and whole, and we are his creation. We were always meant to be perfect, but sin got in the way. Now, we can only submit to the one whose healing work never leaves a scar and whose abiding love makes us whole forever.

Thank you, Creator God, for knowing me so well, and for bringing me complete healing and wholeness. I rest in that tonight.

Do you have scars of brokenness that need healing?

Sound Advice

Listen carefully to wisdom;
set your mind on understanding.
Cry out for wisdom,
and beg for understanding.

PROVERBS 2:2–3 NCV

Grief has a funny way of messing with our heads. It can cause a fog to roll in and settle over our minds. Small decisions feel like monstrous ones, or maybe it's the opposite: big decisions are made hastily because, quite frankly, we don't have the energy to think everything through. So how do we get the wisdom we need for the task set before us? We ask God for it.

Sometimes God provides us with sound advice through family members, friends, or counselors. This can be especially important to seek out when we don't feel like we can see through the fog. Other advisors help us gain the perspective we might be lacking. They can assist us in making an informed decision instead of a hasty one. Use your trusted advisors today.

God, thank you for the people you have placed in my life who can offer me sound advice. Help me to be open to asking for it.

Making your ear attentive to wisdom
and inclining your heart to understanding;
if you indeed cry out for insight,
and raise your voice for understanding.

PROVERBS 2:2-3 NRSV

King Solomon was put in charge of a nation. He knew it was an impossible task to complete without wisdom. He wasn't born the wisest man who ever lived; he acquired his wisdom by asking God to give it to him. James 1:5 says that if we lack wisdom, we should also ask God for it. We can be confident that if God tells us to ask for something, he wants to grant that request.

If God can give Solomon wisdom to run a kingdom, he can certainly give us wisdom to make decisions about big and small things in our lives. Don't hesitate to ask God for understanding. He wants to give it to you if you're willing to listen.

Father, tonight I listen for your wisdom. I need your advice.
Speak clearly to me, I pray.

What do you need wisdom for right now?

Is It Too Simple?

If you confess with your mouth that Jesus is LORD and believe in your heart that God raised him from the dead, you will be saved. For with the heart one believes and is justified, and with the mouth one confesses and is saved.

ROMANS 10:9-10 ESV

How can it be that a humble prayer, a simple and yet astounding desire to lay down one's life and take up a life like Jesus Christ, establishes our eternity in the kingdom of heaven? Is it possible that such an act can really guarantee salvation? Our acceptance into God's family begins with this one act, yet it can feel too simplistic, too easy. We live in a world where, more often than not, we get what we deserve and nothing comes easy.

Paul emphasized how simple the path to salvation really is in his letter to the Roman church: if you believe it, say it. There is no other way. Believe that your simple and earnest prayer assures your acceptance. And it is this simple. God's Word promises that it is.

God, I see all the extra things I try to do to gain your approval. Help me to understand your simple acceptance of me and walk confidently in that.

If you confess with your lips that Jesus is LORD and believe in your heart that God raised him from the dead, you will be saved. For one believes with the heart and so is justified, and one confesses with the mouth and so is saved.

ROMANS 10:9-10 NRSV

Sometimes, because we can't believe that acceptance can come from such a simple act, we reconstruct the gospel. We want to feel like we deserve God's grace, or that we have earned it, or that we've traded fairly. We build another set of requirements: more praying, more giving, more reading, more serving. Quiet time. Worship team. Children's ministry. Bible study. All of these habits are good and Christ-like, but they don't guarantee *more acceptance*. Not from God, anyway.

Trust that God's gift of salvation is really as simple as confessing and believing.

God, I thank you for the simplicity of your gift. I know that Jesus is Lord and I know you raised him from the dead. Thank you that I am saved and accepted because I deeply believe these statements to be true.

Do you find it difficult to believe in the simplicity of God's requirement for acceptance?

Careful Consideration

For I know the plans I have for you, declares the LORD,
plans for welfare and not for evil,
to give you a future and a hope.

JEREMIAH 29:11 ESV

There are two types of people in the world: those who can pack their bags at a moment's notice and take a last-minute vacation to Paris, and those who need months of planning and organization. You may be willing to do either one—it is a trip to Paris, after all!—but under which conditions would you most enjoy yourself? Could you trust that it would be everything you would've planned for yourself if you didn't thoroughly prepare it?

What if a well-travelled Parisian had personally chosen every hotel, restaurant, and attraction based on your individual tastes? Would you relax, knowing that the trip would be exciting yet safe, surprising yet tailored, unexpected yet promising? How does this remind you of the Lord?

God, you know all the things I think I need. Please show me
instead what you think is best for me and for my future.

"For I know the plans I have for you," says the LORD.
*"They are plans for good and not for disaster,
to give you a future and a hope."*

JEREMIAH 29:11 NLT

When we consider the future, it can be difficult to trust that things will work out the way we desire. If only we could know that the plans for our future are certain! Consider that God knows the future, he knows you, and he knows exactly what you need. Read those words carefully… he knows exactly what you *need*.

If you stick to the guidebook, your life might be just fine. You'll be a happy tourist in this world. But if you trust God, the one who knows you and your destination perfectly, you will see the secret places and hidden gems known only to the one who created them. He has a plan that will take you places you never could have imagined. There is no better way!

Father, thank you that you show me special things along the path that I would never see on my own, or even following someone else. You know me, and you love me. I trust your plan for me.

Can you believe that God has the best plan in mind for your life?

Child of God

All who are led by the Spirit of God are children of God.
So you have not received a spirit that makes you fearful slaves.
Instead, you received God's Spirit when he adopted you
as his own children.

ROMANS 8:14-15 NLT

God is a good Father! He loves you with a love that is matchless and unwavering. Our earthly fathers have important jobs; primarily, they guide us to the love of our heavenly Father. Whether a devoted man's guidance models the Father's truly perfect and boundless love, or a flawed man's brokenness leads us to the Father's healing and compassionate love, both lead us home as children of God.

With lives submitted to Jesus Christ, we have the privilege of the Holy Spirit leading us in truth and in action. This Spirit, as Paul describes, is proof that we are adopted into God's family as children and heirs. You can take hold of your claim as God's precious and beloved child.

Thank you, Lord, for adopting me into your family and calling me your own.

All who are led by the Spirit of God are children of God. For you did not receive a spirit of slavery to fall back into fear, but you have received a spirit of adoption. When we cry, "Abba! Father!"

ROMANS 8:14-15 NRSV

God teaches what true fatherhood looks like: loving authority, gentle guidance, unending grace, tender compassion, fierce protection, and perfect faithfulness.

By faith, know that you are a child of God. Walk in the privileges of an heiress: full acceptance, spotless purity, humble confidence, eternal redemption, and an inheritance of life everlasting.

Father I am humbled by your acceptance of me. Thank you for the privileges I enjoy because I am your child. I call out to you tonight and ask for you to be close to me.

How has your earthly father shown you the immeasurable greatness of God's fatherhood?

Under God's Authority

The Spirit himself bears witness with our spirit that we are children of God, and if children, then heirs—heirs of God and fellow heirs with Christ, provided we suffer with him in order that we may also be glorified with him.

ROMANS 8:16-17 ESV

In his amazing power, God appoints us to be ambassadors for his holy kingdom. Our job comes with humble authority and joyous expectations: we will suffer as Jesus did on earth to receive the glory that he does in heaven.

When we first lay our burdens at the cross, we inherit Jesus' authority to overcome sin and death. We can proclaim his name with all its power. When we continue to trust God, our faith is counted as righteousness, and we have the authority of God's new covenant—Jesus will return again to deliver us. As we walk out our faith, we proclaim the truth of the Gospel of Jesus with the same love that he showed to us when he died on the cross.

God, give me grace to walk through suffering so I can also share in your glory.

It is that very Spirit bearing witness with our spirit that we are children of God, and if children, then heirs, heirs of God and joint heirs with Christ—if, in fact, we suffer with him so that we may also be glorified with him.

ROMANS 8:16-17 NRSV

Our prayers, our worship, our hope, our faith, and all of our steps come under God's authority. With the power of the Holy Spirit, we have the authority and honor to suffer with Jesus so that we can be glorified with him. How can we use our authority to bring Jesus glory, even as we suffer for his name? As ambassadors, how can we foster a connection between Jesus and his lost sheep?

Wherever we go, whatever we do, our God's name—and all its love, power, healing, compassion, and grace—goes with us. The authority you have as God's child is a testimony of salvation from sin and your inheritance of glory.

Father, thank you for my inheritance of glory. Help me to live in submission to your authority, trusting you through the suffering.

How does suffering play a part in your opportunity to bring glory to God?

Exceptional Fruit

The fruit of the Spirit is love, joy, peace, patience, kindness,
goodness, faithfulness, gentleness, self-control; against such
things there is no law.

GALATIANS 5:22–23 ESV

Making applesauce with autumn's abundant apple harvest is
a beloved pastime across northern parts of America. Experts
have developed award-winning recipes whose secret, they
say, is combining multiple varieties of apples to produce a
complex flavor profile. The result is a balance of the tart,
sweet, crisp, mellow, and bold flavors for which apples
are so well-loved. Each variety of apple is essential to the
applesauce; their distinct flavors mesh into a delicious thing
of beauty.

In the applesauce of God's ministry, each believer's spiritual
fruit flavor-profile is essential. The fruit of the Spirit looks,
tastes, feels, smells, and sounds different for each of us.
In some, joy is a loud shout of excitement; in others it is
quiet worship. One believer's kindness might feel soft while
another's is firm. Peace can be expressed in as many ways as
there are to use an apple.

God, I can see how we are all made with a distinct flavor to benefit
the whole of your body. Help me to remember that I am unique and
needed.

The fruit of the Spirit is love, joy, peace, patience, kindness, generosity, faithfulness, gentleness, and self-control. There is no law against such things.

GALATIANS 5:22-23 NRSV

When we compare the evidence of our fruit against other believers, lies are whispered to our flesh: *your fruit isn't as shiny, your fruit isn't as fragrant, your fruit is too mushy and flavorless.* A lie is born in thinking that all trees produce the same fruit. That just isn't true.

Your relationship with Jesus Christ is unique. He produces, between you and the Holy Spirit, an exceptional fruit that only grows from *your* branches. You can be who God made you to be. We are all capable and expected to grow fruit that exhibits the fruit of the Holy Spirit. When we come together, according to God's perfect recipe, for his glory, it is truly delicious.

Thank you, Lord, for your perfect recipe. You know how to make exceptional fruit. Help me listen to your guidance so I can play my part just right.

In the past, how have you compared your fruit to others?

Everything Beautiful

He has made everything beautiful in its time. He has also set eternity in the human heart; yet no one can fathom what God has done from beginning to end.

ECCLESIASTES 3:11 NIV

We've probably all heard an older gentleman declare that his wife is more beautiful now than the day they married. And we likely thought, *He needs glasses.* What we fail to recognize in our outward-focused, airbrushed society, is that time really does make things beautiful. More accurately, time gives us better perspective on the true definition of beauty.

Spending time with those we love affords us a glimpse into the depth of beauty that lies within. So while the external beauty may be fading, there is a wealth of beauty inside—and *that's* what the older gentleman was referring to.

Lord God, thank you that you see the beauty in me and in others. Even though my external beauty will fade, you have given me lasting beauty within.

He has made everything suitable for its time; moreover he has put a sense of past and future into their minds, yet they cannot find out what God has done from the beginning to the end.

ECCLESIASTES 3:11 NRSV

God's Word says that he makes all things beautiful in his time. *All* things. Whatever situation you are facing right now, it has the potential to create beauty in you. Believe it! Perseverance, humility, grace, obedience—these are beautiful. But there's more. The beauty God creates in us cannot be fully described in human terms. There is eternal beauty to be found.

When we are met with challenges that cause us to run to God and sit in his presence, we can't help but reflect the beauty of his character.

Father, thank you for challenges that cause beauty in me. Thank you for your promise to make everything beautiful in its time. I believe you for that in my life.

What are you facing right now that could be a catalyst for true beauty?

What Is True

"Sanctify them by the truth; your word is truth."

JOHN 17:17 NIV

Where does belief originate? We can look to scientific evidence of the earth's creation by an intelligent designer, and there are many scientific specialists who can discuss the details passionately and convincingly. We can read the prophecies from Scripture that also point to the truth of God's power, presence, and passion. Then there are scholars, preachers, and authorities who tell you about the prophecies. The historic evidence of the existence of Jesus Christ comes with another set of experts who can explain the proof and compelling evidence.

God created the earth. He spoke the planets, oceans, and trees into being. He imparted to the prophets details of the coming Messiah, and Jesus came and fulfilled those promises in perfect detail. But our very testimonies—our transformation from death to life—are the simple and powerful proof that what we believe is true.

God, I am so convinced that what I believe is the truth because you have shown yourself to me in so many ways. Help me not to be swayed by the philosophies of this world. You are truth.

*"Make them holy by your truth; teach them your word,
which is truth."*

JOHN 17:17 NLT

The humble followers of Jesus who have experienced his
saving grace also give us reason to believe. We were blind, but
now we can see. We were lost, and now we are found. We were
dead in our sins, but now we are alive in Jesus Christ! This is
all we can *know* for certain.

We may not be scientists, theologians, or experts in apologetics,
but we know that we were blind and God enlightened us. We
were lost and God gave us a home. We were dead and he raised
us from our graves and gave us hope. By faith, we know that
what we believe is true.

*Father, thank you for your saving grace. You are truth and life.
I believe in you because you have always shown yourself to be
faithful and true.*

Take a moment to reflect on the undeniable truth that you are
different today than you were before you knew God.

Walking in Boldness

Let us come boldly to the throne of our gracious God. There we will receive his mercy, and we will find grace to help us when we need it most.

HEBREWS 4:16 NLT

We have full access to the throne of God! Is there any throne on earth granting this much access, this little security, so much grace? Imagine walking into Buckingham Palace, unnoticed and unrestricted, without knocking or announcing yourself, and pulling up a chair alongside Her Majesty, the Queen of England. "Hello, Your Majesty. Quite the weather we're having. I was wondering if you could give me some advice on a problem I've been having at home. Do you have some time?"

It's bizarre and ridiculous, obviously. There are procedures to follow, etiquette, protocol for seeing royalty—not to mention the armed guards, alarms, and jail, probably. But just think, this is very much how God wants us to approach him.

God, I am blown away by the reality that you are the King of the Universe and you want me to come boldly before you and ask you for what I need. I ask you today without fear. Thank you for the gifts you have given me.

Let us then approach God's throne of grace with confidence, so that we may receive mercy and find grace to help us in our time of need.

HEBREWS 4:16 NIV

Thankfully, there is a royal throne toward which we can walk with boldness because we have all the credentials we need. There are no guards, no necessary payments, and no barred doors. Its occupant is the God of all creation, and he is eager to help us with anything we need. And his is the only throne that is worthy of our worship.

Approach God's throne, and shamelessly pull up a chair. He loves your company and will never send you away. Walk in boldness as you approach the throne and lift your voice to him.

Oh my King, thank you for your grace. Thank you for allowing me to come into your presence without shame. I approach your throne of grace tonight and ask you for your help.

What guidance are you looking for? His wisdom is yours if you will listen.

I Am Alive!

Such love has no fear, because perfect love expels all fear. If we are afraid, it is for fear of punishment, and this shows that we have not fully experienced his perfect love.

1 JOHN 4:18 NLT

Fear rears its ugly head in lots of ugly ways; the spider waiting in your bathtub, the high bridge you pass going to your favorite park, the loud noise outside your bedroom window in the middle of the night. Fear can be gripping, paralyzing, or terrifying for some. For others, it is motivation to conquer weakness. Those fears are mostly related to phobias, which, one could argue, stem from basic human defense instincts. What about the fears that keep us awake at night? The worries and anxieties that cannot be brushed aside?

Jesus' followers had one such worry: what would happen on Judgment Day? Was Jesus' death enough to cover their sins completely and guarantee their eternity in heaven? John points out their fear as one of punishment. But there isn't room for fear alongside perfect love, and if we are abiding in the love of Jesus, then we have perfect love in us. Fear must surrender.

God, thank you that there is no fear in love. I embrace your perfect love today and walk without fear.

There is no fear in love. But perfect love drives out fear, because fear has to do with punishment. The one who fears is not made perfect in love.

1 JOHN 4:18 NIV

We must surrender to the truth that sets us free: Jesus died and is now alive—so our sin is dead and *we are alive*. We are alive! Death, sin, and fear are overcome! Jesus has overcome!

You can choose not to be fearful, instead living with the resurrection in mind. Jesus has overcome it all; we have nothing to fear and no more debt to pay. Heights and spiders and enclosed spaces might still quicken your heart, but you can rest easy in his perfect love, now and for all eternity. Are you alive with this truth? Fear cannot remain in the presence of perfect love.

Father, I surrender to your truth. You have set me free from fear because you are perfect in your love for me.

How can you train yourself to bask in the love of God?

No Compromise

When troubles of any kind come your way,
consider it an opportunity for great joy.

JAMES 1:2 NLT

The best products are built using the best ingredients. Some companies compromise, and when trouble inevitably comes, their products suffer and they lose money. But organizations dedicated to quality without compromise build things that endure. Oh, beloved, that our faith would be strengthened for endurance! What are we made of? Can we stand the test? Trouble is on the horizon, but we are advised to see it *as an opportunity for great joy*.

Built with quality, we can have *great joy*. Our endurance grows and we are proven *perfect and complete, needing nothing*. We will not compromise. We want more opportunities for great joy! Bring the tests! Grow our endurance! When the final product is revealed, we will shine like pure gold.

God, help me to endure through the testing so I will be found
lacking nothing.

Consider it pure joy, my brothers and sisters,
whenever you face trials of many kinds.

JAMES 1:2 NIV

This isn't easy advice to follow, but in his wisdom, God gave his Word for our benefit. What would we expect him to say? *Dear children, when troubles of any kind come your way, curl up into a ball of despair for all hope is probably lost.* Of course not! God is building us to last!

We would not gain blessing through hopelessness. No, he builds our faith with the highest-quality parts: hope in the promises of God's Word, humility from the grace that he has given us, and love for God who first loved us.

Lord, help me to find joy in the trials that come my way. You know my future and you are building me to last!

In what areas do you find it easiest to compromise?

Lasting Comfort

May our LORD Jesus Christ himself and God our Father, who loved us and by his grace gave us eternal comfort and a wonderful hope, comfort and strengthen you.

2 THESSALONIANS 2:16-17 NLT

There are so many things that we choose to comfort ourselves with: food, entertainment, relationships, music, or even just busyness… We'll choose anything to take our minds off the wave of emotion that is raging inside. It's much easier to grab a pint of chocolate ice cream, or throw ourselves into a project, than it is to face what's really going on. But those comforts just don't last.

When you choose to find your comfort in God, you will not be disappointed. He knows everything you have faced since the moment you were born, and he knows the best way to comfort you right now.

Father, I choose to find my comfort in you today. I need you.

May our LORD Jesus Christ himself and God our Father, who loved us and through grace gave us eternal comfort and good hope, comfort your hearts and strengthen them in every good work and word.

2 THESSALONIANS 2:16-17 NRSV

The apostle Paul said that God is the God of *all* comfort (see 2 Corinthians 1:3). The things we use to comfort ourselves that aren't from God are destined to fail. They can't offer the hope, peace, security, or love found in the presence of God. They can't reach into the deepest places inside us and turn our sorrows into joy.

Will you choose to find your comfort in God tonight instead of the many other things that are demanding your attention?

God, thank you for being the source of true and lasting comfort. I want to find my peace and rest in you.

How do you need to be comforted today?

Good and Faithful Servant

"The servant to whom he had entrusted the five bags of silver came forward with five more and said, 'Master, you gave me five bags of silver to invest, and I have earned five more.' The master was full of praise. 'Well done, my good and faithful servant. You have been faithful in handling this small amount, so now I will give you many more responsibilities. Let's celebrate together!'"

MATTHEW 25:20-21 NLT

By committing our lives to serving Jesus Christ, we commit to investing the treasure he has given us and growing it to an even greater value for his kingdom. When our Master returns, we should have something to show for our years of serving him and proclaiming his name on earth. By faith, we make good on our commitment to Jesus by sharing the gospel, and serving widows, orphans, and refugees in our land. We love as Jesus loved.

Yes, we will make mistakes, and of course God's grace is sufficient for us. Do what you say you will do; after all, God has kept his promises to you. Look forward to the day when you will hear the fulfilment of your commitment: "Well done, my good and faithful servant. Let's celebrate together!"

Oh God, how I desire to hear those words, "Well done." I want to be a good and faithful servant. Give me strength to do that, please.

"Then the one who had received the five talents came forward, bringing five more talents, saying, 'Master, you handed over to me five talents; see, I have made five more talents.' His master said to him, 'Well done, good and trustworthy slave; you have been trustworthy in a few things, I will put you in charge of many things; enter into the joy of your master.'"

MATTHEW 25:20-21 NRSV

We commit to being faithful, honest, and diligent, just as God is. Our lives are a representation of Jesus, and our ability to make good on our commitments illustrates God's faithfulness. We are modeling godliness to a godless world. We demonstrate his truth, love, integrity, and mercy to a world lost in sin. Make good on your commitments to the world in order to shine the light of Jesus in the darkness.

Spend some time reflecting on the faithfulness and dependability of God, and let that be your motivation!

Help me, Father, to be a faithful servant. I want to use the talents you have given me wisely.

What do you find to be the hardest part of keeping your promises?

Shifting Sand

Be my rock of refuge, to which I can always go;
give the command to save me,
for you are my rock and my fortress.
For you have been my hope, Sovereign LORD,
my confidence since my youth.

PSALM 71:3, 5 NIV

The foot traffic in the park was heavy: moms pushing
strollers, joggers huffing over the trails, kids with baseball
gloves and bats heading for open fields, couples meandering
hand-in-hand under the leafy canopy. Observe closely and
one can tell a lot about a person. Their posture, especially, is
revealing. The man on the park bench, shoulders hunched,
seems discouraged. One jogger lifts her head towards the sun,
hopeful, while a mother's eyes dart nervously back and forth.

Write down the things that are distracting you from walking
in confidence. Give them to the Lord and watch him restore
your hope.

God, I don't want to be distracted from walking in confidence.
You love me. I need to know that, to really embrace that, today.

Be to me a rock of refuge,
a strong fortress, to save me,
for you are my rock and my fortress.
For you, O Lord, are my hope,
my trust, O Lord, from my youth.

PSALM 71:3, 5 NRSV

It is obvious when our hopes have sunk into shifting sand; we find no peace, no comfort, and no protective fortress from distress. Our foreheads wrinkle, our steps drift, our distraught hands clasp and wring. Our confidence is lost.

What do you see when you look in the mirror? Worry lines or laugh lines? Are your eyes cloudy with anxieties or bright with possibilities? Are you hesitant or confident? God is the rock on which you can firmly plant your hopes. Lift your eyes to the Son and walk with confidence. The sovereign Lord is the only hope and assurance you need!

Lord, you give me assurance where no one else can. Thank you for saving me. You are my hope.

What is distracting you from walking in confidence?

Unpredictable Life

*A furious squall came up, and the waves broke over the boat, so
that it was nearly swamped. Jesus was in the stern, sleeping on a
cushion. The disciples woke him and said to him, "Teacher, don't
you care if we drown?" He got up, rebuked the wind and said to
the waves, "Quiet! Be still!" Then the wind died down and it was
completely calm. He said to his disciples, "Why are you so afraid?
Do you still have no faith?"*

MARK 4:37-40 NIV

It takes time to adjust to changing situations. Sailors need
time to get their "sea legs," mountain climbers rest in
order to adjust their lungs to altitude changes, and scuba
divers surface slowly to regulate pressure. Even adjusting to
daylight-savings can take some time.

As his child, you are always in his presence. No matter what you
are facing, you can walk confidently. It may take some time, but
he is prepared for everything and will prepare you, too.

*God, thank you that you can prepare me for life's storms. Help me
to listen to your voice and heed your warnings so I am ready for
difficulties as they come along. You are faithful to me and I know
you will be with me through everything I face.*

A great windstorm arose, and the waves beat into the boat, so that the boat was already being swamped. But he was in the stern, asleep on the cushion; and they woke him up and said to him, "Teacher, do you not care that we are perishing?" He woke up and rebuked the wind, and said to the sea, "Peace! Be still!" Then the wind ceased, and there was a dead calm. He said to them, "Why are you afraid? Have you still no faith?"

MARK 4:37-40 NRSV

During their time with Jesus in his ministry on earth, the disciples had to adjust quickly to radical situations. A daughter was raised from the dead, a boy's meager lunch multiplied to feed a crowd of 5,000, a demon was cast into a herd of pigs that threw themselves off a cliff. Could they have woken up in the morning and sufficiently prepared for such things? Then one day, they get in a boat and their limited faith is tested.

It seems as though the disciples never really adjusted to the unpredictability of life with Jesus. Have you? If they struggled while in his very presence, how can we have faith to walk confidently into the unknown? We have his Word and the assurance that his presence is all we need; he is constant in the face of change.

God, I trust that you are steady in the storm and you will not leave me.

What changes are you going through today that make you feel uneasy?

Unlocking Contentment

I have learned in whatever situation I am to be content.
I know how to be brought low, and I know how to abound.

PHILIPPIANS 4:11 ESV

Paul shares with us his beautiful secret, which followers of
Jesus Christ have been surviving on since it was penned,
sealed, and delivered to the Church at Philippi. We are
promised a life of persecution, sacrifice, and rejection.
The key to unlocking contentment amidst the trials is in
trusting that your needs have been met. Trust eliminates the
spectrum between "life is good" and "life is bad." With trust,
all life lived in the strength of Jesus is contentment. All life
is satisfaction. Everything is a fulfillment of his promise that
following him is every gift we need.

What stops you from believing that God truly does meet your
every need? His ways are perfect and good.

God, help me to believe that everything you do is perfect and good.
I am so blessed to be in your family. I want to make it a habit to
focus on all that I have. I want to be content with what you have
given me.

I am not telling you this because I need anything. I have learned to be satisfied with the things I have and with everything that happens.

PHILIPPIANS 4:11 NCV

Contentment grows in the midst of growing discomfort. Joy is found despite the trouble we find around every corner. A life of faith prospers amid the ruins. Find contentment in God. Comfort is found when you trust in your Father for everything. We don't need the trappings and the shimmer of the temporary. Whether we have everything or nothing, we trade it all for the eternal.

God strengthens us to endure these worldly wanderings for the hope and promise of our eternal existence.

Father God, I trust you for everything tonight.

Can you believe God for contentment today?

The Right Path

Make me to know your ways, O LORD;
teach me your paths.
Good and upright is the LORD;
therefore he instructs sinners in the way.
He leads the humble in what is right,
and teaches the humble his way.

PSALM 25:4, 8 ESV

GPS has nothing on God. We use satellites because we want to know where we are going, how long it will take to get there, and how many miles we will travel on our journey. Our lives, however, don't have coordinates recognized by modern-day digital guides.

Only our loving and faithful God leads us in the direction we really need to go. Not only that, but he teaches us his ways as we walk with him. He *instructs sinners* who humbly learn to be *good and upright*.

God, I humble myself and ask you for help. Thank you that you are happy to guide me back to the right path.

Lord, tell me your ways.
Show me how to live.
The Lord is good and right;
he points sinners to the right way.

PSALM 25:4, 8 NCV

The world's guidance can instruct you to take a left—directly into a murky pond. Satellites aren't as accurate as God's perfect instructions. By keeping his covenant and testimonies, we stay on the right path.

With God, both the journey and the destination are worth the effort. We are transformed by travel; we are reinvented by a loving and faithful leader. When mapping out a travel itinerary, won't we look for a path of steadfast love and faithfulness? When we keep his covenant and his testimonies, we receive the promises he gives us in his Word. Trust God to keep you on the right path.

Lord, I do trust you. Show me how to live. I want to walk uprightly before you.

Recall a time when you took a "wrong turn" in your life. Can you see God's faithfulness even in that moment?

Courageous

May he give you the power to accomplish all the good things our faith prompts you to do.

2 THESSALONIANS 1:11 NLT

Courage is often associated with acts of bravery that defy typical human experience: running through flames to save a child, jumping in a raging river to pull someone to shore, or chasing down a thief to retrieve a stolen purse.

But courage doesn't always look so heroic. Courage is standing your ground when you feel like running; it's saying yes to something you feel God is telling you to do even when you aren't sure that you can do it. Ask for courage to make the right choices today.

God, I want to take the first step today and believe that you will give me the courage to continue.

Our God may make you worthy of his calling and may fulfill every resolve for good and every work of faith by his power.

2 THESSALONIANS 1:11 ESV

Courage can be telling someone you don't want to hear their negative thoughts about other people. It can be sharing your testimony with a room full of people… or with one. Sometimes it takes courage just to leave your house.

When we place our trust and hope in God, he will give us the courage we need to do the tasks he wants us to do. If that includes doing something *heroic*, great! But let's not underestimate the importance of walking courageously in the small things as well.

Lord, I admit I don't always feel very brave. Sometimes doing simple things requires more strength than I have. Please be with me tonight. I ask for your courage now.

What are you facing in your life that requires bravery?

Twists and Turns

You are near, LORD,
and all your commands are true.
Long ago I learned from your statutes
that you established them to last forever.

PSALM 119:151-152 NIV

Death and taxes. They say those are the two things we can depend on in life. Of course they don't mention the neighbor who fails to return the cordless drill (again), the empty fuel light blinking when you're late for work (again), and the spontaneous yet cheerful visitor ringing the doorbell when you're still in your pajamas at 3pm (again). Unpredictability is something else we can depend on!

Life will be shaky and unpredictable—*that* you can count on! But by the grace of God you will never have to endure it alone. There is nothing that will cause him to change his dependable ways. Death and taxes will come. So will life's unpredictable twists and turns. But do not be afraid; God is by your side. You can depend on him this morning.

I trust you, God, that you will always be near me. You are the one
I can cling to when all else is shaking.

LORD, you are also near,
and all your commands are true.
Long ago I learned from your rules
that you made them to continue forever.

PSALM 119:151-152 NIV

Through every unpredictable situation, through all disappointments, delays, and disruptions, we can cling even more confidently to the faithfulness of God. He is the one solid rock on which we can firmly stand. He is steadfast and loyal, asking us to trust in his promises.

God says we shouldn't be afraid or terrified; if achieving that weren't possible, he wouldn't ask it of us. He guarantees that he will always be with us, no matter where we go. If it weren't true, he wouldn't promise it.

God, thank you for your promise to never leave me. I am so grateful for your faithfulness this evening. I choose not to be afraid because you are with me.

What things in your life seem dependable? Which seem unpredictable?

Stay the Course

Do you not know that in a race all the runners run, but only one gets the prize? Run in such a way as to get the prize. Everyone who competes in the games goes into strict training. They do it to get a crown that will not last, but we do it to get a crown that will last forever.

1 CORINTHIANS 9:24-25 NIV

Runners are human beings that have honed the evasive skill of self-control. They have the willpower to overcome physical pain and exhaustion. They have the stamina to push past throbbing muscles, breathlessness, and lead feet. They have, first and foremost, the ability to follow through with the plan.

Running may be on the schedule, but, like anyone else, runners have to actually put running shoes on and move their feet along the pavement. Sure, it's more comfortable on the couch. Yes, it's easier to walk, and many runners would rather get together with friends. But they have committed to the plan. And the plan says, *Get dressed, lace up your shoes, and get on the course. Now.*

Father, I determine this evening to get up, get dressed, and put my shoes on. I want to run this race with you, and I am determined to stay the course.

Do you not know that in a race all the runners run, but only one receives the prize? So run that you may obtain it. Every athlete exercises self-control in all things. They do it to receive a perishable wreath, but we an imperishable.

1 CORINTHIANS 9:24-25 ESV

The only difference between runners and non-runners is that runners are determined to put on their shoes and get out the door. This is the only difference between believers and non-believers too. Believers in Jesus Christ have determined to stay the course. Non-believers also run through life, but their direction changes with the wind.

Running this race is the greatest challenge of your life. It requires self-control, motivation, and stamina. It requires submission to the training: saying yes every day to getting dressed, lacing up your shoes, and staying on the course. Determine this evening to run the race so that you will win!

God help me see life through your eyes, and let that motivate me to stay on course.

What is hindering you from putting your running shoes on and hitting the track?

Okay to Fail

It is by grace you have been saved, through faith--and this is not from yourselves, it is the gift of God.

EPHESIANS 2:8 NIV

Sometimes we just need to pick ourselves up, dust ourselves off, and give ourselves the okay to try again. We need to not strive for perfection and accept the fact that we are human— just like everyone else around us.

Sometimes we will miss the mark, but every mistake is an opportunity to learn. To grow. To change. Look for opportunities today to turn mistakes into learning opportunities.

God, you are so gracious, allowing me to fail time and again and still accepting me as your own and desiring to be with me. Help me to learn from my mistakes and grow in maturity.

By grace you have been saved through faith. And this is not your own doing; it is the gift of God.

EPHESIANS 2:8 ESV

Just because you fail, it does not mean you are a failure. We all fail because we are human. But God has grace for our humanity and he loves it when we come to him in humility and ask for another chance.

Love yourself. See yourself the way God sees you. By giving yourself grace, you will begin to know the love that the Lord has for you. He doesn't hold you to your past or shame you for your shortcomings. He lifts you up, brushes you off, and encourages you to go on. He gives you the grace you need.

God, I thank you for your grace. Help me to come to you in humility when I have failed. I know you will forgive me and set me on my feet again.

Can you view your failures as opportunities to learn?

High Vantage Point

My thoughts are not your thoughts,
neither are your ways my ways, declares the LORD.
For as the heavens are higher than the earth,
so are my ways higher than your ways
and my thoughts than your thoughts.

ISAIAH 55:8-9 ESV

In times of war, army strategists benefit from high vantage points. Looking upon the battlefield from above is the best way to formulate strategies for their troops. Before the use of satellite equipment and heat-sensing radar, views were limited to ground level, forcing the use of maps and spies to predict enemy movement and position men. After their invention, hot-air balloons were used by generals in battle to accurately determine the locations of enemy troops.

God has plans for your life, but sometimes they are hard to see. Trust him. He will lead you safely to the where you need to go.

God, please give me your perspective from a higher vantage point.
Lead me in your perfect way.

"For my thoughts are not your thoughts,
*neither are your ways my ways," declares the L*ORD.
As the heavens are higher than the earth,
so are my ways higher than your ways
and my thoughts than your thoughts."

ISAIAH 55:8-9 NIV

Our lives benefit from a higher viewpoint. When we rise
above our circumstances and see life, not from our own
anxious, urgent, sometimes overwhelming perspective,
but from God's, life's battles become less intimidating as
eternity's promises rise into view.

The day-to-day defeats consume us and we struggle to
confidently lift our head above the fray. When this happens,
remember his high thoughts and ways, and believe that he will
lead you. Walk with your head held high, knowing that he sees
everything that surrounds you, and he will guide you perfectly.

Father, thank you for your guidance. Help me not to be distracted by
the many things around me. I want to follow you and you alone.

What decisions are you trying to make that require a higher
vantage point?

Our Influence

Be joyful. Grow to maturity. Encourage each other. Live in harmony and peace. Then the God of love and peace will be with you.

2 CORINTHIANS 13:11 NLT

Light. Joy. Peace. These are things that people crave. Our words do not carry as much weight or influence as our actions do. People want sustenance; they crave authenticity. Our influence can be in the simple, everyday way we handle ourselves.

We can either influence people to live for God or for themselves. They look to us to see what we do. Do we let others go first or do we push ahead to get to the front? Show people what it looks like to serve King who died to save them.

God, I recognize that people look at me to see how I will respond to different situations. Help me to be a good representation of you so others will be drawn to you.

Finally, brothers and sisters, rejoice! Strive for full restoration, encourage one another, be of one mind, live in peace. And the God of love and peace will be with you.

2 CORINTHIANS 13:11 NIV

People are watching the way you handle yourself in stressful situations. Are you gentle with others? Are you compassionate? Are you generous with your time and money? Are you quick to humble yourself and ask for forgiveness if you have hurt someone?

When we live with the love of God in our hearts, we will naturally encourage others and remain calm in the storms of life. We aren't expected to be able to do this all in our own strength—we have to rely on the Lord.

Father God, thank you for your love. I want to show your love to others and encourage them to live for you.

How can you set a good example for someone else today?

Diamonds Emerging

Every valley shall be raised up,
every mountain and hill made low;
the rough ground shall become level,
the rugged places a plain.

ISAIAH 40:4 NIV

Creating a diamond is, for the transforming coal, a long and painful process. Simple carbon undergoes an immense refining pressure that produces a wholly new creation. We might just see a cloudy rock at this stage, but there is another refining step to be taken. After the stone-cutter does his work, a precise shining diamond emerges: magnificent, glittering, brilliant.

The pressure and the pain happen first. The coal cannot avoid this part. But it is the choice, after so much pain, to become more than clear rocks—to see our beauty and joy shimmering beneath the surface—and submit to the shaping and polishing of God's skilled and loving hands.

God, the long and painful process I have been through is difficult.
Help me this morning to see the emerging beauty under the surface
of the hardship.

Every valley shall be lifted up,
and every mountain and hill be made low;
the uneven ground shall become level,
and the rough places a plain.

ISAIAH 40:4 ESV

When we endure hardship, the long and painful process can seem unfair. To the mother with terminal cancer, it seems excessive. To the abandoned wife, it seems unjust. To the orphaned daughter, it seems cruel. But our life stories are written by a compassionate Creator who is crafting a masterpiece. He is refining us, like the diamond, into something entirely beyond our imagination. And we can rejoice in the beauty he is creating. You may not see it now, but it's coming soon.

Let the pressure not be for nothing. Know that you can endure hardship and emerge stronger and brighter than ever when you depend on God to sustain you.

Lord, thank you for creating beauty out of pain. Everything I walk through has a purpose. Help me to trust that tonight.

What painful but beautiful process are you enduring right now?

Established Eternity

We are citizens of heaven, where the LORD Jesus Christ lives.
And we are eagerly waiting for him to return as our Savior.

PHILIPPIANS 3:20 NLT

The question of eternity is a heavy one; some choose to believe that death is the end of existence and the beginning of nothingness. Some believe in a heaven open to everyone, regardless of their life on earth, where we will all exist peacefully. Others believe in the existence of heaven and hell, but that only the most horrible people on earth end up in torment.

What a relief to know the truth! Eternity is a guarantee, one way or the other, and yours can be one of heavenly citizenship. By faith your eternity is established.

God, I long to spend eternity in your presence. I can only imagine the immense beauty and peace you have established there.

Our citizenship is in heaven, and from it we await a Savior, the LORD Jesus Christ.

PHILIPPIANS 3:20 ESV

The Bible tells us that heaven is a real place, inhabited by those who have accepted Jesus Christ as their Savior. Those who haven't trusted him will spend eternity alienated from him, which is the essence of hell: an eternity absent of anything good. But believers in Jesus' death and resurrection for the forgiveness of sins will live and share in his glory. Our bodies will be transformed and everything will come under his control.

You have been promised an inheritance of glory, where all pain, suffering, and weakness will be transformed. All deception, hatred, and greed will come under the control of Jesus Christ as he makes all things new.

Lord, thank you for the inheritance you promise me in eternity because I am yours. Help me to rightly view what goes on in this world. I want to have a kingdom perspective as I live day to day.

What do you look forward to most about eternity?

Believing for More

By faith Abraham obeyed when he was called to go out to a place that he was to receive as an inheritance. And he went out, not knowing where he was going.

HEBREWS 11:8 ESV

Is it a surprise to learn that God can give you all that your heart desires and more? Is it a surprise to know that our human expectations are so limited that they cannot even begin to imagine the fullness of joy in Jesus Christ? We have expectations of glory, but God urges us to come up higher, to stretch our faith. Are we ready for more?

We have been given a very high calling and we cannot achieve it without some exercise. Like it or not, we must get a little uncomfortable, a little sore, a little sweaty. Maybe a lot. But we are capable of so much more than we know. We are braver than we believe. Stronger than we seem. Smarter than we think.

God, stretch my expectations to believe you for even greater things. I want to obey you like Abraham did—following you into the unknown and believing you for the best.

It was by faith that Abraham obeyed when God called him to leave home and go to another land that God would give him as his inheritance. He went without knowing where he was going.

HEBREWS 11:8 NLT

Believing God for more first requires commitment to the challenge; following God into the unknown is strenuous on both mind and strength, and without commitment we'll inevitably give up. It pushes the boundaries of faith, asking that we put aside our limited expectations and believe God's promise of joy. And just when we think we can't endure any more, God reveals the view from the mountaintop and all the strain is suddenly worth it.

We realize that the exercise itself is its own reward; the challenges are worth every drop of sweat and every moment of pain. With expectations stretched, faith is strengthened for God to use us in greater measure.

God, I am ready for a higher climb to a greater height. I know I will find more astonishing joy with you in that place than I can anywhere else.

What do you want to believe God for more of?

The Pilgrimage

With weeping they shall come,
and with pleas for mercy I will lead them back,
I will make them walk by brooks of water,
in a straight path in which they shall not stumble,
for I am a father to Israel.

JEREMIAH 31:9 ESV

The journey of the believer is a lifelong pilgrimage that ends not at a religious temple or city, but in the kingdom of heaven. Our journey's hardships, sacrifices, and struggles are part of our displacement, and they won't end until eternity. Wherever the path leads, we follow. However long and dusty the road, we press on. No matter what storms lay ahead, we continue. With determined steps we press on toward our destination until we are welcomed home.

God knows we were confused and alone for a long time, so he personally leads us. He knows we are thirsty, so there are sanctuaries along the way. He knows we were bruised and broken while stumbling along our old pathways, so he navigates a straight route for our safety. He is a good Father to us and we can trust his leadership.

Father, I trust you. I will follow you wherever you lead me.
That's not an easy thing to say, but I want to commit to that today.

Tears of joy will stream down their faces,
and I will lead them home with great care.
They will walk beside quiet streams
and on smooth paths where they will not stumble.
For I am Israel's father, and Ephraim is my oldest child.

JEREMIAH 31:9 NLT

Before we began this pilgrimage, we were broken, dead in sin, and weeping from our wounds. Our merciful God redeemed us and brought us up out of the mire. It may not always seem like it, but this path he has set us on is full of restoration, nourishment, steadfastness, and love.

The many steps of our pilgrimage are not walked alone, but alongside one who never gets lost, tired, or afraid. Go wherever God leads. Your pilgrimage is a long and beautiful journey, and it's worth every step.

God, give me the determination and strength to stick with my pilgrimage. Help me to keep walking down the path with you even when it seems like I'm doing it on my own.

Where do you feel the Lord leading you in this season?

Show Me More

Let us draw near to God with a sincere heart and with the full assurance that faith brings, having our hearts sprinkled to cleanse us from a guilty conscience and having our bodies washed with pure water. Let us hold unswervingly to the hope we profess, for he who promised is faithful.

HEBREWS 10:22–23 NIV

God is good and he knows all of your needs. He is faithful and he longs to show more of his glory and beauty. *God, show us more of you!* Show us how much you can do through our fellowship and communion. Show us how far your faithful hands can reach and how much love they will pour out upon your Bride. Prepare our hearts to say "yes" to your call. Clear a path and make a way so we can fulfill your plans.

Until Jesus returns, we continue to trust in the faithfulness of God. *We hold unswervingly to the hope we profess* because we have the *full assurance that faith brings*; our hearts are cleansed and we are pure.

Thank you, Father, for your sacrifice that has cleansed me and given me hope.

*Let us draw near with a true heart in full assurance of faith, with
our hearts sprinkled clean from an evil conscience and our bodies
washed with pure water. Let us hold fast the confession of our hope
without wavering, for he who promised is faithful.*

HEBREWS 10:22-23 ESV

We will not lose heart, God! We trust in your faithfulness.
We love you fully, like children chasing after joy. Our love is
pleasing to you, because you delight in your children. You
sing over your children, notes and refrains here and there as
we walk the earth, waiting for you.

One day, your song will be complete, and when we hear its
fullness, we will run to you. We will not give up; instead, we
will ask you to show us more.

*God, I trust in your dependability. You are unchanging and sure.
Thank you for delighting in me, for singing over me, as I walk this
wonderful earth you put me on.*

In what ways have you seen the faithfulness of God
demonstrated in your life?

Many Sins

"Her sins—and they are many—have been forgiven, so she has shown me much love. But a person who is forgiven little shows only little love." Then Jesus said to the woman, "Your sins are forgiven."

LUKE 7:47-48 NLT

It can be hard to trust in complete forgiveness—hard to trust that all of the horrible, shameful, repulsive sins of the past are known by Jesus and yet fully forgiven. If you were the repentant prostitute sitting at the feet of Jesus, would you believe?

Could you confidently listen to your sins, listed in detail for all to hear, and say, "Amen! I have been forgiven! Yes, even of that, hallelujah!" This woman's sins were known to all, and rather than hiding in shame away from the world, she sought Jesus because she believed in his forgiveness. He would not turn from her in disgust, shut her out, or reject her. She was completely accepted, loved, and redeemed.

God, just as this woman was known, loved, and redeemed, so too you know, love, and redeem me. Thank you for forgiveness of my many sins.

"I tell you, her sins, which are many, are forgiven—for she loved much. But he who is forgiven little, loves little." And he said to her, "Your sins are forgiven."

LUKE 7:47-48 ESV

The Pharisee's rebuke of the suffering woman seems so heartless; doesn't he understand that no one could possibly have greater reason to rejoice than this woman? No offering of oil, poured out on the redeemer's feet, could be more pleasing than the one from these humble and grateful hands.

Jesus loves the heights of our gratitude; they are equal to the depths from which we have been saved.

Father, I feel like sometimes I can understand this woman's deep and desperate longing to worship at your feet. Thank you that I am forgiven. Fully, completely, and lovingly.

Can you relate to the woman's cry of shame?

God Is Good

You are a chosen people. You are royal priests, a holy nation, God's very own possession. As a result, you can show others the goodness of God, for he called you out of the darkness into his wonderful light.

1 PETER 2:9 NLT

God is good and he makes all things good. Evil is the absence of God's goodness. Like light and darkness, goodness cannot exist in the same place as evil. The world, however, often seems to exist in shades of gray. Light and darkness tangle together to become something indecipherable and the resulting shadows breed uncertainty.

Politicians, activists, and corporations love uncertainty because it encourages a second look at what once seemed certain. What society believed was good has shifted, but God never shifts. His goodness is certain.

Thank you, God, for choosing to share your goodness with me.

You are a chosen race, a royal priesthood, a holy nation, a people for his own possession, that you may proclaim the excellencies of him who called you out of darkness into his marvelous light.

1 PETER 2:9 ESV

Let's begin with this. *God is good*. Now, decipher the light from the darkness, the good from the evil, knowing that God doesn't change and is always good. He is good in unemployment, in sickness, in despair, in bankruptcy, in another's betrayal, even when it seems like darkness is all around.

God called you out of the darkness into his wonderful light. You belong to him, you are chosen, and you can believe in his goodness and walk in his wonderful light.

Father, you are good and you redeemed me. You never leave me. You reserve a place for me in your eternal kingdom. You are light and there is no darkness in you. I declare that you are good tonight.

List all the things about God that remind you of his goodness.

A Deeper Knowledge

*May God give you more and more grace and peace as you grow in
your knowledge of God and Jesus our LORD.*

2 PETER 1:2 NLT

The fear of failure is one of life's biggest struggles. Failure is
not a great feeling, and yet most successful people will tell
you that failure has been a part of their experience as well.
There is something to be said for the knowledge that comes
from experience.

As your experience of God grows, your understanding of simple
concepts like peace and grace will develop into deep truths.

*Jesus, I want to know you in a deeper way. I ask you to reveal
something of yourself to me today so I can be encouraged with
a fresh understanding of your grace and peace.*

Grace and peace be multiplied to you in the knowledge of God and of Jesus our LORD.

2 PETER 1:2 NASB

The knowledge of God is not a test that you can fail. Every new thing you learn about Christ will add to your faith. Climb the mountains of life with him, test him at his Word, and find his promises to be true.

As you explore the truth, your preconceived notions of peace and grace may challenge you. Treasure this deeper understanding in your heart.

God, show me the purest forms of the most wonderful things. I invite you to reveal yourself to me tonight. Let me experience the joy of discovering a life of fullness in you.

How can you grow in your knowledge of God?

Overflowing with Gratitude

Giving thanks is a sacrifice that truly honors me.
If you keep to my path, I will reveal to you the salvation of God.

PSALM 50:23 NLT

Gratitude makes a lovely countenance. When our cups overflow with gratitude, there isn't room for bitterness or criticism. Gratitude pushes away judgement and disdain and makes room for joy and grace. People walking in gratitude make very pleasant company. Their overflow of thankfulness blesses everyone, from families and friends to the people in line with them at the post office.

Let your life be a testimony of gratitude. Let the aroma of your thankfulness touch the senses of everyone around you—a sweet perfume of God's faithfulness to you. He has blessed you and it is right that you would overflow with praise!

God, I root myself in you. I build my life on you and watch my faith strengthen as I do so.

Those who sacrifice thank offerings honor me,
and to the blameless I will show my salvation.

PSALM 50:23 NIV

When we have an attitude of gratitude, we confirm that we have been blessed. And we have indeed been greatly blessed. Beyond material blessings, beyond the blessing of health and home, beyond even the blessing of family and friends, we have the immeasurable blessing of faith. What a testimony to God's goodness!

By faith, we build our lives on the Word of God, we grow strong as we learn the truth of God. By faith, we *overflow with thankfulness*. Our thankfulness is a gift back to God.

God, let my thankfulness overflow to the furthest reaches of my life, contagious and compelling. Let my countenance reflect your glory.

Tell God how thankful you are today!

Little Lies

Truthful words stand the test of time,
but lies are soon exposed.

PROVERBS 12:19 NLT

Some people are terrible liars. Most children fall into this category. Their made-up stories and far-fetched excuses are sure to draw suspicion even in less-discerning adults. Sometimes we might even find their stories humorous or cute. The dog colored on the wall? Of course it did! The baby took the cookie off the kitchen counter and ate it? Sure thing.

Sometimes telling the truth is hard. Owning up to mistakes, bad decisions, and accidents doesn't come easily. In the end, though, the only thing a lie will do is make the situation worse.

God, help me choose to be honest even when it is difficult. I want to honor you with my words.

Truthful lips endure forever,
but a lying tongue lasts only a moment.

PROVERBS 12:19 NIV

There's nothing funny or adorable about lying. Lies are destructive in every possible way. They can do long-lasting damage to our character and relationships. They destroy trust and stir up doubt. And they certainly don't bring us any closer to God.

A bad liar? That's something you should strive to be. Choose to walk in honesty tonight and be close to God.

Being honest with myself and with others isn't always easy, Lord.
I need your help to be truthful in all things with all people.

How can you make it a point to walk honestly before God and others?

Honored through Grace

The name of the LORD Jesus will be honored because of the way you live, and you will be honored along with him. This is all made possible because of the grace of our God and LORD, Jesus Christ.

2 THESSALONIANS 1:12 NLT

Honor awards are usually given to those who achieve excellence in specific fields. People are honored for their performance in musical, athletic, academic, and professional arenas. Some are honored for their exceptional bravery or intelligence. And rightly so. But if honor is given only for excellent achievement, how on earth can we be considered honorable with our less-than-impressive abilities?

It's crazy to think that we are even capable of bringing honor to God through our lives. We're so *human*, and he's so *perfect*. But that's precisely it—we *aren't* able to walk honorably on our own. We need God's grace to be honoring.

God, I can't achieve the excellence standard you require. It's only by your grace that I am considered worthy of your honor award. Thank you.

The name of our LORD Jesus may be glorified in you, and you in him, according to the grace of our God and the LORD Jesus Christ.

2 THESSALONIANS 1:12 ESV

The secret to living a life that honors God is found in depending heavily on his grace to cover us. We can choose to walk honorably before him by keeping it simple. We do what we know is right, and we don't do what we know is wrong. We don't compromise. We don't chase after the shiny honor awards of the world. And when we get it wrong, we humbly admit our failure, accept God's forgiveness, and keep walking the narrow road.

Evaluate the honor awards you are seeking after right now. Will they ultimately bring honor to the Lord?

Father, I want to bring honor to your name. Help me to live in a way that represents you well.

How can you live honorably before God?

Lasting Hope

May the God of hope fill you with all joy and peace as you trust in him, so that you may overflow with hope by the power of the Holy Spirit.

ROMANS 15:13 NIV

I hope it doesn't rain today. I hope I did well on that final. I hope he didn't forget our anniversary. I hope I get a promotion. Few things that we hope for contain the kind of satisfaction that lasts. Even if we get what we hoped for, what comes next? We have to hope for something else.

When we choose to put our hope in God, we will not be disappointed. Our expectations will be *exceeded.* How often does *that* happen?

God, I see how hope in earthly things is only temporary. Help me to put my hope instead in the eternal reward of living forever with you.

Now may the God of hope fill you with all joy and peace in believing, so that you will abound in hope by the power of the Holy Spirit.

ROMANS 15:13 NASB

While it's not bad to hope for temporary things, the truth is that any of them are disappointing if not met, and all of them only carry brief satisfaction. The one thing we can hope for that has lasting value is our eternity with the Lord. And that's actually exciting!

Think of life without fear, pain, guilt, sorrow, sickness, loss, rejection, or death. Think about an abundance of love, joy, peace, kindness, and beauty. These are worth hoping for.

Father, it's so much more exciting to hope for things that have eternal value. Help me to remember this when temporary things fill my mind.

What are you currently hoping for?

Begin with Humility

Get rid of all evil behavior. Be done with all deceit, hypocrisy, jealousy, and all unkind speech. Like newborn babies, you must crave pure spiritual milk so that you will grow into a full experience of salvation. Cry out for this nourishment, now that you have had a taste of the LORD's kindness.

1 PETER 2:1–3 NLT

Evil behaviors are rooted in ungodly pride. When we come to faith in Jesus Christ, however, we must become like him, a humble servant, shedding our pride and living a life of honesty, integrity, contentment, and kindness. The path to this life begins with humility.

In our spiritual infancy, we are completely humble and fully dependent on God's kindness. Our meals consist of spiritual food; putting off our old lives of sin, crying out for goodness and tasting the pure love of God.

Jesus, thank you for your example of servanthood. I want to be more like you, especially in this way.

Putting aside all malice and all deceit and hypocrisy and envy and all slander, like newborn babies, long for the pure milk of the word, so that by it you may grow in respect to salvation, if you have tasted the kindness of the LORD.

1 PETER 2:1-3 NASB

Nothing is more dependent, more completely humble, than a newborn baby. A precious life, whose only hope is a loving, kind, capable provider, lays waiting for nourishment. If placed in your arms, you alone become solely responsible for meeting her needs, even if all you can do is hand her back to her mother. But while in your arms, she humbly relies on *you* to provide.

Our humble path in life often leads to a tough climb. Through it all, keep the posture of Jesus, who came to lose his life so you could gain the abundant, eternal, glorious life in the kingdom of heaven.

God, help me to walk in humility and grow in servanthood. I know there are areas of pride that I need to work on. I choose tonight to lay down my pride.

What behavior do you need to adjust to ensure that you are walking in humility?

Inspired

The word of God is alive and powerful. It is sharper than the sharpest two-edged sword, cutting between soul and spirit, between joint and marrow. It exposes our innermost thoughts and desires.

HEBREWS 4:12 NLT

Have you ever opened your Bible to a random page, begun to read, and been amazed that the Scripture passage is perfectly appropriate for that exact season of your life? Then at church your pastor uses the same verse as the basis for a sermon. While driving a few days later, a worship song's lyrics match up again to your life. It's like God has a spotlight on you and is aligning the world around you to encourage, direct, or teach you wherever you are. His Word is truly *alive and powerful!*

Reading his Word *exposes our innermost thoughts and desires.* Sound uncomfortable? A bit too vulnerable? We don't usually like feeling uncomfortable, and reading God's commandments brings conviction. Child of God, count this as a blessing! God shines a spotlight on these areas to inspire us toward greater submission to him. When we are submitted, we become more and more like Jesus Christ. And that is what we really want, right?

God, help me to be vulnerable before you. You only want the best for me.

The word of God is living and active and sharper than any two-edged sword, and piercing as far as the division of soul and spirit, of both joints and marrow, and able to judge the thoughts and intentions of the heart.

HEBREWS 4:12 NASB

The Word of God is a marvelously insightful gift. He gave it for our edification, education, and inspiration. Whatever we are going through, the Word of God holds the answer. Whether we are running away from God or toward him, whether we are rejoicing or mourning, however confused or secure we feel, God's Word holds the solution.

Find inspiration in God's Word! It is a gift, alive and powerful, to help you learn, grow, and believe. Ponder the Scriptures and their direct impact on your life tonight, and thank God for his living Word.

Father, I trust you with my deepest thoughts and desires. Thank you for your living Word that breathes life into me and highlights areas for me to grow in. Help me to pay attention to Scriptures that come to mind frequently, and those that jump out at me during my quiet times.

What Scripture verses have been cropping up for you lately?

A Hero

Teach me your decrees, O Lord;
I will keep them to the end.
Give me understanding and I will obey your instructions;
I will put them into practice with all my heart.
Make me walk along the path of your commands,
for that is where my happiness is found.

PSALM 119:33-35 NLT

Adventurous Hollywood tales of heroes have little in common with reality, except, perhaps, the hero. Heroes really do exist. They serve us coffee, walk their dogs down our street. Maybe you are a hero. It doesn't take much really, just being in the right place at the right time. And, of course, doing the right thing. This is what sets a hero apart: a hero does the right thing.

How can you be a hero? How can you walk with integrity? By learning God's commands and keeping them, asking for wisdom and committing to obedience, vowing devotion *with all your heart*, and submitting to walking God's path because it leads to joy.

God, give me more opportunities to share your character with those around me.

Teach me, O LORD, the way of Your statutes,
And I shall observe it to the end.
Give me understanding, that I may observe Your law
And keep it with all my heart.
Make me walk in the path of Your commandments,
For I delight in it.

PSALM 119:33-35 NASB

Heroes put aside their own desires and interests. They have integrity, which means they do what most people wouldn't take the time, risk, or effort to do. David's psalm reads like an oath, a decree for heroes everywhere, spoken as a promise to uphold the integrity of God's goodness and righteousness. *Place your left hand on the Bible, raise your right hand, and repeat after me...*

With God, you are always in the right place at the right time. A person who walks with integrity will do the right thing even when no one is watching.

I like the way it feels to do the right thing, Lord. Help me to make the right choices consistently so I can be a true hero.

When was the last time you felt like you acted with integrity?

Intimately Known

O LORD, you have searched me and known me!
You know when I sit down and when I rise up; you discern my thoughts from afar.
You search out my path and my lying down and are acquainted with all my ways.
Even before a word is on my tongue, behold, O LORD, you know it altogether.
You hem me in, behind and before, and lay your hand upon me.
Such knowledge is too wonderful for me; it is high; I cannot attain it.
Where shall I go from your Spirit? Or where shall I flee from your presence?
If I ascend to heaven, you are there! If I make my bed in Sheol, you are there!
If I take the wings of the morning and dwell in the uttermost parts of the sea,
even there your hand shall lead me, and your right hand shall hold me.
If I say, "Surely the darkness shall cover me, and the light about me be night,"
even the darkness is not dark to you; the night is bright as the day,
for darkness is as light with you. For you formed my inward parts;
you knitted me together in my mother's womb.
I praise you, for I am fearfully and wonderfully made.
Wonderful are your works; my soul knows it very well.
My frame was not hidden from you, when I was being made in secret,
intricately woven in the depths of the earth.
Your eyes saw my unformed substance; in your book were written, every one of them,
the days that were formed for me, when as yet there was none of them.

PSALM 139:1-16 ESV

What more confirmation is needed? Hear the words of your Creator and believe: you are intimately known by him!

Oh God, you know me better than I know myself. Thank you for your interest in me.

Lord, you have examined me and know all about me.
You know when I sit down and when I get up.
You know my thoughts before I think them.
You know where I go and where I lie down. You know everything I do.
Lord, even before I say a word, you already know it.
You are all around me—in front and in back— and have put your hand on me.
Your knowledge is amazing to me; it is more than I can understand.
Where can I go to get away from your Spirit? Where can I run from you?
If I go up to the heavens, you are there. If I lie down in the grave, you are there.
If I rise with the sun in the east and settle in the west beyond the sea,
even there you would guide me. With your right hand you would hold me.
I could say, "The darkness will hide me. Let the light around me turn into night."
But even the darkness is not dark to you. The night is as light as the day;
darkness and light are the same to you.
You made my whole being; you formed me in my mother's body.
I praise you because you made me in an amazing and wonderful way.
What you have done is wonderful. I know this very well.
You saw my bones being formed as I took shape in my mother's body.
When I was put together there, you saw my body as it was formed.
All the days planned for me were written in your book
before I was one day old.

PSALM 139:1-16 NCV

In reading this Scripture again tonight, how do you feel?

Father, when I think about how well you know me, I am blown away. You love me for who I am. You created me and helped shape me into who I am today. I am so grateful.

How do you feel when you consider that God knows every detail of your life?

God Is Just

I will proclaim the name of the LORD; ascribe greatness to our God!
"The Rock, his work is perfect, for all his ways are justice.
A God of faithfulness and without iniquity,
just and upright is he."

DEUTERONOMY 32:3–4 ESV

Being a judge is a weighty calling; if you've ever had to judge a children's art competition, you might understand. Lovingly crafted, covered in heavy-handed brush strokes, glitter, and smiling stick figures, the smudged papers are held below smiling, expectant faces. *Which one is the best?* Could anyone choose a winner, and at the same time create a loser? More than one adult has exclaimed, "I just can't choose, they're all so wonderful!" Truly, being a judge is a calling for God alone.

Thankfully, God is great and perfect—two qualities you want in a judge. And *all his ways are justice*, he is faithful and *without iniquity*. He alone is qualified to judge mankind. He alone will bring about justice with his mighty hand, and it will be eternal. Because he is faithful and without wickedness, we can rest without worry.

God, I choose to trust that you will rule justly in your time.

I will announce the name of the LORD.
Praise God because he is great!
He is like a rock; what he does is perfect,
and he is always fair.
He is a faithful God who does no wrong,
who is right and fair.

DEUTERONOMY 32:3-4 NCV

Winners and losers will be declared when God comes to judge.
There won't be any hesitation or argument. God has seen all
the world's injustice and his judgement will be poured out.
Have faith in that, but in this, as well: *his work is perfect.*

God's works of compassion, love, healing, and grace are
perfect. And his ways of justice are perfect. This isn't true of
us, but it is true of him, and he will make everything right one
day. You can believe that God is just tonight.

Perfect Judge, you examine the hearts of all people and you rule
accordingly. Thank you that I can trust you to act justly in all
situations.

In what situations are you finding it difficult to wait for God's
judgment?

Wholly Loved

"God so loved the world that he gave his one and only Son, that whoever believes in him shall not perish but have eternal life."

JOHN 3:16 NIV

It's likely that we misunderstand, miscalculate, and misinterpret God's amazing love for us because we have nothing quite like it on earth. We get glimpses of it, and indeed we are only capable of loving by any degree because he first loved us, but nothing fully captures God's love. Nothing perfectly embodies his delight; nothing exactly mirrors his infatuation or faithfully interprets his depth of devotion. We fall remarkably short of his marvelous love.

When you feel any shadow of a doubt about how greatly and completely God loves you, you only have to open your love letter from God to be reminded. You cannot be separated from this love. Unlike human love, God's has no limit, always forgives, never cools, and is steadfast.

Father, I choose to take some time to reflect on your words of love today.

"God loved the world so much that he gave his one and only Son, so that everyone who believes in him will not perish but have eternal life."

JOHN 3:16 NLT

No question, earthly love makes mistakes. Our love has limits, holds grudges, grows cold, and loses patience. Our love is blended, inextricably, with our flesh and all its capacity for sin. Human love is a faint whispered echo of the jubilant chorus of love sung out to us by God in all his parts. We can be glad he put in in written form—a love letter to his beloved—so we can carry it with us.

Read your love letter and believe its promise: you are wholly loved by God!

God, there is nothing that can separate me from your love. Thank you for your everlasting Word, your letter of love, that confirms this for me.

What verses in the Bible remind you of God's deep love for you?

Storing up Oil

"All the bridesmaids got up and prepared their lamps. Then the
five foolish ones asked the others, 'Please give us some of your oil
because our lamps are going out.'
But the others replied, 'We don't have enough for all of us. Go to a
shop and buy some for yourselves.'
But while they were gone to buy oil, the bridegroom came. Then
those who were ready went in with him to the marriage feast, and
the door was locked."

MATTHEW 25:7-10 NLT

In the days leading up to Jesus' return, many believers
will walk away. The ones who are unprepared for the pain,
suffering, and sacrifice of those days will walk away from
the truth. Their faith, under severe testing, will falter. Their
lamps will go out.

Begin filling your lamp with the oil of faith now, so that in the
hour of Christ's return you will not walk away because of your
emptiness. Have you stored up enough oil for that long night?

*God, help me to be prepared, I look forward to a long night that
ends with the bridegroom's triumphant return!*

"Then all the bridesmaids woke up and got their lamps ready. But the foolish ones said to the wise, 'Give us some of your oil, because our lamps are going out.' The wise bridesmaids answered, 'No, the oil we have might not be enough for all of us. Go to the people who sell oil and buy some for yourselves.'
So while the five foolish bridesmaids went to buy oil, the bridegroom came. The bridesmaids who were ready went in with the bridegroom to the wedding feast. Then the door was closed and locked."

MATTHEW 25:7-10 NCV

This parable is a warning for all believers. We hope that we will stand strong in the face of evil, but we cannot know how long and desperate the season of Christ's return will be. If even Peter, who walked alongside Jesus and loved him dearly, could deny him three times in one night long ago, then how can we know what we will do during the long night that is to come?

Only by faith will we make it through the night; faith is the oil that keeps the lamp lit. Our perseverance in the age of Christ's return depends on our preparation.

Father, will you show me how to prepare for the long night? I need your wisdom and guidance in times of trouble so I can persevere.

What does it look like for you to fill your lamp, and as many vessels as you can, with the oil of faith?

Prone to Distraction

Now, Israel, what does the LORD your God require of you? He requires only that you fear the LORD your God, and live in a way that pleases him, and love him and serve him with all your heart and soul.

DEUTERONOMY 10:12 NLT

As Israel waits to enter the Promised Land, Moses stops beside the Jordan River. It is the last chance he will have to speak about all that the Lord commands of them. Like parents leaving a grown child at college, Moses imparts as much wisdom as possible with each word, hoping it will stay with them and guide them. It's a commencement address of sorts, spoken to a nation on the verge of independence.

His last words to his people, those he watched grow in faith and humility, are an equation for prosperity: obey God's commandments and you will be a great nation; disobey and you will be brought to destruction. Moses warns them to be careful and stay on the right path, never straying or wandering from God's commandments. We could use those same words as a warning today.

God, I see how important obedience is as a foundation of right living before you. I want to listen carefully to your commands.

*"Now, Israel, this is what the LORD your God wants you to do:
Respect the LORD your God, and do what he has told you to do.
Love him. Serve the LORD your God with your whole being."*

DEUTERONOMY 10:12 NCV

Moses repeats simple wisdom throughout his speech,
knowing better than anyone that God's people are prone to
distraction. They are about to enter a beautiful land, drive
out its people, and take for themselves the cities, homes,
fountains, fields, livestock, and vineyards within. How long
will it take them to forget who it was that brought them out of
slavery and into this great land?

We live amidst great distraction and temptation. God's
commands are the wisdom and knowledge we need to navigate
this foreign land. His commands are for our own good. You
can choose to obey God. He will bring you into a beautiful land
where you will lack nothing, and you will be thankful.

*Distraction is everywhere, Lord. It's hard to set everything aside
and focus on you. Help me navigate life with you as my focus.*

What has God asked you to obey him in recently?

My First Love

"I know you are enduring patiently and bearing up for my name's sake, and you have not grown weary. But I have this against you, that you have abandoned the love you had at first. Remember therefore from where you have fallen; repent, and do the works you did at first."

REVELATION 2:3–5 ESV

All we need is you, Lord. What can the world offer us that will not perish? What can the world give that can withstand God's refining fire? When we are tested, everything else will fall away. Only our love for him will remain. Our salvation cannot be stolen from us. God's love for us cannot be quenched. What, then, takes our eyes away from his faithful gaze?

Remember the early days of your walk with Jesus? His love has not diminished. Return to your first love and walk closely with him today.

God, I choose today, and every day—every hour or minute if needed—to remember the love I had at first, and live as I did then.

You have patience and have suffered troubles for my name and have not given up.
"But I have this against you: You have left the love you had in the beginning. So remember where you were before you fell. Change your hearts and do what you did at first. If you do not change, I will come to you and will take away your lampstand from its place."

REVELATION 2:3-5 NCV

Loving God is a *choice* we make, over and over again, because our hearts are flesh. He holds the universe and everyone on earth; we can scarcely be trusted to hold hot coffee without burning someone. We are fickle and we forget who it was that saved us, who it was that gave us a hope and a future. We have *abandoned the love we had at first*.

Return to your first love. Remember the way your eyes were opened to understanding, how your heart was broken in love, your arms were lifted in praise, and your knees bent in repentance. God misses that. He misses the desperation you had for him, the focused time you spent in his Word, and the joy you found in prayer.

God, you are all I need. Help me to abandon my own desires and live for you.

Do you feel like God is still your first love?

God's Timing

We are saved by trusting. And trusting means looking forward to getting something we don't yet have—for a man who already has something doesn't need to hope and trust that he will get it. But if we must keep trusting God for something that hasn't happened yet, it teaches us to wait patiently and confidently.

ROMANS 8:24-25 TLB

It's hard to wait for, well, anything. We can have almost anything we want immediately. Sometimes even waiting longer than two days to receive our order in the mail seems way too long.

We can gain some great perspective when we think about how life was lived hundreds or even thousands of years ago. Mail took months to travel, items were all made-to order, and food was only delivered to your doorway if it was accompanied by out-of-town guests who were planning on staying for months. We have become pretty impatient, haven't we?

God, I know I am impatient. I try to make things happen quickly when I should be waiting for you. Help me to slow down and trust you.

We were saved, and we have this hope. If we see what we are waiting for, that is not really hope. People do not hope for something they already have. But we are hoping for something we do not have yet, and we are waiting for it patiently.

ROMANS 8:24-25 NCV

It's hard to wait for God's timing. Even when we are waiting for *good* things, we think we shouldn't have to wait for long. Going on a missions trip, starting a job in ministry, leading a small group, marrying the right person… doesn't God want those things for us sooner rather than later? If we don't act now, we might miss out!

Trusting in God's timing means you believe that God won't let an opportunity slip by unless it's not one he wants you to experience. Maybe he doesn't want it for you now, or maybe you're not supposed to have it at all. Can you be okay with that?

Lord, I trust you completely to act at the right time. You won't let me miss out on anything you want for me.

What are you waiting on God for right now?

Such a Time as This

If you keep quiet at a time like this, deliverance and relief for the Jews will arise from some other place, but you and your relatives will die. Who knows if perhaps you were made queen for just such a time as this?

ESTHER 4:14 NLT

Fear of man can be paralyzing. *What might the cashier at the grocery store do if I dare to share the gospel as I check out?* She will probably point and shout, "This woman is a Christian! Get her!" OK, that probably wouldn't happen. Neither is the cashier likely to openly mock, jeer, or get angry and make a scene. Yet the paralyzing fear of these possibilities keeps believers from sharing the loving truth of Jesus. It's understandable, right? Can we really live a life that *desires* persecution?

Well, the answer is *yes*. Take heart! You are not alone in your fears! Esther, Queen of Persia, was also afraid to stand up for her faith. She risked death at the hand of her husband and king, and the fear paralyzed her. But she received wise counsel to speak up. She had nothing to lose and everything to gain.

Father, I want to do the right thing at the right time. Help me to listen carefully to your instructions.

"If you keep quiet at this time, someone else will help and save the Jewish people, but you and your father's family will all die. And who knows, you may have been chosen queen for just such a time as this."

ESTHER 4:14 NCV

Devotion to God brings persecution. When we ask Jesus to be our Savior, we recognize that only he can rescue us. Other people cannot save, redeem, or establish our eternity. Only Jesus has done that. And others don't have the power to take those promises away from us. We were made for "such a time as this" moments.

Remain true to God even in the face of persecution, real or perceived, and boldly proclaim the truth that saves.

God, I need strength to remain true to you in the moments I face persecution. Help me to boldly proclaim you wherever I go whether through my words or actions.

How do you react in situations where you feel like you should share the Gospel with someone, but you don't know what their response will be?

Stubbornly Redeemed

Be steadfast, immovable, always abounding in the work of the
LORD, knowing that in the LORD your labor is not in vain.

1 CORINTHIANS 15:58 ESV

No one enjoys teaching a stubborn child. But stubbornness
redeemed is commitment. In our lives, we can be like
stubborn children, opposing the will of God and demanding
our own way. But we can also be redeemed—stubbornly
devoted to following God and keeping our eyes from
distractions along the way.

In the lives of others, we may be the last ones standing in
defense against the enemy's plans. We need to be stubborn
in prayer, standing firm even when we are last, even when no
one notices, even when we can't see the results.

Jesus, thank you for standing beside me. Please bring brothers and
sisters in Christ alongside me in this battle. Let me be stubbornly
redeemed for your cause.

Be steadfast, immovable, always abounding in the work of the LORD, knowing that your toil is not in vain in the LORD.

1 CORINTHIANS 15:58 NASB

Maybe you feel fatigued and battle weary tonight, or very alone in your stand. Maybe you are tired of being stubborn and want to be stubbornly redeemed. Instead of resisting God, give in to him and watch the beautiful transformation that takes place in your life.

Pray for refreshment and seek out someone who will stand alongside you. Be encouraged that Jesus is the one who brings strength when you need it most.

God, I want to be stubbornly redeemed. I don't want to just be stubborn. Help me to stand firm in the right things and move quickly away from the wrong.

Are you stubbornly redeemed or just stubborn?

Hand in Hand

Though they stumble, they will never fall,
for the LORD holds them by the hand.

PSALM 37:24 NLT

Holding hands is beautiful. Two people choose to join
together, leading, following, or walking as equals. We might
hold hands with a child to cross the street, to help an aging
stranger off the bus, or to embrace even the smallest part
of our beloved while strolling through the park. We grasp
hands for a moment, or many, and offer safety, kindness, or
affection through the simple act.

Can you imagine God's hand extended to those who put their
faith in him? Surely his sons and daughters need the spiritual
comfort, guidance, and fellowship of his hand more than any
other.

God, knowing that you want to walk hand-in-hand with me
through life is comforting and encouraging. I take your hand
today and ask you to lead me.

If they stumble, they will not fall,
because the LORD *holds their hand.*

PSALM 37:24 NCV

We can be certain that God delights in extending his hand to us. The world extends an enticing but dangerous hand. It can offer comfort, guidance, and fellowship. But it can also offer anxiety, burdens, and loneliness.

Take comfort in God's kindness: he is a caring Father and he leads rightly. We cannot fall when we follow his lead because his loving grip will never let us go. As a child trusts the hand that leads them safely across the busy street, so we can trust God. By faith, you will not be pulled away from God by the temptations of the world. He is gentle, thoughtful, and compassionate, delighting over you.

Father, thank you for your tight grip on my hand. Knowing that you will not let me fall gives me confidence to step deeper into my relationship with you.

Will you say "yes" to God's hand, extended gently to you?

A Garment of Praise

Enter his gates with thanksgiving,
and his courts with praise.
Give thanks to him, bless his name.
For the LORD is good;
his steadfast love endures forever,
and his faithfulness to all generations.

PSALM 100:4-5 NRSV

Have you ever looked into a child's grumpy face and demanded that they don't smile? Even the most stubborn child can often be coaxed out of their funk by a few tickles or funny faces. Unfortunately, the same can't be said for adults. Imagine trying to change the attitude of a crotchety older woman with the same method. The picture is somewhat ridiculous.

God doesn't only deserve our praise when life is going well. He is worthy of our adoration every second of every day—no matter the situation. Living this out takes a good dose of faith. If you feel like today is going to be a tough one, decide now to smile.

God, this morning I choose to go about my day with a smile. You are always worthy of my praise and I want others to know that by my actions today.

Come into his city with songs of thanksgiving
and into his courtyards with songs of praise.
Thank him and praise his name.
The LORD is good. His love is forever,
and his loyalty goes on and on.

PSALM 100:4-5 NCV

When life's situations get us down, and all around us lie darkness and depression, it takes a great deal of faith to choose praise. But often that's the only thing that can really pull us out of those dark moments.

When you choose to thank God for his goodness and grace, you can't help but see life in a more positive light. As you praise God, your focus shifts from you to him.

Lord, thank you for walking with me today. I continue to choose a smile this evening and I thank you for all the good you have done in my life.

What does it look like for you to put on a garment of praise today?

My Prayers Are Heard

In the same way the Spirit also helps our weakness; for we do not know how to pray as we should, but the Spirit Himself intercedes for us with groanings too deep for words; and He who searches the hearts knows what the mind of the Spirit is, because He intercedes for the saints according to the will of God.

ROMANS 8:26-27 NASB

It is an amazing and powerful thing that the Holy Spirit within us recognizes the Holy Spirit in another believer. It unites people across geographic, economic, generational, and cultural boundaries. Two souls, surrendered to the same Savior, have plenty in common.

This miraculous connection can also bring us closer to God when we allow the Holy Spirit to show us how. When we are too weak in our flesh to know how or what to pray, we can count on the Holy Spirit to show us the way. What a relief!

God, thank you for your Holy Spirit who helps me communicate with you when I have no words. Help me to rely on you to show me what to pray.

The Spirit helps us with our weakness. We do not know how to pray as we should. But the Spirit himself speaks to God for us, even begs God for us with deep feelings that words cannot explain. God can see what is in people's hearts. And he knows what is in the mind of the Spirit, because the Spirit speaks to God for his people in the way God wants.

ROMANS 8:26-27 NCV

When the words don't seem to come out right or our supplications feel empty, we can submit to the Holy Spirit to intercede for us with prayers beyond mere words. God hears his children. And he hears his Spirit in a language that only the holy can utter.

Believe that God hears your prayers. Just as two people with only Jesus in common can bond over their Messiah, the Holy Spirit in you will never run out of things to mediate to the Father. Cry out however you can, and know that he hears every word.

God, I pour out my heart to you this evening. I know that you are always listening.

What have you been wanting to tell God?

Protection not Perfection

You have been a defense for the helpless,
a defense for the needy in his distress,
a refuge from the storm, a shade from the heat.

ISAIAH 25:4, NASB

In Christ, we are protected. We have a strong shield, a faithful defender, and a constant guardian. Many have mistaken this promise as a guarantee against pain, suffering, or hardship. When sorrows overwhelm us, can we stay faithful to our protector? Will we interpret adversity as betrayal, or embrace a protection that sometimes involves endurance, anguish, and pain?

God's security shelters us according to what we need, not necessarily from what pains us. His hand is upon you though, defending and sheltering you.

God, I see your hand of protection over my life even when things aren't going as I hope. Thank you.

You have been a refuge for the poor,
a refuge for the needy in their distress,
a shelter from the storm and a shade from the heat.
For the breath of the ruthless is like a storm driving against a wall.

ISAIAH 25:4 NIV

Protection does not mean perfection. Can we trust God only when our lives follow a path of ease? Faith gives depth to our expectations; we may not see through the dark clouds of the storm, but we know that God has prepared us for them. No matter how hard the rain falls or how fast the winds blow, we believe in his protection over us as we pass through it.

The storms will rage and the heat will blister, each in their turn and maybe for a long time. Can you believe that he is protecting you through it all? Let no storm shake your faith in this, beloved.

Father, help me to look to you in the storm. I choose to believe that you are protecting me even when the storms are raging.

How is your faith deepened when you recognize that he is with you in the storm?

God Will Provide

"Ask and it will be given to you; seek and you will find; knock and the door will be opened to you. For everyone who asks receives; the one who seeks finds; and to the one who knocks, the door will be opened."

MATTHEW 7:7-8 NIV

Because of God's great and perfect knowledge of you, you can trust that he understands you, from your deepest depths to your highest heights. He knows what lies behind you and he can heal your wounds. He knows what lies ahead of you, and he can prepare you for victory. In Christ, we are given everything we need to shoulder our burdens; we are humble enough to suffer and patient enough to persevere.

God's provisions are personal to each believer. Only you can receive what he offers because you are the one knocking at his door! When he opens it, ask him what it looks like, just between the two of you, to worship? What does devotion look like? How does he want you to overcome sin? By faith, you will receive everything you need.

God, there are so many things I could ask you for. I come to you humbly this morning and ask for your wisdom to guide me throughout the day.

"Ask, and God will give to you. Search, and you will find. Knock, and the door will open for you. Yes, everyone who asks will receive. Everyone who searches will find. And everyone who knocks will have the door opened."

MATTHEW 7:7-8 NCV

God strengthens us in our season of need, not before, and sometimes the strength fades so quickly afterward that we wonder how the feat was accomplished. God asks us to press into him because much prayer is needed for the seasons to come.

Gather the oil of faith now, for days are coming when you will pour out from what you have stored up. And remember that God waits, patiently, for you to cry out for help.

Father, thank you for your provision in the precise moments I need it. I ask you to fill my vessel now so I have enough to last me through the seasons of need.

Why are you knocking on God's door today?

Walking in Purity

Now that you have purified yourselves by obeying the truth so that you have sincere love for each other, love one another deeply, from the heart.

1 PETER 1:22 NIV

Purity in Christ means rejecting judgement, bitterness, gossip, criticism, anger, selfishness, and pride, turning instead to a spotless mindset of love. Replacing the old reflex with one of love, our first reaction becomes gracious and pure. In pureness, we believe the best about one another, bear with each other's burdens, and submit to Jesus for the building up of our character.

This is how we walk in purity: loving as Christ loves and showing the compassion, understanding, encouragement, discretion, grace, patience, selflessness, and humility that is our gift through Christ.

Jesus, I rely on you to be my character builder. I want to love others with your love.

Having purified your souls by your obedience to the truth for a sincere brotherly love, love one another earnestly from a pure heart.

1 PETER 1:22 ESV

The verse today explains a process that begins when "you have purified yourselves." Purification starts with repentance from a sinful past and acceptance of salvation. You obey the truth when you put your faith and hope in God, which produces love for others. It's an impossible gift except through Jesus, whose love is without any blemish or stain.

In contrast, we are full of stains. We judge and criticize and gossip. But with the imparting of Jesus' sincere, pure love, we can reject these habits and instead "love one another deeply, from the heart."

God, I know I am in need of you. I need your forgiveness and your mercy. Help me to reject selfish habits and choose to love others instead.

What do you think of when you hear the word purity?

A Specific Purpose

We are God's handiwork, created in Christ Jesus to do good works,
which God prepared in advance for us to do.

EPHESIANS 2:10 NIV

Very few people know exactly what they want to be *when they*
grow up. We take multiple tests to find out our personality
types, strengths, and spiritual gifts, all to determine what
we should do with our lives. While these tests can be good
indicators of suitable opportunities, the best way to find the
perfect fit is to go directly to the source.

Choose to believe that God has a purpose for your life, and
start asking him to reveal it to you. Don't place limitations on
God. He can do great things through you if you are willing to
trust him.

Thank you, God, that you have a specific purpose for me. You
brought me into the world to do something special, and I want to
walk in it.

*We are God's masterpiece. He has created us anew in Christ Jesus,
so we can do the good things he planned for us long ago.*

EPHESIANS 2:10 NLT

No matter what you may have been told, you were planned
by God. That means that he put you on this earth for a very
specific reason. God's desire is that you will partner with him
in that plan. When you begin to walk in his purpose, you will
find the joy, peace, strength, and grace you need to carry it out.

What makes you excited about the day ahead? Do you believe
God has something special for you to do? It might just be
that what you're passionate about God has placed in you for a
reason. Search it out!

*Lord, you have given me passion for certain things. Help me to look
for ways to use what I am passionate about to serve and honor you.*

What do you really love to do?

Everything I Do

Let us not grow weary of doing good, for in due season we will reap, if we do not give up.

GALATIANS 6:9 ESV

"Look at me! Look at me! Watch this!" Oh how often children seek recognition from just about anyone who will watch. Even though the dive bomb into the water looks exactly the same as it did last time, or the cartwheel is still lopsided after thirty attempts, onlookers continue to encourage the repetitious behavior.

We can choose to search for recognition from others, or we can believe that God sees everything we do. Because he does. He is interested in that project we worked so hard on. He is delighted when we spend our time serving others. He loves it when we do our very best.

God, I want to believe that you really are watching and applauding me. It encourages me to continue on.

Let us not lose heart in doing good, for in due time we will reap if we do not grow weary.

<small>GALATIANS 6:9 NASB</small>

Are we really very different from children who seek attention? Don't we also look for recognition in life? "Look at me; I made dinner every night this week!" "See this awesome presentation I put together for work?" "You should have seen the smiles on the faces of those people I helped today." We want someone to notice our efforts, our charity, our diligence, our excellence. And, though we hate to admit it, we may even get a little upset if nobody does.

Don't waste your time trying to be recognized by others. Share your talents and abilities *without holding back!* Your Father in heaven has his eye on you, and he's not about to look away.

Father, you don't ever stop watching me. Your eye is always on me. Help me not to desire recognition from others. I really only need to be seen by you.

What are the things you most want God to recognize in your life?

I Am Redeemed

"Truly, truly, I say to you, whoever hears my word and believes him who sent me has eternal life. He does not come into judgment, but has passed from death to life. Truly, truly, I say to you, an hour is coming, and is now here, when the dead will hear the voice of the Son of God, and those who hear will live."

JOHN 5:24-25 ESV

Because of Jesus Christ, we get to start over. His grace covers us and we receive his mercies anew each morning. Because of Jesus Christ, we dipped into everlasting pools of healing, baptized by the cool and refreshing presence of the Holy Spirit. We approached the throne humble, expectant, and thirsty because we could no longer shoulder the weight of our sins. Burdens unloaded at the foot of the throne; we were redeemed for freedom and live now in the promise of life everlasting. We have passed from death to life.

Being redeemed means being reinvented, refurbished, and revitalized. Something broken, ugly, or useless is given purpose. We are given a purpose in our redemption: to plead with those still in bondage to break free from their chains. The hour is coming when it will be too late.

God, I believe that you have truly erased every sin I have confessed. Thank you.

"I tell you the truth, whoever hears what I say and believes in the One who sent me has eternal life. That person will not be judged guilty but has already left death and entered life. I tell you the truth, the time is coming and is already here when the dead will hear the voice of the Son of God, and those who hear will have life."

JOHN 5:24-25 NCV

We have the assurance of our redemption, but do we live like the redeemed every day? Do we rejoice like slaves who have been set free? Redeemed, we abandon the path once walked for the one navigated by God.

Slaves cannot determine their steps; they are ordered to walk. But children of God have been ransomed and set free. They must choose to run from the paths of materialism, pride, vanity, and idolatry that have been paved by the world. Choose the path of freedom this evening.

Father, you have redeemed me and set me free. Help me not to pursue things that lead me away from you. I want to walk in freedom and truth.

Spend some time expressing your thanks to God for the redemptive work of his Son in your life.

Rested and Refreshed

Bless the LORD, O my soul, and forget not all his benefits,
who forgives all your iniquity, who heals all your diseases,
who redeems your life from the pit,
who crowns you with steadfast love and mercy,
who satisfies you with good
so that your youth is renewed like the eagle's.

PSALM 103:2–5 ESV

Is it reasonable to believe that a marathon runner can finish a race without a single refreshing cup of water? Would it be fair to expect a doctor, after working a 36-hour shift, to have the energy to perform one last tedious surgery? Can a child be expected not to lick the spatula that mixed the cookie dough? Or should a foreigner be intuitively familiar with the customs of a new land?

Whether you are at peak performance or running on empty, needing renewal now or in the future, God alone can give you what you need for the refreshment of your mind, body, and spirit because he knows your limits and capabilities. He knows that you need time to refuel, space to recover your strength, and that sometimes a little cookie dough goes a long way.

God, you want me to ask you for rest and refreshment every time
I need it. Help me to remember to come to you first.

My whole being, praise the LORD
and do not forget all his kindnesses.
He forgives all my sins and heals all my diseases.
He saves my life from the grave and loads me with love and mercy.
He satisfies me with good things
and makes me young again, like the eagle.

PSALM 103:2-5 NCV

We know that humans have limits. We need to eat and drink
regularly. We get tired and struggle if we don't have enough
sleep. We learn patience and self-control as we get older, but
our emotions can be overwhelmed by life's great upheavals.
The shepherd king David knew this, and understood God's
gracious and loving path of refreshment.

Rest in God when you need to be refreshed. Don't believe
that you aren't strong because you need to rest; you aren't
meant be strong forever. You are designed to lean on the one
whose strength can renew you.

Lord, tonight I feel weak. I need your strength. Bring me your rest
and refresh my spirit. Thank you.

What do you need your strength renewed for today?

Contend for Peace

Don't just pretend to love others. Really love them. Hate what is wrong. Hold tightly to what is good. Love each other with genuine affection, and take delight in honoring each other. Do all that you can to live in peace with everyone.

ROMANS 12:9-10, 18 NLT

These are very convicting directions from God's Word. Unless you have completely mastered loving everyone you meet, Paul's words to the Roman church might leave you feeling a little squeamish. How can we determine to really love each other? In the same breath we can *hate* what is wrong and then *do* what is wrong. We are holding tightly to what is good, but at the smallest distraction we let go and grab hold of something shinier. Someone we genuinely love and delight to honor can become an easy target for our criticism and jealousy.

Ask for God's love for others to overwhelm your heart so you can really love them. Ask for his mindset to replace yours, and cling tightly to his good Word.

God, give me your heart of love and forgiveness toward people I need to make peace with today.

Your love must be real. Hate what is evil, and hold on to what is good. Love each other like brothers and sisters. Give each other more honor than you want for yourselves.
Do your best to live in peace with everyone.

ROMANS 12:9-10, 18 NCV

We are flawed. Deeply and truly we are flawed, but not hopelessly. If God commands that we do all that we can to live at peace with everyone, we can believe that he has made a way for us to achieve it. Begin with confession and repentance. Cry out to God for his Holy Spirit to change you from the inside—your thoughts, your opinions, your outlook—so that your words and deeds will also be transformed.

Read and meditate on Scripture, day and night, so that it is painted on the walls of your mind. Contend for peace in all relationships by putting off old habits and adopting God's heart of love.

Father, start transformation in my heart so I can change from the inside out. I want to have your thoughts toward people and treat them with love. I need peace in my relationships, and you're the only one who can make it last.

Which relationships in your life need peace right now?

Reliability

When they call to me, I will answer them;
I will be with them in trouble,
I will rescue them and honor them.

PSALM 91:15 NRSV

There's something to be said for a reliable car. It starts *every* time you turn the key over. It *never* breaks down and leaves you stranded in the middle of a highway. It *always* blows heat in the cold of winter and cold air in the heat of summer.

Our perfectly reliable God is always near. He doesn't forget about our important plans or our hopes and dreams. He won't be caught off guard when it's our birthday, anniversary, graduation day, important final interview, or anything in between. Thank God for his reliability this morning.

God, you want what is best for me and you have the means to
see it happen. I place my focus on you today because I will not be
disappointed.

When he calls to me, I will answer him;
I will be with him in trouble;
I will rescue him and honor him.

PSALM 91:15 ESV

If we want our cars to be reliable, we want people to be even more so. They *always* show up when they say they will. They *never* forget to finish their part of an important project. *Every* time you call, they pick up the phone.

We all know that neither cars nor people are completely reliable. What we do know is that both cars and people will fail us at some point in our lives. It's inevitable. Aren't you glad to be in relationship with the God who cannot fail you because it is not in his nature to fail—*ever*?

Father, thank you for your reliability. You are always near and always good.

What are you hoping for from God today?

Other Opinions

Yes, the LORD is for me; he will help me.
I will look in triumph at those who hate me.
It is better to take refuge in the LORD
than to trust in people.

PSALM 118:7-8 NLT

God created you for relationship with him, just as he created Adam and Eve. He delights in your voice, your laughter, and your ideas. He longs to fellowship with you just as he did with his first son and daughter. But, like Adam and Eve, we are sometimes persuaded by the opinions of others instead of listening and obeying the commands of our Father and greatest friend.

When life gets difficult, we can run to him with our frustrations. When we're overwhelmed with sadness or grief, we can carry our pain to him. In the heat of anger or frustration, we can call on him for freedom. He is a friend that offers all of this—and more—in mercy and love, and he is worthy of our friendship.

Thank you for loving me so much, Father, that you want to share in my everyday moments. I ask you to walk with me throughout this day.

The LORD is with me to help me,
so I will see my enemies defeated.
It is better to trust the LORD
than to trust people.

PSALM 118:7-8 NCV

It is understandably tempting to share our grievances, triumphs, problems, or desires with friends and loved ones we can easily call on the phone or meet for coffee. God has given us wonderful relationships! But we run the risk of listening first to their opinions rather than God's, and this risk can trap us in sin.

Don't let others' opinions of you matter more than God's. Train your heart to run first to God with your pain, joy, frustration, and excitement. His friendship will never let you down!

God, what you think of me matters most. I want to remember this when I am sharing with others. I don't need to impress people or hide the truth from them because only your opinion truly matters.

How much value do you place on the opinions of others?

Developing Maturity

We know how much God loves us, and we have put our trust in his love. God is love, and all who live in love live in God, and God lives in them. And as we live in God, our love grows more perfect. So we will not be afraid on the day of judgment, but we can face him with confidence because we live like Jesus here in this world.

1 JOHN 4:16-17 NLT

Responsibility is something that is sorely lacking in the world. We have excuses for everything. We even have excuses for excuses. Nothing is anyone's fault, and we are encouraged to live solely for ourselves.

As we work on developing love for others, we recognize God's heart and we begin to carry compassion and a desire to help. As we love God, we gain better understanding of his love for us, and we become more aware of our need for his grace. This is the maturity that he desires for us: closeness to him, and relationship with others.

Lord, give me your heart. Help me to become more aware of your maturing work in my life.

So we know and rely on the love God has for us. God is love. Whoever lives in love lives in God, and God in them. This is how love is made complete among us so that we will have confidence on the day of judgment: In this world we are like Jesus.

1 JOHN 4:16-17 NIV

Without responsibility, how can we expect to grow in our relationship with God? We can't live oblivious to our fault or the needs around us. God calls us to a higher level of living. He asks us to love him first and our neighbor next. He tells us to respect each other, to consider others as more important than ourselves. It's so counter-culture that we have to really work at developing it.

Spend some time this evening pondering how you can grow in maturity in your relationship with the Lord. Begin thinking of ways you can show awareness of others' needs and set aside your own.

God, I know I think of myself far too often. It's what the world tells me to do. I don't want to listen to the advice and trends of the world, though. I want to consider others and love them well.

What areas in your life are lacking a sense of responsibility?

Second Chances

You, O LORD, are a shield about me,
My glory, and the One who lifts my head.

PSALM 3:3 NASB

Picture a young girl running a race. She leaps off to a great
start when the gun sounds. She pushes her way to the front of
the pack in no time and sets a pace that is tough to compete
with. As she rounds the final corner with the finish line
in sight, she stumbles. She tries desperately to regain her
balance, but it's too late. She crashes to the ground. Trying
to be brave, she jumps up and sprints the final yards to
complete the race. Fourth place.

Have you ever had one of these days? You were off to a good
start and then everything came crashing down around you? Let
God be the author of a second chance for you. Don't give up.

Father, sometimes I feel like I can't look up. I need your words to
wash over my wounds and bring healing to my heart, soul, and
mind today.

You, O L<small>ORD</small>, are a shield around me;
you are my glory, the one who holds my head high.

<small>PSALM 3:3 NLT</small>

Head hung low, skinned knees burning, and vision blurry, the young girl walks over to her coach. He gently lifts her chin to the sun, and brushes away the tears that have spilled over. As her bottom lip begins to quiver, he reassures her that everything is going to be okay. That life is full of painful moments that creep up unexpectedly, but it's also full of second chances. "Don't give up on yourself," he says, "I haven't given up on you."

When we've given up, run away, lost the plot, or stumbled and fallen, God doesn't give up on us. When we come to him with our heads hung low, he lifts our chins, looks deep into our eyes, and whispers tender words of compassion that reach the deepest places in our hearts.

God, whisper to my heart tonight. I need to hear from you.

How do you think God feels about you in this moment?

Free Advice

"Don't store up treasures here on earth, where moths eat them and rust destroys them, and where thieves break in and steal. Store your treasures in heaven, where moths and rust cannot destroy, and thieves do not break in and steal."

MATTHEW 6:19-20 NLT

There are many so-called experts ready and willing to give you advice (usually for a price) about any problem you have. Whether you are dealing with health issues, money matters, relationship woes, career dilemmas, car troubles, housing hassles, or pet problems, there is an expert out there ready to diagnose and treat it. If you lived in the neighborhood of Galilee two-thousand years ago, you would've had access to the world's greatest advisor. His advice was free... sort of.

Eternal treasures are a reward worth seeking, and Jesus' instructions are advice worth taking. Take Jesus' perfect advice and seek after that which brings eternal reward.

Jesus, thank you for your perfect advice. I want to follow after that which brings an eternal reward.

"Don't store treasures for yourselves here on earth where moths and rust will destroy them and thieves can break in and steal them. But store your treasures in heaven where they cannot be destroyed by moths or rust and where thieves cannot break in and steal them."

MATTHEW 6:19-20 NCV

Jesus asked that you be willing to give up everything you had to follow him. Your job, your family, your house and wealth—all were given up for the sake of following Jesus the Messiah. If he were advising you today, would you listen?

In Matthew 6, Jesus teaches us to forsake all earthly gain because it is temporary and vulnerable. Real treasures, he instructed, should be stored in heaven where they are safe. When we pray quietly, for God's ears only, he hears and will reward us. When we give to the needy in private, without telling others about it, God sees our sacrifice and will reward us. The praise and approval of the world is fleeting and worthless compared to the treasure that God stores up for us as we forsake earthly gain.

God, give me the right perspective on treasure and worth. Your rewards are best.

Evaluate the things you spend your time on. What has eternal reward attached to it?

Discovering Beauty

The whole earth is filled with awe at your wonders.

PSALM 65:8 NIV

Have you ever looked at a spider's web covered with dewdrops? What about the iridescence of a hummingbird wing, a glistening canyon covered in ferns, a breathtaking sunset, or a chubby-faced giggling baby? Our hearts soar overlooking the snowcapped mountains and listening to birdsongs on a summer's afternoon.

Each day we are presented with the beauty of God's world. You may be surprised to find it on your daily drive or by listening a little closer to one of your co-workers.

Lord God, help me to see the world around me with new eyes of amazement.

Even those people at the ends of the earth fear your miracles.
You are praised from where the sun rises to where it sets.

PSALM 65:8 NCV

God's beauty is all around us; it includes the people he has put under our care. Beauty can be seen in the little girl with a darling lisp as well as the pierced and tattooed teen with purple hair and attitude. It emanates from every person God created.

All of us are wonders of God's creation. Sometimes we need to slow down a bit to look for the beauty and diversity of the world around us. Break your habit this evening and take time to appreciate the beauty of God's creation.

Father, I am in awe of your wonders. I want to see and appreciate the miracles you have placed right in front of me.

What beauty do you see as you look around this evening?

Taking Hold of Promises

Understand, therefore, that the LORD your God is indeed God.
He is the faithful God who keeps his covenant for a thousand
generations and lavishes his unfailing love on those who love him
and obey his commands.

DEUTERONOMY 7:9 NLT

God's promises are so good! Is there one that is better
than another? He promises to protect, heal, comfort, love,
forgive, provide, equip, overcome, abide, listen, delight,
guide, fulfill, understand, reward, renew, refresh, bless,
lead, redeem… the list goes on longer than these pages. But
promises get made and broken every day. How can we trust
that God's promises are true?

God has been faithful to his covenants since he promised
Adam and Eve that nothing good would come from eating the
fruit of that tree. He continues his faithfulness to you, his
daughter and his delight.

God, I come to you this morning to sit in your presence and dwell
on your goodness. Help me to believe that your promises are for me.

Know that the LORD your God is God, the faithful God. He will keep his agreement of love for a thousand lifetimes for people who love him and obey his commands.

DEUTERONOMY 7:9 NCV

All of God's promises are as true for you as they were for Noah, Abraham, Joseph, and David. He can rescue you from disaster, make you flourish in the wilderness, redeem you from despair, and knit your heart together with his in deep friendship and devotion. If you will only believe.

Don't ever let go of his promises. Take hold of them and overcome!

Father, it seems impossible that you have the same promises for me as you did for Noah, Abraham, Joseph, and David. I stand on your promises this evening because I know your Word is truth and you are faithful.

Do you struggle to believe that God's promises are for you?

What Is Best

Those who know the LORD trust him,
because he will not leave those who come to him.

PSALM 9:10 NCV

Why don't parents let their children eat candy for breakfast, lunch, and dinner? The answer is obvious. It wouldn't be good for them. But ask the children what they think, and they could probably come up with a pretty convincing argument that candy is good for them.

In life, situations come along that seem good. We think that man would make the perfect husband, or that job would be the best jumpstart to our career, or that adventure would be the ultimate experience. The problem is we don't have the vantage point that God does. All those opportunities might be "candy," but what we really need is a good, nutritious meal.

Father, show me when I'm chasing after candy. I want a solid meal that will sustain me instead.

Those who know your name put their trust in you,
for you, O LORD, have not forsaken those who seek you

PSALM 9:10 ESV

When we let go of the idea that we know what's best, and choose to believe that God actually does, we will find what is truly good. How wonderful it is to know that we don't have to feel the pressure of making all the right choices on our own.

God has an amazing way of nurturing us even when we choose to eat candy. We just have to admit that his way would have been better and move forward in his grace. Can you do that tonight?

God, I need your grace to cover my bad choices. I admit my fault and ask you to show me the better way.

What experiences in your life seemed good, but turned out being less than God's best for you?

Stand on the Truth

Your words are true from the start,
and all your laws will be fair forever.
I am as happy over your promises
as if I had found a great treasure.

PSALM 119:160, 162 NCV

The world shouts, "Truth is relative!" "Truth is what I believe!" "Truth is what I want it to be!" We cannot entertain these lies. Truth is found in God's Word alone. Truth is absolute. It has not changed since the beginning of time and it will not change on into eternity.

Stand together with those who believe and declare that God's Word is the definition of truth itself.

Father, help me not to listen to the world's definition of truth. Only your Word is truth. You are truth.

The sum of your word is truth;
and every one of your righteous ordinances endures forever.
I rejoice at your word
like one who finds great spoil.

PSALM 119:160, 162 NASB

Because God's Word is true, we can believe everything it says. It's by far not the most popular thing to stake our morals, beliefs, and decisions on, and we can be sure to expect a good amount of opposition and ridicule when we do. This is why it's important to surround ourselves with others who also believe wholeheartedly in the absolute nature of God's Word.

Spend some time this evening in the truth. Absorb it and let it bring you life.

God, I stand on your Word tonight. I believe everything that is written in Scripture. I know it is truth. Help me to find others who believe the same.

What does it look like for you to stand on the truth of God's Word in this season of your life?

Truly Understood

This High Priest of ours understands our weaknesses, for he faced all of the same testings we do, yet he did not sin.

HEBREWS 4:15 NLT

My Daughter,

Don't lose heart. Guard your faith and listen to my voice. I understand your love for me. You may think it's small or diminishing, but I feel its strength and fullness. You love like a child—believing and carefree. Keep your eyes fixed on me, beloved. I understand your needs. I am a refuge and strength for you; only I can and will sustain you.

My care is what is right for you: I am your stream of water, your living sacrifice, your good shepherd. I am your comfort and my mercy is complete. I understand your heart and all its pains, sorrows, longings, and disappointments, and I comfort you. I never leave you or forsake you. I love you so much.

Father, your love is overwhelming. I bask in its warmth today.

We do not have a high priest who is unable to empathize with our weaknesses, but we have one who has been tempted in every way, just as we are—yet he did not sin.

HEBREWS 4:15 NIV

Whatever you need, you can ask him and he will answer you; he already knows your heart and what you long for. Nothing is a surprise to him!

Know that God truly understands your heart. He knows the test you are facing, and he gives you the mercy you need to endure it. When you need it most, his grace is there.

Jesus, you understand me because you have faced similar trials. Thank you for your mercy that helps me get through each day.

Write a letter to God, expressing your gratitude for his deep understanding of your heart.

Every Situation

Then you will understand what is right, just, and fair,
and you will find the right way to go.
For wisdom will enter your heart,
and knowledge will fill you with joy.
Wise choices will watch over you.
Understanding will keep you safe.

PROVERBS 2:9-11 NLT

All of life is a test. As we live each day, the tests we face teach us valuable lessons. It may seem backwards: usually lessons are learned to prepare us for a test. But in life, the test often comes first. Through the lessons, God gives us the wisdom we need for the next test.

It's a safe bet that the tests will keep coming. Thankfully, our hearts gain understanding every time. Tension and uncertainty melt away; joy blossoms. Solomon's advice is that we listen to wisdom, apply it, and learn as we go. Then we will have understanding; we will find the right path with wisdom in our hearts and joy from knowledge.

Thank you, God, for giving me the opportunity to make wise choices.

*Then you will understand righteousness and justice
and equity, every good path;
for wisdom will come into your heart,
and knowledge will be pleasant to your soul;
prudence will watch over you;
and understanding will guard you.*

PROVERBS 2:9-11 NRSV

Gaining wisdom doesn't guarantee that you won't stumble and fall on your face or stick your foot in your mouth. You will still make mistakes, say the wrong thing at the wrong time, and wish you could go back in time and do it right. It stings.

Even when we fail the test, we learn a lesson and gain wisdom. If we humble ourselves, we can trust that God will give us wisdom in every situation. Another test is just around the corner, waiting for us to pass with flying colors!

Father, even though I fail your tests often, I thank you that I can take joy in the wisdom I gain from those tests. You don't expect me to get it right the first time, and you even have grace if I fail it the second time. Thank you for continuing to be patient with me while I learn.

What valuable lessons have you learned from life's tests?

Aching to Belong

"Those the Father has given me will come to me, and I will never reject them."

JOHN 6:37 NLT

We all long to feel part of a community or group because we were created to be in close relationships with each other. The Lord knit in us the desire for friendships that are close and life giving. But sometimes we can feel left out from a group and we ache to belong.

It can be very painful to feel unappreciated and unwelcome. Feeling unloved is a lonely place to be. Sometimes we go to great lengths in order to feel acceptance from others. You belong to God and he will never reject you. Let his acceptance of you give you peace today.

Father, I would love to know what you think about me. Help me to remember that I don't need to do anything to be accepted by you. I can just be who you made me to be.

"All that the Father gives me will come to me, and whoever comes to me I will never cast out."

JOHN 6:37 ESV

God wants you to know that you are perfect the way you are. You do not need to change who you are to feel his acceptance. He knows you completely and loves you deeply.

When you feel that ache to belong, go to God, let him fill it with the knowledge that you already do belong. You belong to him. His arms are open and ready to embrace you—just as you are.

Thank you, God, for the sense of belonging that I get when I am with you. Let that feeling flood through me tonight.

What about yourself do you feel like you need to change in order to be accepted by others?

Adoration

"You are a people holy to the LORD your God. The LORD your God has chosen you to be a people for his treasured possession, out of all the peoples who are on the face of the earth."

DEUTERONOMY 7:6 ESV

You are like a precious flower. You are absolutely the apple of your Father's eye. He loves and cherishes you beyond comprehension. You are adored.

Because God adores us, he allows us to go through some things that don't always feel good. But God is perfect. He is good, loving, and protective. We can trust that in those difficult moments, he is shaping and molding us to be more like him—to grow fully into who he wants us to be.

Father, to be adored by you is too wonderful to describe. I want to be who you want me to be. I submit myself to your molding and shaping, knowing that you are completely trustworthy.

You are a holy people, who belong to the LORD your God. Of all the people on earth, the LORD your God has chosen you to be his own special treasure.

DEUTERONOMY 7:6 NLT

When you adore something, you don't just love it; you watch it, protect it, and handle it with great care. Your Father doesn't want to miss a thing. He wants to know every detail of your life. He handles you with such great care because he wants you to fully become who he intended you to be.

Can you see how you have become a richer person through some of the difficulties God has allowed to cross your path? Do you recognize his goodness even in those times?

God, thank you for adoring me. I see how you have grown me in moments of difficulty and I am grateful for your loving care.

What are some ways you feel God adores you?

Response to Anger

"Don't sin by letting anger control you." Don't let the sun go down while you are still angry.

EPHESIANS 4:26 NLT

There are many things in this world that make us angry, that should make us angry. Sometimes all it takes is turning on the five o'clock news and being confronted with injustice and hardship; it causes our blood to boil.

Even though anger sounds bad, anger in itself is not wrong. God created us to feel deeply in a wide range of emotions. It is the way we respond in our anger that matters greatly. If we allow our anger to get the best of us, it could destroy relationships or cause heartache and deep pain.

God, help me to have the right response to anger. I don't want to ruin relationships with anyone because I can't control my angry emotions. Give me grace for others and self-control.

"In your anger do not sin": Do not let the sun go down while you are still angry.

Ephesians 4:26 niv

In our anger we always have a choice. We could lash out and be destructive, or we could allow our anger to evoke change in an unjust situation. It is possible to feel angry, yet exercise restraint and self-control when encountering unpleasant or unfair circumstances.

We can take comfort that God knows how we are feeling in every moment—in every situation—and that he cares deeply. He will help us choose to be loving and grace-giving if we feel like our anger is spiraling out of control. All we have to do is ask him.

Father, there are many things that upset me. Sometimes I am right in my assessment of a situation and others times I am not. Help me to seek your wisdom before I respond in anger.

What's the best way you have found to control your anger?

Signs of Anxiety

Cast all your anxiety on him because he cares for you.

1 PETER 5:7 NIV

Your stomach feels like it's doing flips, your mind is stuck on repeat, everything feels more intense than usual, and sleep doesn't come easy. These are all signs of anxiety. Anxiety can be difficult to deal with, and sometimes it can begin taking over the way you do life.

If you ever find yourself in this state, immediately go to God. He does not want you to struggle with anxiety. When he sees you with so much mental and emotional weight, he wants to give you rest. He can take all of your anxiety and replace it with peace.

Choosing to cast my anxiety on you, Lord, is not easy. It sounds like it should be, but I have a hard time letting go of the many thoughts in my mind. I need your peace today, God.

Give all your worries and cares to God, for he cares about you.

1 PETER 5:7 NLT

Tell God all the things that are overwhelming you. Go through each thing and picture yourself giving it to him. Ask him to help you stop the thoughts that play over and over in your head. Ask for peace. Your heavenly Father loves you and he wants to comfort you. When unhealthy levels of anxiety arise, go to the Lord and allow him to lift you up. He will carry you through the situation and give you peace.

What things are causing you to be anxious? Take some time to give those things to the Lord and ask him to bring you comfort and peace tonight.

God, so many things cause anxiety if I dwell on them. I need your peace and rest tonight. Help me take control of my thoughts and give my cares to you.

Are you struggling with anxiety?

Honest and Authentic

"God sees not as man sees, for man looks at the outward appearance, but the Lord looks at the heart."

1 SAMUEL 16:7 NASB

Honest and genuine relationships are priceless. When we hide who we are, it becomes almost impossible for those who love us to enter into our lives and truly know us. A shallow friendship is empty and lonely. In order to have solid friendships, we need to let our guards down and let others into the hidden areas in our lives.

It can be scary to be open and transparent, but by doing so we are able to create true relationships that encourage and strengthen us in our weakest areas. Living an authentic life allows us to see that we aren't alone in our struggles. We need each other.

God, thank you for giving me friends who can encourage and strengthen me. I want to be authentic and show them my struggles as well as my victories.

The LORD does not look at the things people look at. People look at the outward appearance, but the LORD looks at the heart.

1 SAMUEL 16:7 NIV

There is much joy and freedom to be found in being who we are. This includes our relationship with God. Sometimes we forget that he already knows the inner workings of our hearts. Even though we may try, it is impossible to hide our struggles and shortcomings from him. Yet, he still loves us despite our faults and embraces us even more. He should be our standard for all other relationships.

Are you the same when you are alone as you are when you are with other people? Do you struggle to show your true beautiful colors to those around you? Let God show you today how much he loves you just for who you are!

Father, thank you for loving me for who I am. Help me to be real with others. I don't want to hide who I am.

What do you think will happen if you let others in?

Definition of Beauty

Don't be concerned about the outward beauty of fancy hairstyles, expensive jewelry, or beautiful clothes. You should clothe yourselves instead with the beauty that comes from within, the unfading beauty of a gentle and quiet spirit, which is so precious to God.

1 PETER 3:3-4 NLT

God's definition of beauty can become clouded in the face of the world's description. You can't open up a magazine or social media window and not be bombarded with images of pretty women: photoshopped and scantily-clothed.

The danger of these images is that we try to compare ourselves with them. We size up our appearance and feel ugly in comparison. Thoughts begin to worm themselves into the core of our beings. We begin to claim ownership to lies instead of embracing the truth that God wants us to know and live by.

Father, I want to truly know and believe that you think I am beautiful on the inside and out.

Do not adorn yourselves outwardly by braiding your hair, and by wearing gold ornaments or fine clothing rather, let your adornment be the inner self with the lasting beauty of a gentle and quiet spirit, which is very precious in God's sight.

1 PETER 3:3-4 NRSV

You are beautiful. From the top of your head to the bottom of your feet. Knowing you are truly beautiful begins with you absorbing what God thinks of you. Not only are you outwardly beautiful in your Creator's eyes, but inwardly too.

We all possess a beauty that it not easily seen on billboards or on TV. We harbor a beauty that surpasses any worldly definition. Our grace. Our patience . Our compassion. Our generosity. Our kindness. All of these things make us beautiful in God's eyes.

God, help me to embrace the unfading inner beauty of a gentle spirit. I want to place more importance on being beautiful on the inside than I do on being outwardly beautiful.

What do you see when you look in the mirror?

Boldness Defined

I remind you to fan into flame the gift of God… for God gave us a spirit not of fear but of power and love and self-control.

2 TIMOTHY 1:6-7 ESV

Any new situation can be daunting. A new job. A new group of friends. A new adventure or opportunity. All of these things can cause our knees to buckle and our heart to race.

Sometimes we need boldness for the concrete and tangible fears we face; an angry family member, a disgruntled friend, a failed test. Or maybe we need boldness to defend the weak and rise up for the forgotten. Sometimes we simply need boldness to do what we know is right. God made you a warrior. Warriors don't run from scary situations; they march forward and battle on.

God, show me just how brave I can be when I depend on you.

I remind you to rekindle the gift of God that is within you through the laying on of my hands; for God did not give us a spirit of cowardice, but rather a spirit of power and of love and of self-discipline.

2 TIMOTHY 1:6-7 NRSV

Many times, we just want to cower and hide, but hiding doesn't make fears disappear. Instead, they are allowed to fester and grow. Before we know it, fear takes control of our lives.

You may wish that you were braver. You can be. God has equipped you with everything you need to conquer any situation. He has given you the weapons to fight with—chin up and shoulders squared. You never have to go into any situation afraid. You can have full assurance that God will give you the boldness you need in the exact moment you need it.

Father, give me boldness to carry out that which you have asked of me. I need you.

What situations can you think of that require you to be bold?

Greatest Comforter

You have given me many troubles and bad times,
but you will give me life again.
When I am almost dead,
you will keep me alive.
You will make me greater than ever,
and you will comfort me again.

PSALM 71:20-21 NCV

As Christians, we are never promised that we will go through life seeing no trouble. In fact, it's quite the opposite. We're told time and time again in the Bible that there will be tough times, that we will be persecuted for our beliefs, and we won't always have a life of ease.

But there is good news despite all that. We have someone we can always turn to in our times of pain. God is waiting for us to run to him. He is the greatest comforter we could ever find. He wants to restore us, refresh us, and bring us contentment amidst the darkness of our anguish.

Thank you, God, that there is hope and life in you.
You are my Comforter.

You who have made me see many troubles and calamities
will revive me again;
from the depths of the earth
you will bring me up again.
You will increase my honor,
and comfort me once again.

PSALM 71:20-21 NRSV

You can always turn to Jesus during times of trial. He will open his arms and welcome you, helping you find your way through it all. If you feel burdened by what life has offered you, pray for his peace today. He will restore you over and over again.

Be encouraged by the Psalmist's response. In the midst of his trouble, he gave himself to the Lord. He knew that was the only way to life, comfort, and joy.

Father, you have kept me safe from myself. Help me to run to you for comfort when I need it most.

In what areas do you need God's comfort today?

Follow Through

You desired faithfulness even in the womb;
you taught me wisdom in that secret place.

PSALM 51:6 NIV

Commitment, follow-through, and faithfulness are all words
that mean about the same thing. They are character traits
that God desires in you. Some things we commit to because
they seem fun or easy. Other things deserve our commitment
because they are the right things to do. These are the
commitments that are often more difficult to stick with.

Faithfulness is one of the nine fruits of the spirit written in
Galatians 5:22-23. It holds great value before God. As his
child, you are an example and a light to many. When God calls
you to be faithful, it means that you do what you say you are
going to do even when it is inconvenient. You stick with it
because others are depending on you.

Thank you, Lord, for your commitment to me today.

You delight in truth in the inward being, and you teach me wisdom in the secret heart.

PSALM 51:6 ESV

By learning to be a more faithful person, you will find that others trust and respect you deeply. Jesus was faithful to his Father in the most difficult commitment imaginable—being crucified on the cross for our sins.

Because of Jesus' faithfulness to his commitment, we are able to be in relationship with the Father. That is something to be extremely grateful for.

God, help me to go against the grain of my culture and begin following through on my commitments.

How can you show faithfulness in areas you have committed yourself to?

Full Confidence

The LORD will be your confidence
and will keep your foot from being caught.

PROVERBS 3:26 ESV

It is so amazing to think there is only one you in this entire world! Only one with your laugh, your face, your quirks, and your specific talents. No other person can be you better than you. God made you with great intention—every inch of you inside and out—and he doesn't make mistakes.

Seek the Lord and he will reveal more of who you were created to be. You may see talents come forth that you never knew you had. There is a mission for you in life: love and accept yourself for who you are. Be you; nobody can do it better!

God, thank you for making me who I am. I want to know more
about who you created me to be. Help me to grow in confidence
as I develop the talents you have given me.

The LORD will be at your side
and will keep your foot from being snared.

PROVERBS 3:26 NIV

You are beautiful in God's eyes, and he created you for a purpose. The only way you can fully accomplish his purpose for your life is to get to know yourself and accept the beautiful person you are. When you do this, you wear an outfit called confidence. It's the kind of clothing that shines bright and attracts others to its light.

Are there areas in which you feel insecure? Pray for the Lord to bring you full confidence in who you are tonight.

Father, where I feel insecure help me to rely on you. I trust you to be my full confidence tonight.

What are some talents you feel God has given you?

Contentment

I know how to live on almost nothing or with everything. I have learned the secret of living in every situation, whether it is with a full stomach or empty, with plenty or little. For I can do everything through Christ, who gives me strength.

PHILIPPIANS 4:12-13 NLT

Have you ever looked at someone else's life and wistfully thought, *I wish I had what they had?* It seems harmless enough, but when those thoughts grow and multiply (as they are known to do), they become dangerous. When we allow discontentment to foster in our lives, we allow our joy to be taken from us.

Discontentment gives our hearts permission to wander in directions that are not good. Our priorities are in danger of becoming hazy. Choose to be content with everything you have today.

Thank you, Father, that I can choose to be content with the many or few things I have. You take care of my needs and for that I am grateful.

I know what it is to have little, and I know what it is to have plenty. In any and all circumstances I have learned the secret of being well-fed and of going hungry, of having plenty and of being in need. I can do all things through him who strengthens me.

<small>PHILIPPIANS 4:12-13 NRSV</small>

Instead of partaking in a friend's joy over their successes and accomplishments, when we're not content we begin to envy and resent them. There are no winners in a comparison game. We become so focused on what we want or don't have that it becomes impossible to notice and be thankful for what we are blessed with.

Discontentment makes us unhappy and miserable. It inhibits us from enjoying and embracing every moment of life. Don't let it steal your joy this evening.

God, sometimes the only way to battle discontentment is to continually number my blessings, and thank you for your goodness. I choose to do that tonight.

What things in life are you thankful for?

Courage to Do the Unusual

"So do not fear, for I am with you; do not be dismayed, for I am your God. I will strengthen you and help you; I will uphold you with my righteous right hand."

ISAIAH 41:10 NIV

The Bible is chock full of courageous women. Esther faced possible death or severe punishment from her husband the king just for asking him to dinner. Ruth followed her mother-in-law to a new country where life was full of unknowns because she felt it was the right thing to do.

Hannah gave up her son because she knew he belonged in the house of the Lord. Noah's wife got on a boat when there wasn't a drop of water to be found anywhere and everyone thought she was crazy. They all obeyed God's commands no matter what it looked like to others. Would you be able to do the same?

God, these women in the Bible showed more courage than I feel like I could muster up in a lifetime. I need your strength today to do what is right.

"Don't be afraid, for I am with you. Don't be discouraged, for I am your God. I will strengthen you and help you. I will hold you up with my victorious right hand."

ISAIAH 41:10 NLT

In your lifetime, you will come upon many situations where you will need to muster up your courage. Whether it's standing up for what's right, taking a leap into the unknown, or making a change in your life, you can do it if you take hold of the Lord's hand and ask for his strength.

God is willing to walk you through anything if you'll ask him to. Ask for his help and he will give you strength.

Father, you say that you are always with me. Help me to be able to do everything you ask of me. I want to be obedient to you.

Do you need courage today?

Work of Art

He has filled him with the Spirit of God, with wisdom, with understanding, with knowledge and with all kinds of skills.

EXODUS 35:31 NIV

Everyone has a creative streak. God made us to create in various mediums. We could be defined as writers, musicians, painters, builders, athletes, dancers, chefs, photographers... the list is endless. Have you ever created something and then stepped back to admire it? You might have even been filled with pride and admiration. Artists go to great lengths to make sure their work is not only seen, but also preserved.

This is how God looks at you. You are his greatest work of art, created for a wonderful purpose. He doesn't focus on your flaws; he sees his perfect creation, and he thinks it is wonderful. He thinks you are wonderful.

Creator God, thank you for creating me uniquely. Help me to understand how precious I am to you.

*He has filled him with the Spirit of God, with skill, with
intelligence, with knowledge, and with all craftsmanship,*

EXODUS 35:31 ESV

Sometimes you might feel like you aren't worthy. You may
look at yourself with disgust, wishing you had a different gift,
talent, or personality. This breaks God's heart. If only you
could see yourself the way God sees you.

You would be completely blown away if you knew just how
much your Creator admires you. You are not a mistake. Your
hair color, your smile, your interests, your abilities, they were
all orchestrated by God. No piece of artwork is the same; none
can be duplicated. Each is unique and special to the artist.

*God, sometimes when I look at myself all I can see are my flaws.
Help me to see what you see—a beautiful masterpiece that you love
dearly.*

How do you look at yourself: as a masterpiece or as a flawed
piece of art?

Created for Delight

"He will rejoice over you with gladness,
He will quiet you with His love,
He will rejoice over you with singing."

ZEPHANIAH 3:17 NKJV

Did you know that the mighty God, Creator of heaven and earth, is a proud Papa? That's right! He is a loving Father who delights in you—his daughter! He created you not just so you can enjoy him, but also that he may enjoy you.

God delights in the way you see things, the sweet thoughts you have, the things that make you laugh, and the way you represent him. He delights in your hard work and what makes you determined in life. He delights in you because he made you. He is not looking for perfection; he just wants a relationship.

God, I love that you enjoy the little things about me. I want to enjoy you, too. Help me to think of you whenever I laugh today.

"The LORD your God is with you,
the Mighty Warrior who saves.
He will take great delight in you;
in his love he will no longer rebuke you,
but will rejoice over you with singing."

ZEPHANIAH 3:17 NIV

Every good thing that is in this world is from God and teaches us about his character. Humor and laughter are a part of who he is. Art and creativity are a part of who he is. Peace and quiet, along with excitement and surprises, are all a part of who he is. There are many things that he enjoys, but we are at the top of his list.

Like a parent delights in their child, so your heavenly Father delights in you. You are his. He loves you, and nothing can change that.

Father, thank you for delighting in me. Thank you for blessing me
with surprises, laughter, and creativity. What a wonderful God
you are!

List some things about you that you feel God delights in.

Dignified

She is clothed with strength and dignity;
she can laugh at the days to come.

PROVERBS 31:25 NIV

When Proverbs 31 describes the perfect woman, one of the key ways she is described is as being dignified. What exactly does it mean to be dignified? It means having pride in who you are, and it's a quality that commands respect.

Would people looking at your life from the outside see dignity? Would they describe you as being worthy of respect? Do your actions and decisions show you to be one who takes pride in who you are?

God, I want to exemplify strength and dignity. Help me to make choices that honor you and show me to be dignified.

Strength and dignity are her clothing,
And she smiles at the future.

PROVERBS 31:25 NASB

God calls us to clothe ourselves in dignity, or to wrap ourselves up in it so completely that we become the very essence of the word. Think of a woman you would describe as having dignity. What makes you think of her that way?

Take a look at your life and your day-to-day actions. Do you believe that the way you are presenting yourself to the world is respectful? As you get dressed, envision yourself first putting on dignity. Wrap yourself up in it.

Lord, help me to put on dignity every day. I want to be clothed in decorum, grace, and honor.

How can you make dignity a part of your being?

Working Diligently

The plans of the diligent lead to profit
as surely as haste leads to poverty.

PROVERBS 21:5 NIV

Success is hard to measure. Who is successful? The one who tries her very best and gives it her all? Or the one who puts forth just enough effort to get the job done? Do you ever wonder why you should do things with all your heart? Why you should finish every single project well? Why you should even bother?

Nothing good comes out of not trying our best. There's no success or sense of pride and accomplishment. There is no reward in cutting corners. Who wants to be known for their lack of attention to detail, their careless ways, or lazy, half-hearted attempts? Work diligently so you have a sense of accomplishment when your project done.

God, help me to work diligently in everything I have been given to do. I want my completed work to show my diligence and hard work.

Good planning and hard work lead to prosperity,
but hasty shortcuts lead to poverty.

PROVERBS 21:5 NLT

Perhaps the project you are working on now seems insignificant or unimportant. It could very well be possible that no one will ever see or acknowledge your efforts. It could be a tedious and unpleasant task—one that might not seem worth your time or attention. There is much value in diligently putting your all into it anyway.

Being diligent every day takes a lot of effort and energy. It also takes discipline. But through it all, our characters are being shaped and strengthened. Even if the reward isn't immediate, the day will come where we will be able to see the fruit of our labor.

Lord, help me not to seek attention for my diligence now. I really only need you to see and acknowledge my hard work. Help me to remain committed to the tasks at hand.

Are you committed to be diligent in every task even if your efforts go unnoticed?

Good Enough?

By his divine power, God has given us everything we need for living a godly life. We have received all of this by coming to know him, the one who called us to himself by means of his marvelous glory and excellence.

2 PETER 1:3 NLT

When we think about doing things with excellence, we think of doing them to the best of our ability. To excel is to never stop or settle for less, but always grow and get better.

God doesn't want you to settle for "good enough." He wants you to go forward in life, always putting your heart and mind in a position to learn and grow. He doesn't want or expect perfection; he just wants you to desire to live with excellence. He can help you with the rest.

Lord, I don't want to settle for anything less than excellence. You have given me everything I need to walk out my faith excellently. Show me how to do that today.

His divine power has given us everything we need for a godly life through our knowledge of him who called us by his own glory and goodness.

2 PETER 1:3 NIV

Excellence is what the Lord desires for us—in our walk with him and our attitudes toward others. He desires us to have a hunger to pursue him and a heart that is willing to be taught by him.

When things are done with excellence, whether in music, sports, friendships, studies, or otherwise, we have an understanding that there is always more to learn and achieve. This is the attitude our Father wants us to have regarding our walk with him.

God, I know that good enough is not really good enough at all. I desire excellence because you desire it as well. Give me the strength I need to live with excellence as my goal.

What areas, in your walk with the Lord, do you need to adjust in order to walk excellently?

Complete Faith

Now faith is the assurance of things hoped for, the conviction of things not seen.

HEBREWS 11:1 NASB

When a storm arose on the lake where the disciples were, they were filled with fear as their boat rocked back and forth. Jesus began walking toward them on the water. As Peter witnessed this incredible sight, he gained quite a bit of confidence and his faith grew. Peter asked Jesus if he too could walk on the water, and Jesus agreed. Peter got out of the boat and began to walk on the water. But as soon as the waves came, Peter started to sink.

Peter's faith was shaken because of his circumstance. We can be a bit like Peter and lose faith when our circumstances become difficult. It's our faith that determines our outcome. When we place all our faith in the Lord, he shows up in a huge way.

God, I place all of my faith in you because I need you to show up for me today.

Faith is confidence in what we hope for and assurance about what we do not see.

HEBREWS 11:1 NIV

Faith can be challenging at times. When things are going well, it's easy to have faith, but when things are not going as planned, we can be easily shaken. At times, our faith can weaken according to our circumstance, just like what happened to Peter when he stepped out of the boat.

Step out in faith and continue to keep your eyes on Jesus as you walk through your circumstances. Give all your concerns to God and have full faith that he is working on them!

Father, help my faith not to be determined by circumstance. I want to believe you when I step out on the water and as I walk. Help me not to look at the things around me to determine my level of faith. Help me to just believe.

Are you struggling to have complete faith in a particular area of your life?

Family Blessing

My child, listen to your father's teaching
and do not forget your mother's advice.
Their teaching will be like flowers in your hair
or a necklace around your neck.

PROVERBS 1:8-9 NCV

If someone were to take a group of people all different ages and genders, put them in a house, and say, "Okay you are a family now. Get along, and love each other!" it would be incredibly difficult. It may even be a disaster. Thankfully, that is not the way families are designed. Family is created by God. He designed each of us a certain way and thought very hard about which family we would belong to.

Your family is your own personal training ground. It was given in love and it is to be treated with love. Go ahead and enjoy the gifts that have been specifically chosen for you. A gift from God is always one to treasure, respect, and take very good care of.

God, thank you for each member of my family. I ask that you
would bless them richly today.

Hear, my child, your father's instruction,
and do not reject your mother's teaching;
for they are a fair garland for your head,
and pendants for your neck.

PROVERBS 1:8-9 NRSV

When we are placed in a family, whether through birth or adoption, we are specifically chosen by God to be placed right where we are. Each person within the family is a gift. That's right! Your sister who borrows things and never gives them back, or your little brother who teases you incessantly are gifts from God.

It is important to look at each member in your family as a gift from God. Each helps the other grow. Maybe that annoying little brother was put there to help you with patience, or the borrowing sister teaches us to be less selfish with our stuff.

God, you know where you want to take me, and you know
everything I need to walk through before I'm ready for you to take
me there. Help me view my family as a blessing and not a nuisance.

List each member of your family and write down at least one way they are a gift to you.

Afraid of What?

"Be strong and courageous. Do not fear or be in dread of them, for it is the LORD your God who goes with you. He will not leave you or forsake you."

DEUTERONOMY 31:6 ESV

Some people are afraid of spiders, others are afraid of the dark. Fears are not uncommon, but we don't usually like talking about them. Sometimes we don't share our fears because we are embarrassed or because we feel like we will look weak and silly.

If we bottle up our fears, they have the tendency to grow into huge obstacles that are challenging to overcome. God does not want us to conquer difficulties alone. Ask him today to help you face them.

God, thank you for being so faithful. I want to be free from the fears that are holding me back from living a joy-filled life. Please show me how to do this.

"Be strong and bold; have no fear or dread of them, because it is the LORD your God who goes with you; he will not fail you or forsake you."

DEUTERONOMY 31:6 ESV

Fear has a way of strangling our hope and courage. It can keep us from living a free and joy-filled life. It can stop us from pursuing our dreams. It can even inhibit us making wonderful friendships and experiencing new things. Fears can grip us if we don't give them over to God.

God is our light in the scariest of places. With him by our side, we can face whatever causes us to be afraid. If we lean on him and ask him to help, he will give us a boldness we have never known before.

God, give me the boldness I need tonight to conquer my fears.

What are you most afraid of? Can you give it to God today?

Harboring Resentment

Be gentle and ready to forgive; never hold grudges. Remember, the LORD forgave you, so you must forgive others.

COLOSSIANS 3:13 TLB

It might temporarily feel good to harbor resentment and bitterness toward someone that has hurt us, but eventually the walls that we build to protect ourselves will only cause us pain. The walls say that the offender doesn't deserve to be forgiven. That somehow, in our own brokenness, we are more deserving of God's love and grace.

It is amazing how in our own hurt we can easily forget how we have sinned and desperately need God. Are you secretly harboring resentment toward someone? God knows how you feel. Ask him to help you forgive, and let him heal your brokenness.

Father, you have forgiven me for so much. Help me to extend the same forgiveness toward others. I don't want to harbor resentment toward anyone. Show me where I am doing that in my heart.

Bear with one another and, if anyone has a complaint against another, forgive each other; just as the LORD[has forgiven you, so you also must forgive.

COLOSSIANS 3:13 NRSV

If we ask God for the ability to see our offenders the way he sees them, we gain empathy and a bit of understanding in the midst of our hurt. If we refuse to extend forgiveness, not only are we refusing to love one another the way God wants us to, we are also standing in the way of God's restoration. We are declaring ourselves the judge—a position of authority that no one but God has a right to.

How wonderful that our Judge is one who is fully of mercy and compassion for us! We can trust that he will lovingly make all of the wrongs right. Trusting him completely eliminates our need to withhold forgiveness.

God, I trust in your judgment. It sets me free from the weight of bitterness and allows me to experience the healing that I need from you. I need that tonight.

Give your resentment to God today and walk in freedom.

Freedom from Sin

We have freedom now, because Christ made us free. So stand strong.

GALATIANS 5:1 NCV

Sin is ugly. We don't feel good after we sin, yet we continue to struggle with it. The tough part about sin is that Satan tempts us, roots for us to fail, and then beats us up with shame and guilt. All of this spiritual and emotional chaos makes it hard to receive the freedom offered by God.

When you sin and then repent, it is finished. God doesn't keep a record of your wrongs. You don't need to rehash, revisit, and recall all the sin. When you entertain your shame, you put spiritual handcuffs on. Your heavenly Father can't wait to make it all right. Receive his forgiveness so he can set you free.

God, I ask for your forgiveness this morning. Set me free from the bonds of guilt and shame, and help me to walk in freedom from sin.

For freedom Christ has set us free. Stand firm, therefore, and do not submit again to a yoke of slavery.

GALATIANS 5:1

You are forgiven. The things you struggle with and the sin that entangles you no longer have power over you. You are set free! When you struggle with sin but have a repentant heart, you are forgiven because of the work Jesus did on the cross. And the cost of forgiveness has already been paid by and through him.

Take some time tonight to truly let go of the things you've been beating yourself up about, and receive the freedom that comes from God's forgiveness.

Heavenly Father, I receive your forgiveness tonight. Thank you for the peace that your freedom brings to my heart.

Is there something that you have been beating yourself up about? Let it go.

Two Are Better

Two people are better off than one, for they can help each other succeed. If one person falls, the other can reach out and help. But someone who falls alone is in real trouble.

ECCLESIASTES 4:9-10 NLT

God created the concept of friends in the beginning. He first created Adam for himself, and then Eve for Adam. Community is what God desired in the Garden of Eden. He knew that there was much joy to be found in relationship. He knew that we would need companions.

Life is lonely without good friends to confide in, to laugh with, cry with, and learn with. It's true, two people really are better off than one. Be a good friend to someone you love today.

Father, thank you for surrounding me with friends who can help me on the journey of life. I know I need to continue to be in relationship with those you have placed in my life. Help me to value those relationships dearly.

"Two are better than one, because they have a good reward for their toil. For if they fall, one will lift up the other; but woe to one who is alone and falls and does not have another to help".

ECCLESIASTES 4:9-10 NLT

When you isolate yourself from the people who love you, you feel alone in the moments you most need a friend. When you hurt, you hurt alone. When you fail, you fail alone. When you celebrate life's triumphs, you celebrate alone.

Being alone was never God's intention for you. He wants you to be friends—first with him, and then with others. Feel his nearness tonight as you spend time with the best friend there is.

God, please give me some creative ideas for how I could show my close friends how much I appreciate them today.

What friends are you thankful for today?

A Gentle Answer

A gentle answer deflects anger,
but harsh words make tempers flare.

PROVERBS 15:1 NLT

Most people don't like conflict. Unfortunately, conflict is unavoidable. We all have our own ideas and opinions, so it's not unusual to come up against different viewpoints. We may even find ourselves in disagreement with people we love— like parents, siblings, and best friends.

Our hearts in every conflict should have peace as the end goal. We may not ever come to full agreement, but we can resolve every conflict with gentleness and love. Being gentle means putting yourself in someone else's shoes. It means listening to their feelings. And it means responding softly— with kindness and grace.

God, I will be the first to admit that seeking peace in the midst of conflict is really hard. I know it's the right way to do things, but I need your help to be gentle in my responses. Please give me grace so I can give it to others.

A gentle answer turns away wrath,
but a harsh word stirs up anger.

In the heat of an argument, it is tempting to bite with our
words. This is especially true when we feel like we are right,
or when we have been wronged and feel justified in our
emotions. But fighting doesn't resolve anything; in fact, it
only makes the situation worse. Words are powerful: they can
be used to love and affirm, or they can be used to hurt.
We shouldn't let them flow free without thought.

Responding with a gentle answer can be difficult because
strong emotions are often involved in conflicts. If we take
deep breaths, and try to step back for some perspective,
we can choose to respond in love.

God, I don't want my words to inflict pain and stir up anger.
Soften my heart, Lord, and help me to give a gentle answer in
response to conflict.

How do you normally respond in conflict?

Gift of Grace

To each one of us grace was given according to the measure of Christ's gift.

EPHESIANS 4:7 NKJV

Grace can be one of the hardest things to give. We tend to grip it tightly in our hands. We crave justice and can go to great lengths to obtain it. We easily forget the grace God gives us is the same grace he wants us to give others.

When we uncurl our fingers and offer grace, we not only free them from hurt, we free ourselves. Grace is such a beautiful gift to give and to receive.

Father, why do I hold on to injustice and hurt so tightly. It does me no good! I want to offer the beautiful gift of grace to others instead.

He has given each one of us a special gift through the generosity of Christ.

EPHESIANS 4:7 NLT

As hard as it can be to give others grace, it can be even harder to give it to ourselves. Sometimes the person in our life that needs the most grace is us. We can be so unkind. We berate ourselves for our mistakes and beat ourselves up over our shortcomings. How many times have we called ourselves stupid? Or worthless?

Instead of punishing yourself for your mistakes, why don't you give yourself a little grace, like your heavenly Father gives you. Accept that you will make mistakes and move along.

God, I know I need to give myself grace. Help me to look past my mistakes and see what you see.

How does it look to give yourself a bit of grace today?

Even More than Jonah

I, with shouts of grateful praise, will sacrifice to you.
What I have vowed I will make good. I will say,
"Salvation comes from the LORD."

When you're young, your parents give you constant reminders to use good manners. One of the most popular phrases in a growing family is, "Say thank you!"

There's a reason why parents want to teach the lesson of showing gratitude to others. There is simply nothing better than doing something for someone when you know that they are thankful for it.

God, I am so thankful for all you have done for me. Help me to show gratitude in my daily life, so people will know me as being someone who is always thankful.

"I with the voice of thanksgiving will sacrifice to you;
what I have vowed I will pay.
Salvation belongs to the LORD!"

JONAH 2:9 ESV

We thank our friends for a ride, thank our grandma for a birthday gift, and thank someone for having us over for dinner. But when was the last time you thanked God for all that he's done for you?

Our Father in heaven wants to know you are thankful for your many blessings too. Even Jonah, sitting in the stinky, dark belly of a giant fish, showed his gratitude to the Lord. And if Jonah can be thankful from the pit of a fish, surely we can be thankful for all that we have.

Lord, I certainly have more to be thankful for than Jonah did sitting in the belly of a fish. Tonight, I want to ponder the many things you have provided for me. I am thankful.

Make a list of all that you've been given, and spend some time thanking the Lord for his many blessings.

Burden of Guilt

*You were taught to put away your former way of life, your old self,
corrupt and deluded by its lusts, and to be renewed in the spirit
of your minds, and to clothe yourselves with the new self, created
according to the likeness of God in true righteousness and holiness.*

EPHESIANS 4:22-24 NRSV

Do you ever lie awake at night, thinking of all the ways in
which you fell short during the day? Guilt consumes you,
making you feel bad about all the poor choices you've made.
You toss and turn, unable to sleep because you cannot forgive
yourself. It's like a burden you're carrying, weighing you
down and making it difficult to breathe.

That's not the life God wants for you! Read the Scripture for
today again. You are made new. You are created in the likeness
of God—true and holy! Embrace your renewed self today.

*God, it's hard for me to forget about my past way of life when
things pop up every day. Help me to renew my mind and focus on
your holiness instead.*

Put off, concerning your former conduct, the old man which grows corrupt according to the deceitful lusts, and be renewed in the spirit of your mind, and that you put on the new man which was created according to God, in true righteousness and holiness.

EPHESIANS 4:22-24 NKJV

Do you have a burden you're carrying with the shame of guilt? Give it to God. Apologize to those you've wronged, make up for your mistake, release it to the Lord, and move on. He forgives you, so you are free to forgive yourself!

We are full of mistakes, but we don't need to carry that burden around. If that were the case, then Jesus died for nothing. He died so that he could shoulder our deadweight for us, and we were made new in that moment!

Jesus, the work you did on the cross is a debt I can never repay. Thank you for releasing my burden of guilt and shame again tonight.

How does it feel to release your burden of guilt to God?

Momentary Gain

The LORD detests the use of dishonest scales,
but he delights in accurate weights.

PROVERBS 11:1 NLT

Honesty is a struggle for most of us. We like to bend the truth to get out of a potential consequence, or maybe we don't honestly answer a question because we don't want to offend people even though we know it's something they should hear.

God teaches us to always be honest. There is freedom in honesty. Lies are a breeding ground for more lies. Bigger lies. The more we lie, the easier it becomes, and suddenly, we find ourselves lying about serious things. Put an end to the lies today and embrace the truth.

Oh God, help me to speak honestly. I don't want to bend the truth or avoid being honest. You are truth itself and I want to be like you.

Dishonest scales are an abomination to the LORD,
But a just weight is His delight.

PROVERBS 11:1 NKJV

When we get away with something because we lied, we often still reap the consequences of the lie in our hearts; we feel convicted about not telling the truth. Honesty brings things to the light and removes the shackles of lies.

Though there may be consequences for telling the truth, it is much better to live a life of freedom from guilt than it is to live for the momentary gain of a lie. That moment never lasts very long.

God, I confess that I have lied. Forgive me. I want to value honesty over the momentary gain of a lie.

Is there something you have not been honest about recently?

Honored Above You

Be devoted to one another in love.
Honor one another above yourselves.

ROMANS 12:10 NIV

Your world is probably filled with many people that come
from different walks of life. Some have a lot of money,
some do not; some are considered cool and others not so
much. There are people who have talents that make them
popular, while others have important talents that are hardly
recognized. Have you noticed who most people choose to be
friends with?

It is easy to honor, love, and be friends with those that are
like us, but it is Christ-like to look for those who may need a
friend and make them feel loved and respected by honoring
them above yourself.

God, there are people around me who need to feel loved and
respected. Help me to be someone who lifts them up in honor today.

Be kindly affectionate to one another with brotherly love,
in honor giving preference to one another.

ROMANS 12:10 NKJV

When we think about Jesus and his friends, we remember
that he befriended the underprivileged, the tax collectors,
and the not-so-popular people. When these individuals got
to know Jesus as a trusted friend, they felt honored and loved
for who they were.

Jesus honored others above himself. Because of this, their
lives were forever changed. Is there someone in your
workplace or neighborhood that you feel needs to be shown
more honor, love, and respect? Think about how you could do
that tonight.

*God, I know I need to work on being devoted to others. It's easy to
put myself first in so many areas of my life, but that's not what
you call us to. Help me to be honoring of those around me.*

How might you honor someone above yourself?

Hope in the Right Place

The LORD takes pleasure in those who fear him, in those who hope in his steadfast love.

PSALM 147:11 ESV

Hope is expecting an ideal outcome against all odds. People can put their hope in many different things, but the return of that hope won't be very successful if it's not rooted in Christ.

God asks us to put our hope in him. When the ground is being shaken beneath us and things seem out of our control, we make our requests known to the Lord and then believe with full confidence that he has heard.

God, I know you want to bring me closer to you. Thank you for hearing my requests and lavishing your love on me.

The LORD delights in those who fear him,
who put their hope in his unfailing love.

PSALM 147:11 NIV

Placing our hope in the Lord begins with giving him the desires of our heart and then truly trusting him with those desires. He honors the hope we have in him and he knows how weak our hope can be.

Sometimes it can be scary to place great hope in God for fear of being disappointed. This is where we need to trust and accept that our loving Father knows what is best for us. If we hope for something that is not to our benefit, then he won't grant our request—for our good!

Father, I trust that you know best—about everything. Help me to have a good attitude when things don't turn out the way I want them to.

Hope big and trust in God. He always wants what's best for you.

The Gift of Talents

When pride comes, then comes disgrace,
but with humility comes wisdom.

PROVERBS 11:2 NIV

Our talents are a gift from God. We all have different talents and we should take good care of them. We can use them to bless others and bring glory to God. Often when people have been gifted with a talent, they like to receive the credit and bring attention to themselves. This is the absolute opposite of what God asks of us.

It is important that we view our talents not as our own, but as a tool to bring honor and glory to God. It can be tempting to be proud and boastful, but the more we walk in humility with our talents, the more we allow God to reach others through our talents.

Father, I have nothing without you having given it to me.
Help me to act in humility with the talents you have given me.

Pride leads to disgrace,
but with humility comes wisdom.

PROVERBS 11:2 NLT

Humility comes when you are confident in God's opinion
of you, so you don't use your talent to seek attention from
others. It comes when you choose to use your talent to honor
God simply because he is worthy of it. It comes when you
recognize that you have no talent without God.

Are there ways in which you can act more humbly in your
God-given talents? Thank him for the gift of your talents
tonight.

God, I really do care what you think of me. Thank you for the
talents you have given me. I want to use them to glorify you and
bless others.

Make a list of how you can start using your talents to bless
others!

Who You Are

To all who believed him and accepted him,
he gave the right to become children of God.

JOHN 1:12 NLT

Based on the sheer volume of quizzes found online, it is easy to determine that we are a culture desperate to know who we are. We try so hard to be identified by our personalities, our hobbies, and our interests. Are we intellectuals? Writers? Artists? Musicians? Engineers? We spend so much time on a crusade to discover who we are, even letting others—sometimes people we don't know—speak into our lives and define our identity.

Truly, you are so many things. But above all, you are a child of God. Knowing who you are is the anchor for getting you through difficult and confusing situations in life. You belong to God. You have a place in his family and an identity that is highly valued.

God, help me to find my place in your family. I want to know who I am in light of who you have called me to be. Thank you for a place to belong.

To all who did receive him, who believed in his name,
he gave the right to become children of God,

JOHN 1:12 ESV

Do you desperately want to discover your identity? Let the truth pierce your heart. You are the child that God loves so much, he would go to the ends of the earth for you. Like a loving father watches over his child, God watches over you.

Are you afraid? Don't be. You are a child of God. Do you feel lost and alone? You aren't. You are a child of God. Make a list of who God says you are. Start with these: you are the daughter of a King, you are loved, you are wanted, you are valued, you belong, you are known. Wrap yourself in these truths tonight.

Father, thank you for giving me renewed hope in who I am. I am
valued, treasured, and cherished. I belong to you.

Are you searching for who you are? Look no further.
You are a child of God.

Influence

"No one lights a lamp and then puts it under a basket. Instead, a lamp is placed on a stand, where it gives light to everyone in the house. In the same way, let your good deeds shine out for all to see, so that everyone will praise your heavenly Father."

MATTHEW 5:15-16 NLT

When our lives are captured by God and completely changed, we can't help but want access to a microphone to declare his goodness to the world. But we don't always have to be standing up in front of a class, shouting God's word for everyone to hear in order to be an influence.

Our influence can be even more impacting and valuable by simply following God. If we allow him to direct our lives, people can see firsthand how life-changing God is. Follow him closely today and watch it change others around you.

God, I want my light to shine for you. Help me not to hide it but to place it on a stand for all to see.

"Nor do they light a lamp and put it under a basket, but on a lampstand, and it gives light to all who are in the house. Let your light so shine before men, that they may see your good works and glorify your Father in heaven.

MATTHEW 5:15-16 NKJV

Our influence will be our unshakeable joy in trials. It will be the way we defer to the weak and lonely with a compassion that only comes from knowing God's compassion in our own lives. It will be in the way we include the unloved and outcast. It will be in the way we give our money to those who need it. It will be in the way we visit the sick and care for the widows.

Be encouraged that God is using you, even when you aren't shouting from a street corner. The platform we have is a strong but subtle one. Use that platform this evening to draw people to God through you.

Father, thank you for making me a light in a very dark world. Help me to show people your love simply by serving them and being compassionate toward them.

Don't be afraid to shine for God.

Inspired by Thoughts

One generation shall praise Your works to another,
And shall declare Your mighty acts.
I will meditate on the glorious splendor of Your majesty,
And on Your wondrous works.
Men shall speak of the might of Your awesome acts,
And I will declare Your greatness.

PSALM 145:4-6 NKJV

With technology and social media right at our fingertips, it's difficult to be inspired by the things God intended for inspiration. Minute by minute, our heads are down trying to connect with others. But what about the magnificent beauty that's also at our fingertips?

Gifts from God are all around you. Lift up your head and allow yourself to be inspired. As you go about your day, look for God's beauty. Write down what aspects of God's creation inspire you the most. Then thank him for them!

There are so many beautiful things around me that you have created, God. Help me to notice the things in your creation that inspire me the most.

Parents will tell their children what you have done.
They will retell your mighty acts,
wonderful majesty, and glory.
And I will think about your miracles
They will tell about the amazing things you do,
and I will tell how great you are.

PSALM 145:4-6 NCV

God made us to be creative and he wants to inspire our creativity. That's why he gave us towering mountains, hand painted skies, starry nights, rippling rivers, amazing wildlife, and the changing of seasons. What he made was well thought out and it was all made with us in mind.

God knows we need his beauty not just to inspire us, but also to feed our spirits in a powerful way. He wants to meet with us in the quiet moments and teach us more about himself.

God, breathing in your creation does fill me with awe and wonder. You feed my spirit and inspire my soul. Help me to meet with you tonight and be taught more about you in my quiet moments.

It's in the sweet places that God wants to tell us he loves us.

Straight and Narrow

People with integrity walk safely,
but those who follow crooked paths will slip and fall.

PROVERBS 10:9 NLT

Do you live confidently and carefree? When you choose to live with integrity, you will. We have nothing to fear when we live in the truth, but when we choose dishonesty, we spend our days in constant fear of being found out.

God doesn't want us stumbling about our days unsure of our footing and watching out for every step we take. He wants us to live free of the cares and burdens we carry when we keep secrets and live in the shadows. He wants us on the secure path of truth.

God, I don't want to lie and constantly worry about being found out. Help me to choose integrity and honesty in everything I do.

Whoever walks in integrity walks securely,
but whoever takes crooked paths will be found out.

PROVERBS 10:9 NIV

It's a lot of work to hide the real story from others. Stories have to be kept straight, details have to be remembered, and it's a battle to think of the lies we've told. In the end, we are always discovered.

Pray that you will remain on the path of honesty, honor, and virtue. Put one foot in front of the other, secure in the knowledge that you will not stumble. Stay off the crooked path, and keep your eyes on the straight and narrow one ahead of you!

God, I want to remain on the path of honesty. Help me not to stumble into deceit and lies. You are the God of truth and I want to honor you in all I do.

What are you often tempted to lie about? Choose integrity today!

Infusing Happiness

Splendor and majesty are before him;
strength and joy are in his dwelling place.

1 CHRONICLES 16:27 NIV

There is a significant difference between feeling joy and feeling happy. Joy goes beyond the basics and infuses happy with some extra oomph. And it can only truly come through Christ our Lord. He is the source of our great pleasure!

Experiencing the Lord's joy doesn't mean you'll never feel sadness again. Hard times come to everyone regardless of our maturity in faith. Pray that you will feel great pleasure in your life no matter what comes your way.

God, I want to experience your joy again today. Help me to sense your presence as I make my way through this day.

Honor and majesty surround him;
strength and joy fill his dwelling.

1 Chronicles 16:27 NLT

Happiness is a temporary feeling. Joy stays with us. Happiness flees in the midst of tough times, but joy is there regardless of our circumstances. It's a fruit of the Spirit, produced only by God's work in us. It's a gift from him!

When we are aware of God's grace and favor, then joy can truly come. Put your trust in him. He loves you, and wants to share all of his gifts with you.

Father, thank you for the everlasting joy that you give me. I don't always feel happy, but I know I can be full of joy because you live in me.

Take some time to ask God for the spirit of joy today!

Injustice

"I, the LORD, love justice;
I hate robbery and wrongdoing.
In my faithfulness I will reward my people
and make an everlasting covenant with them."

ISAIAH 61:8 NIV

"It's not fair! How did she get away with that?" We may have thought this when someone hurts us or is dishonest about something and doesn't get caught. Sometimes things are unfair, and it's hard to ignore them. We want justice, and we want it now!

We have a hard time waiting for justice. We don't want to wish it on others; however, it is comforting to know that if we do not see immediate consequences for wrongdoing, we can rest assured that our loving and protective God saw it, and he will make it right.

God, give me patience in waiting for justice. Help me to love others even when they hurt me. I want to be an example of your love and mercy to those around me.

I, the LORD, love justice.
I hate robbery and wrongdoing.
I will faithfully reward my people for their suffering
and make an everlasting covenant with them.

ISAIAH 61:8 NLT

There is a lot of injustice in this world, and it can be frustrating, sad, and confusing to think about. There is hope. God teaches us in his Word that he is just. This means he stands for justice. All who have greatly wronged others will either be led to repentance or will receive the appropriate consequence in the end.

God sees and knows it all. He is quick to love and slow to anger, but those who hurt his children and do not repent will be punished.

God, change my heart toward those who have hurt me. Help me to extend mercy and grace to them tonight.

What are some ways you can make things right with people you have wronged or people who have wronged you?

A Good Leader

"I am the good shepherd.
The good shepherd lays down his life for the sheep."

JOHN 10:11 NIV

What do you look for in a leader? If we are to bring others into a relationship with Christ, we are all called to become leaders ourselves. One of the best examples we could ever ask for in leadership was Jesus himself. And he called himself a good shepherd.

Shepherds needed to nourish, comfort, lead, correct, and protect their sheep. And most importantly, a good shepherd would encourage those in their care to follow his example and stay with him.

Father, thank you that you love your sheep and guide them through life, protecting them as they listen to you.

"I am the good shepherd.
The good shepherd sacrifices his life for the sheep."

JOHN 10:11 NLT

Though a shepherd in Jesus' time was not a job that many aspired to, it called for special skills. A shepherd had to guide his flock of sheep without scaring them into submission. Sheep are known to make poor choices when operating under fear.

Are you a leader for Christ's kingdom? Are you encouraging others to follow your example, comforting them in times of need and correcting them gently when the situation calls for it? Be a good leader to those around you tonight.

God, I want to encourage others in their walk with you. Help me to be able to comfort and encourage as well as correct when needed. I take my example from you.

Spend some time today writing down all the ways you can display leadership.

A Living Sacrifice

Therefore, I urge you, brothers and sisters, in view of God's mercy, to offer your bodies as a living sacrifice, holy and pleasing to God— this is your true and proper worship.

ROMANS 12:1 NIV

Sacrifice. That's not a very comfortable word is it? We don't think of it as being easy or as the popular choice. What does it mean to be a living sacrifice?

As God's followers and children, we should live in a way that honors and blesses him. It is so difficult to live that kind of life with all the temptations of this world and everything at our fingertips. In fact, we can't live a holy and pleasing life *and* give in to the temptations of this world. Ask God to help you to be honoring to him today.

God, I understand that sacrifice isn't supposed to be easy. Help me to let go of the things that hinder me from drawing close to you.

I plead with you to give your bodies to God because of all he has done for you. Let them be a living and holy sacrifice--the kind he will find acceptable.

ROMANS 12:1 NLT

We often fall into the trap of doing what we want: buying too much stuff, gossiping about others, being ungrateful—these are just a few things we need to watch out for when it comes to

If you practice each week to work on an area in your life that you feel hasn't blessed the Lord, then you will feel something change, and you'll receive the confidence that only your heavenly Father can give. By living this way, you are sacrificing your desires and truly worshiping him. This is pleasing to God.

Father, a sacrifice for you isn't really a sacrifice at all. You have given me so much; this is the least I can do for you.

What sacrifices can you make that would please God?

Never Truly Alone

A man of many companions may come to ruin,
but there is a friend who sticks closer than a brother.

PROVERBS 18:24 ESV

Most of us are not strangers to feeling lonely from time to time. We know what it feels like to be sad, without a friend to call on for comfort and company. We can feel lonely in our grief. We can feel lonely in our accomplishments. We can even feel lonely in a room surrounded by people.

Do you know that you are never truly alone? God is with you always. Even in times when you feel the most alone, he is there. He promises never to leave or forsake you. Your Father cares deeply for you.

Father God, thank you that even when I feel alone, I never truly am. You are always with me. Help me to feel your nearness today.

One who has unreliable friends soon comes to ruin,
but there is a friend who sticks closer than a brother.

PROVERBS 18:24 NIV

Feeling like no one cares or understands us is difficult.
Sometimes all we wish for is someone to be there. Someone
to listen to our needs and genuinely care.

When you feel loneliness pressing in, before you even call
out to God, he is already there. There is much comfort in
knowing that in all our journeys we do not travel alone. Do
you feel lonely tonight? Reach out to God and ask for his
presence to comfort you.

This evening, Lord, I need to feel you all around me. You are a
wonderful comforter and you genuinely care about me. Help me to
rest in your presence now.

How does it feel to know that God is always with you?

Struggle to Trust

Trust in the LORD with all your heart,
And lean not on your own understanding;
In all your ways acknowledge Him,
And He shall direct your paths.

PROVERBS 3:5-6 NKJV

There can be seasons where things don't work out in your favor and life seems harder than normal. It could be related to relationships, work, sports, or even family dynamics. When things are tough in these areas, it tends to greatly affect our feelings, our mindset, and even our trust in God. We might feel like we're in the desert all alone.

The good news is that God knows just where we are. We are not lost. Many times when we are walking through difficult situations, the Lord has allowed us to experience those difficulties to test what is in our hearts. He is refining and maturing us.

God, I know you are trying to teach me something. I want to be willing to learn. Please give me strength.

Trust the LORD with all your heart,
and don't depend on your own understanding.
Remember the LORD in all you do,
and he will give you success.

PROVERBS 3:5-6 NCV

The next time you find yourself in one of these seasons, don't stop trusting God! Go to him immediately and ask him what he wants to teach you. Though it may feel like he is far away, he's actually close by, molding and shaping you like a potter does with clay.

When you make yourself vulnerable to God, he will reveal the things he is working on, and assure you that there is purpose to your season in the desert. Trust in him and he will carry you through!

God, I admit I don't like being in the desert. But I want to grow and mature in my relationship with you, so teach me while I'm here.

Are you struggling to trust God in this season?

Led by Truth

Lead me by your truth and teach me,
for you are the God who saves me.
All day long I put my hope in you.

PSALM 25:5 NLT

When we think of truth, we often think of confessing something we've done that was not wise. But truth is also shown in the encouraging words we say to others and the life we live as representatives of God.

God loves when you stand for him, especially during difficult times. He sees what you do and say during those times, and he knows how hard it is for you. It blesses him beyond measure to see your boldness. As you continue to walk in truth, he will use you in great ways, and he will prepare a beautiful place for you in heaven!

God, you are truth. I want to be bold for you and walk in your truth. Thank you for saving me. I put my hope in you.

Lead me in your truth and teach me,
for you are the God of my salvation;
for you I wait all the day long.

PSALM 25:5 ESV

Living a life for truth means to live in a way that stands for truth in all circumstances. It can be difficult to speak truth when there is a chance we may offend someone, be met with awkward silence, or stand with the minority.

You may find yourself in a situation where you feel the need to stand for what is right, but you're unsure you can find the courage to do so. Likely the Holy Spirit is nudging you to speak out in truth. If you listen to that nudge and obey it, you open a door for God to touch others.

Father God, tonight I ask that you would help me to find courage to speak into situations that you are asking me to speak into. Open doors for me to speak your truth to others.

In what areas do you feel you need to be living a more truth-focused life?

Real Value

"For where your treasure is, there your heart will be also."

MATTHEW 6:21 NIV

Status, titles, popularity, and expensive houses are some common things valued by society. It's difficult not to value these ourselves. But what has true value?

God wants us to focus on valuing things that are of him— things like love, generosity, righteousness, and honesty. These bring lasting value because they add to the kingdom of heaven. Titles and popularity are temporary; they can be taken away in a single day. Think about the things you value today.

God, I know there are things that I have been valuing too greatly. Help me to reevaluate the actual worth of what I am pursuing.

*"Wherever your treasure is,
there the desires of your heart will also be."*

MATTHEW 6:21 NLT

If you happen to be popular, or can afford that expensive house, that's fine, but the moment you find yourself being motivated by, and becoming focused on, those things, you have given it too much value. You can't place equal value on homes and righteousness; it just doesn't work that way.

God is not impressed by status. He is, however, very impressed by the love he sees in your heart, the honest words you speak, and the generosity you display. Be aware of what you find valuable because that is what your heart will spend the most time going after.

*Father, help me to place the right value on the right things.
I want to chase after real treasure.*

What do you think is valuable in life?

Not Beyond Repair

He heals the brokenhearted and bandages their wounds.

PSALM 147:3 NLT

Sometimes when we look closely at ourselves, all we see is a broken and shattered remnant of what we once were. Sin, tragedy, rejection, or heartbreak can leave us feeling terrible. We wonder how we can pick up the pieces and be made whole again.

In our brokenness, it's easy to feel hopeless. We try so many methods to fill the void. We may look to relationships, things, or drugs to fix us. They can make us feel better temporarily, but eventually we realize that despite all our efforts, we still feel broken and incomplete.

Jesus, I don't know how you do it, but I thank you for loving me in all of my brokenness. I ask you to make me whole today.

He heals the brokenhearted
and binds up their wounds.

PSALM 147:3 ESV

God is faithful. He doesn't leave us alone in our brokenness, instead, he meets us in our ugliness, takes our broken pieces, and tenderly puts us back together again. Why? Because he loves us too much to leave us in the state we are in. He wants us to experience healing and restoration.

In him we find wholeness that the best doctor or medicine can't provide. He is the only one that can heal our pain completely. His love is so deep it can even remove scars.

Father, I need you tonight. Only you can heal the inner parts of me that feel like they are beyond repair.

Trust God in your brokenness today.

Different Wisdom

If you need wisdom, ask our generous God, and he will give it to you. He will not rebuke you for asking.

JAMES 1:5 NLT

Have you ever made a decision because most people around you thought it was truly a good idea, but it somehow didn't feel right to you? On the flip side, have you ever made a decision about something that made others think you were crazy, but deep down you knew it was the right thing to do? These are examples of two different kinds of wisdom. The first decision was made with worldly wisdom; the second with Godly wisdom.

Don't be intimidated by what others think and say. Trust in the wisdom of God. Everything he does is for your good. He cannot wait to share more of his heart with you. Take the leap and walk in God's wisdom. You will not be disappointed!

God, I know I need more of your wisdom. Help me to act on what I know to be right instead of going along with what the world says.

If any of you lacks wisdom, let him ask God, who gives generously to all without reproach, and it will be given him.

JAMES 1:5 ESV

The Bible teaches us that God's wisdom looks foolish to those who don't have a relationship with him. It also says the things that seem wise to the world are often foolish in the eyes of God. It seems a little confusing. The good news is that we don't have to have it all figured out. God gives us the Holy Spirit to help guide us.

That voice that you hear deep inside is often the Holy Spirit guiding you closer to the plans that God has for you. The more time you spend with your heavenly Father, the louder the voice of the Holy Spirit becomes within you. And the more you choose to walk in that Godly wisdom, the more Godly wisdom you will receive. Soon you will feel confident and certain when he speaks because you will recognize his voice.

Father, help me to rely on you for your wisdom. You give it generously, and I want to receive it humbly.

How do you feel God is leading you to walk in his wisdom?

The Point of Worry

"Can all your worries add a single moment to your life?"

MATTHEW 6:27 NLT

It's easy to worry about the future. How am I going to do on my review? Am I going to get that promotion? What will she say when I confront her? How am I going to pay down my debt? These are a few examples that can send our minds racing.

What is the point of worry? Has worry ever helped anyone feel better? Has it ever solved the problem? No. Each day has enough problems of its own. It is better to take each day one step at a time and let God lead us through it. The things that are for tomorrow will still be there tomorrow, and that's where they should stay for now. Then, when the time comes, we can ask God for help.

God, I take rest and comfort in knowing that you are for me and you are more than enough. Let those thoughts eliminate the worry that tries to creep into my mind today.

"Can any one of you by worrying add a single hour to your life?"
MATTHEW 6:27 NIV

Everything you walk through with God is not going to be easy, but worry does not have to be part of it. If you seek God during tough times, you can have confidence that he has heard you, and he will work out his good and perfect will.

We often rehash things and stir up all kinds of new worry. Don't go there. Let God take care of it, and allow yourself to let it go. Everything is not always going to land in your favor, and everyone isn't always going to be thrilled with you. You can try your best, but the real work belongs to God. Let him do it.

Father, tonight I place all my concerns in your hands and let them go. Thank you for taking them from me.

Where are your most common areas of worry, and how can you let God carry you through them?

Not a Mistake

You created my inmost being;
you knit me together in my mother's womb.
I praise you because I am fearfully and wonderfully made;
your works are wonderful,
I know that full well.

PSALM 139:13-14 NIV

God doesn't make mistakes. Take a deep breath, and then read that again. God doesn't make mistakes. He just doesn't. When we read in the Book of Psalms that he created us from the very beginning of our existence, from fingertips to toes, we know that he did it with purpose, and that he did it flawlessly.

You are worthy because God made you worthy through his Son. Repeat this to yourself today: "I am enough because I am his."

Thank you, God, that I am enough because I am yours. You don't make mistakes. You planned every part of me and you love me.

It was you who formed my inward parts;
you knit me together in my mother's womb.
I praise you, for I am fearfully and wonderfully made.
Wonderful are your works;
that I know very well.

PSALM 139:13-14 NRSV

It's so easy to let the things of this world dictate how we feel about ourselves. If we don't have enough of such and such, or our circle of friends feels too small, or if we don't have the latest item, it feels like we are not quite worthy enough.

But you were created to be a masterpiece! You are lovely and you are loved simply because that is how God made you. Because you belong to the Lord, you are enough.

Father, I belong to you. I don't need what everyone else has.
I just need you.

Can you see yourself as a masterpiece today?

The Struggle Will End

Let your roots grow down into him and draw up nourishment from him. See that you go on growing in the Lord, and become strong and vigorous in the truth you were taught. Let your lives overflow with joy and thanksgiving for all he has done.

COLOSSIANS 2:7 TLB

In the weeks leading up to Thanksgiving, the theme of gratitude becomes all but inescapable. This can be wonderful, reminding us of all the good in our lives, but it can also be painful. What if we're in a season where thankfulness eludes us? What if counting our blessings seems to take no time at all?

If this is you, you are not alone. Pore over his Word, and let his love and truth pour over you. The struggle will end. The blessings will come. All will be well.

Lord, today help me to be full of gratitude even if I'm finding it hard to be thankful. You are always good and faithful.

Having been firmly rooted and now being built up in Him and established in your faith, just as you were instructed, and overflowing with gratitude.

COLOSSIANS 2:7 NASB

There will always be times when struggle seems more prevalent than blessing, when gratitude seems like an impossible requirement, and faith, once so familiar, has gone into hiding.

Release your heart from any guilt bubbling up inside, and sink your roots into Jesus. Let gratitude and faith overflow from one into the other, and may all your roots intertwine in the rich, fertile soil of God's love and truth.

Thank you, God, that I can depend on you for a heart of gratitude. It doesn't always come naturally, but it is possible to dwell on the many blessings I have and create an underlying attitude of thankfulness.

Begin speaking out all the things you are grateful for.

Declared Holy

He brought out his people with rejoicing,
his chosen ones with shouts of joy.

PSALM 105:43 NIV

Have you ever felt captive to the dark thoughts inside your head? Do you sometimes feel trapped by the poor choices you've made? Has life been overwhelming you with all you've endured?

Rejoice, my friend, because you no longer need to feel imprisoned by it all. The Bible tells us that we are set free from what would enslave us. God has set aside his chosen ones, and that includes you!

Oh God, the joy I feel because of you is indescribable. I'm so
thankful you have set me free from all that burdened me.

So he brought his people out with joy,
his chosen ones with singing.

PSALM 105:43 ESV

God has brought us out of bondage and into joy. He chose to rescue us and as he does, he sings over us!

Release your feelings of guilt—and your burdens—and instead be glad. There is great joy in being able to relieve yourself of the heaviness you've been carrying around. And you can do so because our God and Savior has wiped your slate clean. It's time to party—you are free!

Father, I pray I'd continue to shake off the chains of sin and remember you came to release me from all that would keep me captive and set me free into joy.

Do you feel God's joy over you as he leads you out of bondage?

Rejoice in God's Gift

Let the righteous be glad;
Let them rejoice before God;
Yes, let them rejoice exceedingly.

PSALM 68:3 NKJV

There are those that would have us believe that a life lived according to God's will means a life of doom, gloom, and not much fun at all. And oh, how much they're missing when they live under this misconception!

When you are given the gift of salvation, and live under the grace of God, there is great reason for celebration, and so much to rejoice about.

God, I delight in knowing you. I pray I'd come to know you in a deeper way each day. May your joy fill me to the brim.

Let the godly rejoice.
Let them be glad in God's presence.
Let them be filled with joy.

PSALM 68:3 NLT

When you truly begin to know this good, good Father of ours, then you begin to see how worthy he is of praise and rejoicing.

There is a joy in knowing him that cannot be matched by anything else you'd find on this earth, no matter how hard you may search for it. God is simply the best; he is perfect in all that he does.

Father, I rejoice that you love me the way you do. My heart is full of gladness because of you!

Spend some time rejoicing in the Father's goodness tonight.

Reap Joy

Those who sow in tears
Shall reap in joy.

PSALM 126:5 NKJV

Loving God and having a real relationship with him doesn't mean we won't go through times of trial. There are things you will experience that may bring you to your knees with sorrow and sadness.

Our work here on earth needs to be done regardless of what we are feeling emotionally as we do it. As we struggle, we can rest assured, knowing that our time of jubilation is coming.

Lord, thank you for getting me through times of trial with your promise of joy in the days to come.

Those who plant in tears
will harvest with shouts of joy.

PSALM 126:5 NLT

The Bible says that when we sow in tears, we will reap in joy. What exactly does this mean? How can we reap something opposite to what we are sowing?

We are promised the greatest joy we will ever know with our Lord and Savior. Although we may weep through the sowing of our day-to-day tasks and duties, a joyful harvest is coming. The tears may fall, but the day is near when they'll turn into joy. Only God is able to turn our sorrow into joy. Trust that he will do that for you tonight.

God, it's only because of you that I can push through and work, knowing that you're the giver of the greatest joy anyone can ever experience.

Have you experienced joy from sorrow in your lifetime?

New Opportunities

You know that when your faith is tested, your endurance has a chance to grow.

JAMES 1:3 NLT

It's kind of hard having trouble be an opportunity for joy, isn't it? In fact, it's our instinct to feel just the opposite. And yet we are asked to view it that way despite those instincts.

That's because, when times of trouble come our way, we become stronger in the long run. We are stretched in new ways, learning and growing as we go. Growing endurance is something to rejoice over!

God, it's hard to look at times of trouble in a positive light. Help me to trust you with what you are doing in my life.

The testing of your faith produces endurance.

JAMES 1:3 NASB

If we always stayed just the way we are today, we'd never experience personal growth. But when we look at tough times as an opportunity to change for the better, we can begin to feel thankful for those times.

Try to delight in your rough patches, relying on the Lord to get you through it all.

Help me to find joy in the midst of suffering, and to know that as I grow emotionally, I am turning into the person you have created me to be.

What testing are you going through now that is producing endurance?

Source of Happiness

Come, everyone!
Clap your hands!
Shout to God with joyful praise!

PSALM 47:1 NLT

When you're feeling euphoric, doesn't it make you want to sing with gladness? Your feet start tapping along, and soon your whole body is getting into the feeling. David felt the same way all those years ago as we wrote what we now know as the Psalms.

Take a look at his words. Don't they feel like they could have been written in a modern-day song? Spend some time this morning shouting to God with joyful praise!

Father, I've never known exhilaration like the feeling that comes from knowing your love. I praise you this morning because you are so good.

Clap your hands, all peoples!
Shout to God with loud songs of joy!

PSALM 47:1 ESV

Knowing the true joy that comes from a loving relationship with God isn't something new. People have been clapping their hands with glee for thousands of years. And yet the joy of the Lord feels just as fresh and new every time we experience it as if it were happening for the first time.

So go ahead and sing if you're feeling the joy of the Lord. He's a good Father—and worthy of your praise tonight!

God, thank you for the incredible gift of your overwhelming joy. I want to sing your praises all the days of my life.

Sing a new song of joy to the Lord tonight.

Quiet Strength

The meek shall inherit the land
and delight themselves in abundant peace.

Psalm 37:11 NIV

Our culture follows the motto "If you've got it, flaunt it!" Riches, beauty, cute kids, desirable status, and beautiful vacations are continually posted online. Real-time updates of everyone else's amazing lives parade around in our mind, causing unrest and discontentment. The Bible talks a lot about meekness; it is not surprising that this is a word we don't hear or understand in our culture.

Meekness means quiet strength. It is humility that models the humility of our Savior. God says the meek are those who will have what everyone really desires—delight and abundant peace!

God, help me to find delight in you, and to quit the comparison
game. I want that quiet strength that is found in humility.

The meek shall inherit the land
and delight themselves in abundant peace.

PSALM 37:11

Do we really think that what we see on social media is the entirety of someone's life? Look more closely and you will see they face the same struggles you do. We are human after all.

True blessing is having the joy of the Lord: a spiritual prosperity incomparable to earthly riches. Take some time tonight, that you might have spent scrolling social media, and give it to the Lord. Ask him to reveal areas of your life that are breeding discontentment and pride, and instead seek to model meekness and humility.

Lord, I repent of discontentment that I have allowed to rob me of your peace. Help me to demonstrate gratitude for my life, just the way it is.

What's the best way for you to practice meekness?

Keep Your Eyes Open

Let the heavens be glad, and let the earth rejoice;
Let the sea roar, and all it contains;
Let the field exult, and all that is in it.
Then all the trees of the forest will sing for joy.

PSALM 96:11–12 NASB

Look around you. If you keep your eyes open, you can see the entire world rejoicing in the knowledge that our God is good. You can hear in the rolling thunder during a rainstorm, as it booms loudly and the skies come alive with lightning.

Sounds of praise are all around you. Join in the chorus with the rest of the earth today!

Father, I'm awed by the world you've put together for us.
I can't help but feel joy as I take it all in!

Let the skies rejoice and the earth be glad;
let the sea and everything in it shout.
Let the fields and everything in them rejoice.
Then all the trees of the forest will sing for joy.

PSALM 96:11–12 NCV

You can see the world rejoice in the gentle sway of the long grass in the pasture, or listening as the animals munch on their lunch. As the tide laps against the shore, it sings a soothing love song to the Lord over and over again.

Each and every place our sight lands should be a reminder of the great beauty God has put together for us. Let's sing a joyful song and rejoice together in the knowledge that we are loved greatly.

God, thank you for the chorus of praise that your creation sings.
Help me to keep my eyes and ears open for thanksgiving.

What did you observe today that could have been interpreted as the earth giving praise to God?

Pursue God

A joyful heart is good medicine,
but a crushed spirit dries up the bones.

PROVERBS 17:22 ESV

We all have a medicine cabinet at home. It's the spot you go to for the bumps and bruises, the aches and pains that life brings our way. Bloody knee? Slap a Band-Aid on it. Feeling a headache coming on? There's a pill for that. Tummy troubles? There's a cure for that too.

But there's a medicine that's even better than any over-the-counter pharmaceutical you could take. And it's available at any time—you'll never run out! Ask God for a joyful heart today and feel it soothe your aches and pains away.

Lord, there's no better medicine for my soul than turning to you.
I want to sing with joy because of your great love.

A happy heart is like good medicine,
but a broken spirit drains your strength.

PROVERBS 17:22 NCV

The joy that comes from a deep and real relationship with the Lord is like medicine to your very soul. There's no better cure for the aches and pains that sorrow can bring you like turning your face to him and soaking in his love for you.

You can rejoice in knowing God is for you. He wants you to know elation like you've never known before! Tonight, before you go to bed, smile. Start the process of having a happy heart.

God, I'm so glad you make yourself so available to the ones who seek you out. Help me to have a happy heart.

Even if it seems crazy, smile at your life right now.

Full Potential

Make my joy complete by being of the same mind, maintaining the same love, united in spirit, intent on one purpose.

PHILIPPIANS 2:2 NASB

These words, written so many years ago, really say it all, don't they? You can experience happiness without allowing the Lord into your life, but your true joy cannot be complete until you're living in accordance with him and his desires for you.

Even better, these words were written by a man living in prison at the time. Paul was a man who knew what joy was, despite his circumstances. Can you walk in joy today despite what you are going through?

O Lord, I want my joy to become complete through you. It's my heart's desire to give myself over to you fully.

Make me truly happy by agreeing wholeheartedly with each other, loving one another, and working together with one mind and purpose.

PHILIPPIANS 2:2 NLT

When we're united together as Christians, intent on the purpose of spreading the love of our Savior together, our joy knows no limits. It becomes complete as we let him into our lives, opening up our hearts to him, and relying fully on him for everything we need.

Working with others in a peace-filled, loving environment is something you won't find in many places. Make it your goal to agree wholeheartedly with the people around you this evening.

God, help me to encourage other believers to be of like mind, so that together we can change the world for your kingdom.

Are you in wholehearted agreement with those around you?

Long for the LORD

Restore to me the joy of your salvation
and grant me a willing spirit, to sustain me.

PSALM 51:12 NIV

Picture a mountain of calorie-free chocolate cake, served up to you at the end of a delicious dinner. Or maybe you prefer salty over sweet, and a big bowl of salsa with chips is what beckons you. Isn't your mouth just salivating at the thought of it?

Imagine indulging at any time, knowing that it's good for you and doesn't come with any repercussions. You know what's even better than any of that? The sweet taste of the joy that comes from the Lord.

Lord, I want to taste the sweetness of the joy that comes from knowing you. As each day passes, I crave more of you!

Restore to me the joy of your salvation,
and make me willing to obey you.

PSALM 51:12 NLT

The joy of the Lord is better than the most delicious meal you could ever imagine. It fills us up to overflowing and pours hope and peace over others as they come into contact with you.

Just like the imaginary treats at the table, you can dive in to God's joy any time without worry. It tastes great and it's good for you (it's like an advertiser's dream come true!). The best part is that you'll never run out of the great joy that the Holy Spirit brings, and you'll continue to crave more with every passing moment.

God, I dive into your joy this evening. I thank you for the sweetness that it brings to my life.

Have you tasted the sweetness of the joy of the Lord?

Go Deeper

His anger lasts only a moment,
but his favor lasts a lifetime!
Weeping may last through the night,
but joy comes with the morning.

PSALM 30:5 NLT

When you're in the middle of a painful situation, it can feel as if it's taking forever for it to pass. Time almost stands still as you wait for the pressure to ease up. And yet, we have something to look forward to.

Joy is coming! The pain of the night may bring you to tears, but there is light ahead. And that light is bringing with it a time of rejoicing for you.

Lord, thank you for providing me with the hope that joy is coming,
despite my current circumstances.

His anger is but for a moment,
His favor is for a lifetime;
Weeping may last for the night,
But a shout of joy comes in the morning.

PSALM 30:5 NASB

Have you ever experienced the worst kind of sorrow? There is hope for you. Joy is headed your way. While your problems may never disappear altogether, you will begin to see bright spots in the midst of the pain as you look to the Lord to guide you through.

Trust your Father in heaven. He wants you to know his joy!

Father, I could not walk through this life without you by my side, loving me through the worst that this world can throw my way.

Press deeper into the Lord today and let him guide you through your difficulty.

Abundance of the Holy Spirit

If anyone cleanses himself from what is dishonorable, he will be a vessel for honorable use, set apart as holy, useful to the master of the house, ready for every good work.

2 TIMOTHY 2:21 ESV

Wouldn't it be great to have been a fly on the wall (or an angel on the wall as the case may have been) as God dreamed us up? Picture it. He was deciding exactly how he wanted us to be, and along with the color of our eyes and the shade of our skin, the texture of our hair, and all of our personality traits, he made sure to leave room for us to be filled up. Wait, what? Yes. He created us to be vessels.

Spend some time this morning thinking about what you would like your vessel to be filled with. Ask the Lord to fill you to overflowing!

Lord, fill me to the brim. I want your joy to overflow in me, spilling out onto everyone in my life.

If anyone cleanses himself from these things, he will be a vessel for honor, sanctified, useful to the Master, prepared for every good work.

2 TIMOTHY 2:21 NASB

As vessels, we can try to fill ourselves up with everything this world has to offer. And there's a lot that's tempting. But when we fill ourselves to the brim with God's joy and peace, it comes bubbling up and spilling over so we can share it with others.

We're a vessel without a top, made to overflow so God's joy can be seen by everyone. Continue to ask God to fill you tonight.

God, I thank you for creating me to be a vessel that can be filled by you. I ask for you to fill me with your peace as I lay down to sleep this evening.

What do you want God to fill you with today?

Cast Off Your Worries

Do not be anxious about anything, but in everything by prayer and supplication with thanksgiving let your requests be made known to God.

PHILIPPIANS 4:6 ESV

Do not be anxious about anything. Goodness, that's a hard one to wrap our minds around, isn't it? At times, it seems as if our world is falling apart. There's so much to feel anxious about! And yet, it's possible to let it go through God's grace.

Have you ever heard it said that worry doesn't change anything? It's so true. But giving it to God through prayer and supplication changes everything. Give him your anxiety today and leave it behind.

O Lord, I praise you for carrying my burdens. I give you my anxiety and I'm grateful to be free from it!

Don't worry about anything; instead, pray about everything.
Tell God what you need, and thank him for all he has done.

PHILIPPIANS 4:6 NLT

It's amazing the peace you feel when you hand over your worries to the Lord. This Scripture tells us to simply tell God what we need and thank him for everything he has done. This is supposed to be the key for not worrying. God has always been faithful and he will continue to be.

It doesn't mean you won't think about difficult situations anymore, or that you won't have any concerns. Instead, God will take the burden from you and carry it for you— if you allow him to!

God, I'm so thankful I can be at peace during the trials in life, because I know you will supernaturally help me to do so.

What do you need God to take from you today?

Satisfied

Because your love is better than life,
my lips will glorify you.
I will praise you as long as I live,
and in your name I will lift up my hands.
I will be fully satisfied as with the richest of foods;
with singing lips my mouth will praise you.

PSALM 63:3-5 NIV

There are times in our lives when we really need answers
or a breakthrough, and sometimes we just want to be blessed.
Our loving Father says to simply ask.

God wants to give us good gifts. He knows what is best for us.
His love is better than life itself, and he knows exactly how to
satisfy us.

Lord, there are many things that I need and many things I want.
I ask you for them now because I know that you are a loving Father
who wants to answer me today.

Because your love is better than life,
I will praise you.
I will praise you as long as I live.
I will lift up my hands in prayer to your name.
I will be content as if I had eaten the best foods.
My lips will sing, and my mouth will praise you.

PSALM 63:3-5 NCV

You might not want to ask God for things because you feel they are too much, or they're too specific. God is able to handle your requests—he won't give you things that will bring you harm or that you will use for selfish gain.

The truth is that God wants us to ask him for everything. He is delighted when we trust in him for the smallest and the largest of things. Trust him for whatever it is that you need tonight.

God, I trust you for the small requests and the large ones tonight. I know you will provide everything I need at the right time and in the right measure.

Can you be fully satisfied with all the Lord has given you?

I Belong to You

I still belong to you;
you hold my right hand.
You guide me with your counsel,
leading me to a glorious destiny.

PSALM 73:23-24 NLT

Parents are usually insanely proud of their children. It doesn't seem to matter what particular gift a child might have, a parent will always find something in that child to praise.

A parent's love is not about what the child can do, but about who they are. They see a beautiful heart and amazing potential. The same is true of your heavenly Father. He sees the potential you have to do great things for him. Ask him to show you what those things are today.

Father, sometimes I forget that you love me for who I am,
not what I do. You see my heart and you rejoice over me.

I am continually with you;
you hold my right hand.
You guide me with your counsel,
and afterward you will receive me into glory.

PSALM 73:23-24 ESV

If we could only picture ourselves holding God's hand all the time, we would probably save a lot of stress and tension in our lives. When we trust that we belong to God and he is watching over us like a proud Dad, it gives us the confidence we need to move forward in what he has planned for us.

Our heavenly Father is not only present, he's also protective, proud, and loving. Can you imagine him tonight, being so happy to be near you that he sings and rejoices over you! You are deeply loved.

God, give me the confidence to walk through life with the knowledge that I have a heavenly Father who delights in me so much that he can't help but sing!

What song do you hear the Lord singing over you?

Starting Over

Praise the LORD!
Oh, give thanks to the LORD, for He is good!
For His mercy endures forever.

PSALM 106:1 NKJV

Have you ever wished you could have a do-over? It would be so great to turn back the clock, reverse a decision, and do it differently. There is wisdom in looking back, but we can't change what was done in the past.

When we embrace God's mercy that is new every morning, there does not need to be any carryover of yesterday's mistakes. Our part in the transaction may require repentance of sin or forgiving someone, perhaps even ourselves. Bathed in his mercies, we can begin each day squeaky clean!

Lord, I am so grateful that your love and your mercies never end.
You extend them to me brand new every morning. Great is your
faithfulness!

Praise the LORD!
Oh give thanks to the LORD,
for he is good,
for his steadfast love endures forever!

PSALM 106:1 ESV

There are some things we can do over, like tweak the recipe or rip the seam, but most often, the important big decisions can't be changed… except when it comes to spiritual things.

God tells us that we can start over every morning because his mercies will be there. Whatever went awry the day before, whatever mess we made from poor choices, we can begin the next day with a completely clean slate! Praise the Lord for that tonight!

Father, thank you for a clean slate. I am so grateful for your mercy that allows me to start over each day.

Look forward to a new day with new mercy tomorrow.

Found Delightful

Let those who delight in my righteousness
shout for joy and be glad
and say evermore,
"Great is the LORD,
who delights in the welfare of his servant!"

PSALM 35:27 ESV

Despite this season of thanksgiving, it can be a struggle to find delight. If the holiday spirit isn't quite abundant, take delight in God's righteousness. Shout for joy and be glad! And hold fast to the promise of his delight in you. His delight isn't circumstantial.

Thank God for past triumphs and current struggles that lead to a future of strength. You are delightful to God. Believe that today.

God, you see all of me and still find me delightful. Thank you.

Give great joy to those who came to my defense.
Let them continually say,
"Great is the LORD,
who delights in blessing his servant with peace!"

PSALM 35:27 NLT

Regardless of your situation today, God finds you delightful. It isn't a patronizing delight, like an adult chuckling while a toddler throws a temper tantrum; rather, he sees right past whatever emotion we are expressing to the depths of who he knows us to be.

It's humbling to think that God finds us delightful, even when we are acting immaturely, or we struggle with the same sin over and over again. He delights in us and offers us peace from the striving.

Father, I am humbled to be found delightful by you. Thank you for being so patient with me and for seeing past my actions right into my potential.

Take a moment to rest in God's delight over you today.

Worthy

"You are worthy, O LORD,
To receive glory and honor and power;
For You created all things,
And by Your will they exist and were created."

REVELATION 4:11 NKJV

Worship is our natural response to the goodness of God. It's not simply an emotional reaction—worship is also the act of offering back to God the glory that he rightly deserves.

When we stop to think about God's power, majesty, and creativity, we cannot help but glorify him because he is so worthy of the highest form of honor.

Creator God, I want to look for you in everything, so I can give praise back to you for all you've done.

"Worthy are you, our LORD and God,
to receive glory and honor and power,
for you created all things,
and by your will they existed and were created."

REVELATION 4:11 ESV

Imagine being able to say that you created *everything*. Stop and think about that for little while. Our God created the entire world—by his will. There is no one else worthy of receiving all glory, honor, and power.

By glorifying God in our daily lives, those around us will take notice and some will ultimately be led to join us in praising him.

God, help me to praise you in the way that you are worthy of.
Help me to respond to you with honor, appreciation, and worship.

Thank God today for all that he has created.

Sacrifice of Thanksgiving

Offer to God a sacrifice of thanksgiving
Call upon Me in the day of trouble;
I shall rescue you, and you will honor Me.

PSALM 50:14-15 NASB

The Israelites in the Old Testament had a complicated list of rituals and sacrifices to follow. Among the five special offerings, one was the peace offering, or the sacrifice of thanksgiving. God asked that an animal without defect be offered to him from a heart that was full of gratitude for his grace.

It's not always easy to be thankful. In times of great difficulty when everything in the natural screams "I don't like this!" gratitude comes at great sacrifice. It is a denial of the natural response, dying to one's own preference, and in submission saying, "God, your way is best and I thank you."

Lord, today I want to say thanks for being my God. As I call out to you, I know you will be my deliverer and get all the glory in the process!

"Give an offering to show thanks to God.
Give God Most High what you have promised.
Call to me in times of trouble.
I will save you, and you will honor me."

PSALM 50:14-15 NCV

When Jesus came, old requirements were replaced by the new so that our worship could be an expression of our hearts directly through our lips. No need for complicated rituals and sacrifices—just a thankful heart.

Having a grateful heart gives us the privilege of calling on God in our day of trouble and the assurance of his deliverance.

God, thank you for the grace you show me each day. I offer my sacrifice of thanksgiving today and every day, especially when it's difficult to have a heart of gratitude.

Can you offer God your sacrifice of praise tonight?

Stored Goodness

How abundant are the good things
that you have stored up for those who fear you,
that you bestow in the sight of all,
on those who take refuge in you.

PSALM 31:19 NIV

David, who enjoyed a great friendship with God, makes many wonderfully startling claims about God. God is storing up goodness! What exactly is that goodness? Is it safety and security? Is it peace in trials? Is it a quiet heart in the middle of a storm? Is it joy in the midst of mourning?

Yes, it would seem that God's goodness could be all of these and much more. Ask him to reveal his goodness to you today.

Help me, God, to trust in your goodness. Thank you that you see
my faith even when it's weak, and you store up goodness for me.

How great is the goodness you have stored up
for those who fear you.
You lavish it on those who come to you for protection,
blessing them before the watching world.

PSALM 31:19 NLT

God has so much goodness that he actually has to store it up, so he doesn't drench us in it all at once. But there is a caveat. The goodness referenced in this passage is reserved for a special group of people—those who fear God. It is for those who humbly come to him because he is the King and they are not.

Rest assured, God will reward you more than you could possibly imagine when you fear him rightly and come humbly before him.

God, thank you for your endless supply of goodness. You are the definition of goodness itself. Help me to rightly fear and honor you tonight.

What does it mean to you to fear God?

Water of Life

"Whoever drinks of the water that I shall give him will never thirst. But the water that I shall give him will become in him a fountain of water springing up into everlasting life."

JOHN 4:14 NKJV

Sometimes, we need "extra." Our spiritual requirements are never met by earthly experiences. When these experiences occlude our spiritual opportunities, we leave off from them, thirsting.

Jesus says that he is the living water. His living water is an endless fountain. We can reach up to him, relying on him to fill us with eternal life.

Jesus, I praise you. Thank you for being good to me and loving me. Please pour your "extra" into my thirsty soul as I pour your holy Word into my life.

"Whoever drinks of the water that I will give him will never be thirsty again. The water that I will give him will become in him a spring of water welling up to eternal life."

JOHN 4:14 ESV

Life as expected derails at times—whether from internal failures or external events—and this creates great inner struggle. The verve inside us may dwindle in the face of such difficult challenges. Where will we get joy and strength to continue?

Jesus says he brings us abundant life *wherever* the enemy has tried to steal, kill, or destroy. He is just that faithful.

Lord, envelope me in your presence, and train me to stand in you as a relentless and immoveable child of your joy.

Spend time drinking in the refreshing water of life tonight.

Receive Life

*"You gave me life and showed me kindness,
and in your care you watched over my life."*

JOB 10:12 NCV

To say that Job went through a rough patch would be putting it lightly. He lost everything he had, from his family, to his wealth, friends, and more. And yet, even in the worst of it, he could still see that God was good.

Job knew that he was cared for in his darkest hour, and that the God he loved was one of kindness. Can you have the same confidence in God today?

*Father, I pray I'd see your kindness even on my darkest days.
I know how much you care for me, and I'm so thankful for that.*

You gave me life and showed me your unfailing love.
My life was preserved by your care.

JOB 10:12 NLT

In our own times of darkness, our God is watching over us. He cares about every detail of our lives, no matter how big or small. In our moments of despair, we can look to him and be comforted, because he wants us to see his kindness. He gave us life!

He doesn't sit high above us, laughing as we stumble and flail; rather he is a friend to us who walks us through everything we encounter.

You're a kind and loving God, and I'm in awe of you. Thank you for being with me and blessing me with life.

Do you sense God's nearness even in the darkness?

Washed in Kindness

At one time we too were foolish, disobedient, deceived and enslaved by all kinds of passions and pleasures. We lived in malice and envy, being hated and hating one another. But when the kindness and love of God our Savior appeared, he saved us, not because of righteous things we had done, but because of his mercy.

TITUS 3:3–5 NIV

Whether you grew up in the church, or just learned the good news of salvation through Christ as recently as last week, there comes a point in your life when you have a decision to make. Will you continue on living according to the whims and desires of the flesh, or will you give yourself over to the Lord and become new through him?

When you make the choice to be reborn in Jesus, you realize the incredible gift of kindness he has given you. Thank him again for that kindness today.

Lord, I want to be more like you. I'm thankful for the renewing you've done in my heart.

In the past we also were foolish. We did not obey, we were wrong, and we were slaves to many things our bodies wanted and enjoyed. We spent our lives doing evil and being jealous. People hated us, and we hated each other. But when the kindness and love of God our Savior was shown, he saved us because of his mercy. It was not because of good deeds we did to be right with him. He saved us through the washing that made us new people through the Holy Spirit.

TITUS 3:3–5 NCV

God saved us! He rescued us from our own nature and instilled in us the ability and desire to become more like him. We can look back on our foolish past and determine not to repeat our silly mistakes.

You have been washed clean and renewed through the kindness and grace of God. Thank him tonight for his incredible love.

God, you have shown me such kindness. Thank you that you saved me and washed me clean of my past. Help me to continue seeking after you.

Can you sense the kindness of the Lord today?

Just Because

Honor the LORD for the glory of his name.
Worship the LORD in the splendor of his holiness.

PSALM 29:2 NLT

It isn't your birthday, but there's a gift on the counter with your name on it. You haven't done anything particularly special lately, but a card arrives in the mail to let you know you are loved—just because. It feels wonderful. It feels even better when you are on the giving end.

Meditate this morning on God's holiness, his perfection, his splendor. Let it bring you to your knees in gratitude. Worship and honor him for being your Lord.

Lord, above all other names, I worship yours. I love you for who you are and I thank you for who you are helping me become.

Ascribe to the LORD the glory due his name;
worship the LORD in the splendor of holiness.

PSALM 29:2 ESV

When was the last time you worshipped God just for being God? He loves to receive spontaneous gifts of love, honor, and praise just as much as we do. When you give God glory just because he deserves it, it delights his heart.

Spend a few moments this evening thanking God for being who he is. Let your praise and thanksgiving flow freely as you honor him.

God, I have so much to be thankful for. You are worthy of my honor and praise.

What are you especially thankful for today?

Celebrate His Goodness

I remain confident of this:
I will see the goodness of the LORD
in the land of the living.

PSALM 27:13 NIV

When something great happens to you, don't you just want to shout about it to everyone you know? You want to share the good news. "Did you hear what happened to me?" we ask our friends. "Let me tell you all about this fabulous thing!" Our excitement cannot be contained.

Expect good things from God. Remain confident that you will see his goodness. Look for it all around you today.

Lord, thank you for being the good and merciful God that you are. I want to tell everyone I know the many things you have done for me.

I would have despaired
unless I had believed
that I would see the goodness of the LORD
In the land of the living.

PSALM 27:13 NASB

There is nothing better than telling others about the many good things the Lord has done for us and given us. We should be itching to share the good news, and to tell all those with whom we come in contact about his mercies and kindness. He deserves all our praise, for he is a good God.

When you feel as though you are in the pits of despair, choose to believe in the goodness of the Lord. You might even need to choose that tonight.

Thank you, God, for giving me hope when all else seems dark and discouraging. You are good and you will continue to be good. I believe it tonight!

How has God demonstrated his goodness to you lately?

Receive Mercy

Who is a God like you,
who pardons sin and forgives the transgression
of the remnant of his inheritance?
You do not stay angry forever
but delight to show mercy.
You will again have compassion on us;
you will tread our sins underfoot
and hurl all our iniquities into the depths of the sea.
You will be faithful to Jacob,
and show love to Abraham,
as you pledged on oath to our ancestors
in days long ago.

MICAH 7:18–20 NIV

Time and time again, the people of Israel rebelled against the Lord and sinned. They deliberately turned their backs on him and made foolish decisions. Today, we do the same thing. We turn our backs, and time and time again we sin against the Lord.

The good news is that our God is a forgiving one; he doesn't hold a permanent grudge against us. He doesn't stay angry forever. Instead, he wants to show us his mercy.

Father, I'm sorry for the many ways I have sinned. Forgive me again today.

There is no God like you.
You forgive those who are guilty of sin;
you don't look at the sins of your people
who are left alive.
You will not stay angry forever,
because you enjoy being kind.
You will have mercy on us again;
you will conquer our sins.
You will throw away all our sins
into the deepest part of the sea.
You will be true to the people of Jacob,
and you will be kind to the people of Abraham
as you promised to our ancestors long ago.

MICAH 7:18–20 NCV

God remains faithful, even when we're not. All we have to do is ask for his grace. He remains true to us, dedicated to help us mature in our walk with him.

God is waiting to give us the gift of compassion if we'll just turn to him and admit we need him.

God, I'm thankful for your daily mercies. Your faithfulness knows no bounds. I turn to you this evening and seek your compassion.

How does it feel to know God throws your sins deep into the sea?

Glorify and Worship

Not to us, O LORD, not to us,
but to your name
goes all the glory
for your unfailing love and faithfulness.

PSALM 115:1 NLT

It's easy to be caught up in the admiring words of others. When you achieve a certain goal, or something great happens to you, you want to take the credit. After all, you're a hard worker. You deserve some accolades, right?

It's tempting to hope you'll get all the glory. But there is only one who deserves to be glorified. Turn to him and give him the honor he deserves this morning.

God, you have been so faithful in the gifts you have given me, and the things you've done for me. I pray I'd glorify you and give you the praise when I'm tempted to be puffed up with accolades.

It does not belong to us, LORD.
The glory belongs to you
because of your love and loyalty.

PSALM 115:1 NCV

Compliments are great, and there's nothing wrong with receiving one. But when we put our stock in what we achieve and think we've done it on our own, we lose sight of the one who gives us everything we have.

God should be glorified for all he's done, and all he's given us. Every good thing comes from him, and it's important that we never forget it. He is faithful in his generosity, and he deserves our praise and worship.

Thank you, God, for all the things you've helped me to accomplish. I couldn't have done any of it without you.

What have you been complimented on recently? Can you honor God for it?

Never Changing

For his unfailing love for us is powerful;
the LORD's faithfulness endures forever.
Praise the LORD!

PSALM 117:2 NLT

If there is one thing we know, it's that nothing stays the same. Life is an uncertain thing, changing from moment to moment. However, no matter what changes you go through in life, no matter how it ebbs and flows, there is one thing you can count on—the Lord and his faithfulness.

Simply put, God's faithfulness endures forever. He is always there for you, and he's devoted and true.

Lord, I am amazed by your faithfulness. I know that, when the rest of my life feels wobbly and unsteady, you are someone I can count on to be a constant.

For great is his steadfast love toward us,
and the faithfulness of the LORD endures forever.
Praise the LORD!

PSALM 117:2 NRSV

We can put our faith in God because he is steadfast. He never changes, and he tells us he will be faithful. Because of that, we know it to be true. After all, he's a God who keeps his promises.

When you are filled with worry or fear about upcoming changes, you can rest assured that God will be faithful to show you his unfailing love.

God, thank you for loving me without fail, and for remaining faithful forever.

What does devotion look like to you?

Abiding Love

Satisfy us in the morning with your unfailing love,
that we may sing for joy and be glad all our days.

PSALM 90:14 NIV

Early morning sun streamed in the window. The steam from her coffee cup caught the light on its way upward. Peace settled in as she whispered a soft, "Good morning, Lord." These quiet moments of solitude in his presence were her strength.

The pause, the simple escape from the fast pace that defined the rest of her day, was life giving to her. She turned the soft pages in the well-worn Bible and read the words that would keep her going for whatever was ahead of her that day.

Turn my heart to you, Lord, first thing. Let me think about you
when I wake up before I think of anything else.

Satisfy us in the morning with your steadfast love,
that we may rejoice and be glad all our days.

We all have different times of the day that we open the Word, but there's something about the evening, something about giving him the last minutes of your day.

It's like putting the entirety of your day safely into God's hands. Finish your day with the presence of the Lord, and you'll find a joy that keeps you singing and peace that settles the worries of the night.

Lord, my heart overflows with thankfulness as I consider all you've done for me. I sink my roots down right here, into my love for you.

Do you take time to satisfy your soul in God's presence?

I Will Look Up

My voice you shall hear in the morning, O LORD;
In the morning I will direct it to You,
And I will look up.

PSALM 5:3 NKJV

Have you ever stood in the middle of a thick forest, with dense evergreens on all sides and a rich carpet of coppery pine needles? As you look around, all you can see is trees. There is no glimpse of what is beyond them, just dark layers of pine.

If you stop for a moment, and look up to the place where the trees narrow and the light breaks, you are profoundly reminded of how much more is out there. It doesn't matter how hidden you are, there is a big sky and a great God who is always there.

Thank you, Jesus, that it is as simple as looking up. Remind me that I'm not alone and that no matter how thick the troubles might stand around me, you are with me and you are guiding me.

In the morning, LORD,
you hear my voice;
in the morning I lay my requests before you
and wait expectantly.

PSALM 5:3 NIV

Let the Lord stop you right in the middle of your life. If you find yourself looking around frantically, focusing in on the trials that you can't see past, you will lose sight of what is outside of them.

Stop, and look up. Let your eyes adjust and take in the light. Drink in God's presence. When you wake up in the morning, before walking forward, before weaving your way through whatever the day might bring, look to his light and speak of his goodness.

God, I drink in your presence today. Help me to see your light as I lift my head and look up.

Are you looking up to God and waiting expectantly for him to meet with you?

The Greatest

Now these three remain: faith, hope and love.
But the greatest of these is love.

1 CORINTHIANS 13:13 NIV

Because we are human, it can be really hard to think of God's
love in any other way but how we know it with other people.
And with other people, it can often feel like there are strings
attached. If you let someone down, if you don't live up to their
expectations, you may see them start to slip away or reject you.

Do you believe that God loves you unconditionally? Or do
you somehow feel that there are strings attached? If so,
close your eyes and picture a giant pair of scissors snipping
right through all of those strings. They don't exist in your
relationship with God.

God, thank you for your unconditional love that remains longer
than anything else.

So now faith, hope, and love abide, these three;
but the greatest of these is love.

DEUTERONOMY 7:9 ESV

Though we may find it hard to believe, rejection is never
the case with the Lord's love. It is unconditional. There is
nothing you can do to make him turn away from you.

God designed you before you were ever a wisp of your
mother's imagination. You are one of his chosen people, and
he is faithful to those he loves!

Father, thank you for choosing me. Your love remains forever
and I am so grateful for it.

Thank God today that he loves you through the good and the
bad.

Nothing Compares

Wisdom is far more valuable than precious jewels.
Nothing else compares with it.

PROVERBS 3:15 TLB

Solomon had a chance to ask God for anything. Instead of riches and glory, he asked for a heart to hear God. God gave him all the wisdom, knowledge, and intellect available. Solomon used this understanding to establish a legal and judicial system unrivaled in his time. He had foreign policy success and a healthy economy at home.

We need to ask God for wisdom. Too often we ask for things. When we gain insight, it is easy to know what is and is not important.

Lord, sometimes I feel foolish and don't know what to do.
Help me seek your wisdom.

Wisdom is more precious than rubies;
nothing you desire can compare with her.

PROVERBS 3:15 NLT

Solomon had riches beyond comprehension, but he favored wisdom. He knew that good judgment and understanding was worth more than gold or jewels.

With knowledge, priorities reveal themselves, and good judgment allows us freedom from making poor choices. Ask God for continued wisdom in your life.

Father, I want to use good judgment in all that I do.
Give me insight to improve my thinking.

Do you rightly value wisdom?

Demonstration of Obedience

Blessed are all who fear the LORD,
who walk in obedience to him.

PSALM 128:1 NIV

Why is obedience to God so important? Simply put, our obedience is a demonstration of our love for him. Though good works don't give us eternal salvation (only a relationship with Jesus can do that), if we truly love God, then we have a desire to follow him and live a life of good deeds. We will want to follow the example set by Christ and live our lives modeled after him.

It may not be easy, but it is possible to begin to desire to walk on the path God sets for us. Ask him to give you a heart change, so that you want to walk in obedience.

Thank you, God, for giving me an amazing model of obedience
and for transforming my life.

How joyful are those who fear the Lord—
all who follow his ways!

PSALM 128:1 NLT

There are times when everything in us wants to rebel against what we're told to do—whether it's to clean our rooms, stay away from bad influences, or complete a project on time. But a life in Christ is one that is transformed.

If you feel like rebelling today, set that feeling down before the Lord. Seek his blessing by fearing him tonight.

Help me to be humble, God. I know you desire humility, and rebellion isn't humility. Continue to transform me, Jesus.

Make a list of the many ways Jesus obeyed his Father when he was on the earth.

Waiting Patiently

Live a life worthy of the Lord and please him in every way: bearing fruit in every good work, growing in the knowledge of God, being strengthened with all power according to his glorious might so that you may have great endurance and patience, and giving joyful thanks to the Father, who has qualified you to share in the inheritance of his holy people in the kingdom of light.

COLOSSIANS 1:10-12 NIV

One of the hardest things to do is to wait. The countdown to something fun can feel like it takes a million years. The time spent waiting for big news may feel like an eternity.

Are you waiting patiently for something? Pray that you can experience joy through the waiting. Ask the Lord to fill your heart with true happiness and patience until the day you are hoping for finally comes.

God, I believe that you are going to answer my prayers.
I thank you for giving me patience and joy in the waiting process.

Then the way you live will always honor and please the LORD, and your lives will produce every kind of good fruit. All the while, you will grow as you learn to know God better and better. We also pray that you will be strengthened with all his glorious power so you will have all the endurance and patience you need. May you be filled with joy, always thanking the Father. He has enabled you to share in the inheritance that belongs to his people, who live in the light.

COLOSSIANS 1:10-12 NLT

Paul knew the difficulty of waiting even back in his day, thousands of years ago. He implored the people of Colossia to be patient, and to feel a spirit of joy even while they waited for what they wanted.

This kind of joy can come only from the Lord. It's much too hard to find it on our own. Ask him for this kind of joy tonight.

God, thank you for strengthening me with endurance, and helping me find thankfulness and joy in the middle of waiting.

Can you wait patiently, knowing that there is joy in the waiting?

Empty Tank

"Submit to God and be at peace with him;
in this way prosperity will come to you."

JOB 22:21 NIV

Did you know that God designed our bodies to require rest?
It seems like a luxury to have rest in this day and age, and the
ability to truly enjoy it becomes difficult. Our minds think about
the things that we need to get done, or perhaps we get distracted
by other people and things clamoring for our attention.

Maybe it's an hour on the couch, or a quick prayer and a deep
breath in the breakroom at work. Either way, the key is to
seek God first and not as a last resort after total burnout. Find
time for rest today.

God, I do need your rest and peace. Help me to make it a priority to
spend time with you and get away from the busyness of life.

*"Submit to God, and you will have peace;
then things will go well for you."*

JOB 22:21 NLT

Like a car that needs to be filled with gas and have the occasional oil change to operate correctly, our body, mind, and spirit need peace and rest to operate well. The peace that God wants to give us is a supernatural peace. It's a peace that feeds us in all areas of our lives and restores our souls. All that is required of us is to recognize that we *need* his peace, and then take the time to slow down and meet with him.

Our bodies will start shutting down if we are not aware of our need for rest. We have to stop plowing forward with so little gas in our tanks, and go to God. He is abundant in peace and faithful to give it when we ask.

Father, thank you that you want me to rest and refuel my tank. I come to you this evening and ask you to fill me up as I rest.

Is there a particular area in your life where you need God's peace?

Against the Crowd

Whoever walks with the wise becomes wise,
but the companion of fools will suffer harm.

PROVERBS 13:20 ESV

History shows us that we tend to follow the masses. It is natural to want to fit in, to be included, to feel part of something bigger than ourselves. But we need to be careful who we are trying to fit in with.

We need to guard our hearts and listen to that tiny voice of reason deep within us. When we don't, we can find ourselves in situations that are over our heads. God gave us wisdom to make good decisions. That tiny voice that seems so relentless and strong? That is the Holy Spirit given to us by God to help us choose wisely. Decide to listen to that voice today.

God, I don't want to ignore my beliefs in order to be accepted by others. Help me to set my heart on walking with you and not behaving the way others do just to fit in.

Walk with the wise and become wise;
associate with fools and get in trouble.

Proverbs 13:20 NLT

Often the hardest part of resisting to go along with the crowd is the precise moment we need to say no. When we gather the courage to stand up for our values and morals, a feeling of peace will rush in. That peace is worth every moment of feeling uncomfortable. We may be temporarily mocked for walking away, but the choices we make today could have a huge impact on our future. It might seem fun and harmless to join the crowd in the moment, but the damage done to our futures could be devastating.

God wants to help you resist temptation. With him you are stronger, braver, and wiser than you think. When you choose to walk with God, you won't stumble because he is with you every step of the way.

Father, please guide me and help me to make wise decisions.
I want to hear your voice and obey it. Fill me with peace when
I have to go against the crowd to make the right choice.

Do you feel pressured to be someone you are not?

The Final Prize

We are surrounded by a great cloud of people whose lives tell us what faith means. So let us run the race that is before us and never give up. We should remove from our lives anything that would get in the way and the sin that so easily holds us back. Let us look only to Jesus, the One who began our faith and who makes it perfect. He suffered death on the cross. But he accepted the shame as if it were nothing because of the joy that God put before him. And now he is sitting at the right side of God's throne.

HEBREWS 12:1-2 NCV

If you are an athlete, then you know what it means to persevere. Pushing yourself past your wall, breaking down what you thought were your limits, and hanging on to the end are all a part of an athlete's way of life.

Are your eyes on the prize of life with the Lord? As you spend time with God today, ask him for his assistance in helping you through the tough times.

God, I pray for the ability to persevere. I know the prize waiting for me at the end is going to be worth it!

Since we have so great a cloud of witnesses surrounding us, let us also lay aside every encumbrance and the sin which so easily entangles us, and let us run with endurance the race that is set before us, fixing our eyes on Jesus, the author and perfecter of faith, who for the joy set before Him endured the cross, despising the shame, and has sat down at the right hand of the throne of God.

HEBREWS 12:1–2 NASB

Our lives as Christians are like a marathon. There is the world's greatest prize waiting for us if we can push through and endure until the end. When we cross the finish line, we get to run into the arms of Jesus.

Hardship will come, but we can get through it if we just keep our eyes on that prize. If you're feeling low on energy and perseverance tonight, ask God to fill your empty vessel. He loves to help us when we ask him to.

Father, I need you tonight. It's hard to persevere in life sometimes and I feel like I'm scraping the bottom of the barrel for motivation. Give me your perspective and fill me up with renewed vigor.

What do you look forward to most about the final prize?

My Protector

"Because he loves me," says the LORD, "I will rescue him;
I will protect him, for he acknowledges my name.
He will call on me, and I will answer him;
I will be with him in trouble,
I will deliver him and honor him.
With long life I will satisfy him
and show him my salvation."

PSALM 91:14-16 NIV

At some point in your life, there will come a time that you will look around and suddenly realize that you've found yourself in an uncomfortable situation. You may not even be sure why it is that you feel so icky, but you know that you don't feel good about what's happening.

In these times, you can call a parent, or you can call a trusted friend. But before you call anyone else, you should first call on God for protection. Ask him for his protection over you as you start your day today.

Father, when uncomfortable situations arise in my life, help me to run first to you to get the protection I need. You love me and you are always with me.

"Because he has loved Me, therefore I will deliver him;
I will set him securely on high, because he has known My name.
"He will call upon Me, and I will answer him;
I will be with him in trouble;
I will rescue him and honor him.
"With a long life I will satisfy him
And let him see My salvation."

PSALM 91:14-16 NASB

God wants to protect you and keep you safe. The Bible tells us several times that he is our protector. While this doesn't mean that harm will never befall you, it does mean that he will deliver you. The way he brings you through it might look different than you expected it to.

Pray for protection over your life tonight. Ask God for his help when tricky situations arise, and he will deliver you.

Thank you, God, for your protection. You hear me when I call out to you, and you rescue me.

Make a plan to pray for protection now, so when the time comes, you will be ready!

Foolish Wisdom

"I will destroy the wisdom of the wise; the intelligence of the intelligent I will frustrate." Where is the wise person? Where is the teacher of the law? Where is the philosopher of this age? Has not God made foolish the wisdom of the world?

1 CORINTHIANS 1:19-20 NIV

Our culture is one that values intelligence and an educated mind; philosophers and the great thinkers are among the highly esteemed. It can be easy to get caught up (or left behind!) in debates of religion, politics, and philosophy.

The problem with worldly wisdom is that it is self-generated; it exists in the context of a finite mind that cannot grasp the mysteries of God. Thank God today that you are pursuing spiritually intelligence which is worth far more than human intelligence.

Father, when I feel like I am unable to answer the intellectual bullies around me, help me to look at the source of their wisdom. I only want to trust in your wisdom that is eternal and life-giving.

"I will destroy the wisdom of the wise; the intelligence of the intelligent I will frustrate." Where is the wise person? Where is the teacher of the law? Where is the philosopher of this age? Has not God made foolish the wisdom of the world?

1 CORINTHIANS 1:19-20

When Jesus came into the world, he upset the Scribes and the Pharisees—the most learned people of that time. He turned their ideas and assumptions upside-down and frustrated their intelligence.

God's wisdom is for those who are humble enough to accept his ways. This is how he makes the foolish wise. Ask God for his wisdom tonight.

God, you are full of wisdom and life. I want to pursue your will for me and understand your ways. Help me to trust in your wisdom tonight.

Do you trust the wisdom of God over the wisdom of man?

You Have Purpose

Whether, then, you eat or drink or whatever you do,
do all to the glory of God.

1 CORINTHIANS 10:31 NASB

Too often we measure our worth based on what we do or on what our status is. We love to label ourselves because it gives us a sense of self-worth. We all have this need to know what drives us: to know why we wake up in the morning, so we cling to labels as if our lives depend on them. If our current situation does not meet up to our expectations, we feel worthless and insignificant. A life without meaning is a sad one without hope.

Our purpose is to love God, abide in him, know him, and serve him. We just have to embrace it. It is simplicity at its finest. Too often we complicate the subject and go wandering in search of our life's purpose—we already have an opportunity to live purposefully every single day!

God, thank you for giving me purpose right where I am.
I want to embrace your purpose for me today.

*The answer is, if you eat or drink, or if you do anything,
do it all for the glory of God.*

1 CORINTHIANS 10:31 NCV

The good news is that we all have purpose. Every single one
of us has purpose that cannot be measured: young or old,
employer or employee, mother or daughter, doctor or janitor.
If we live for God, we are exactly where God wants us to be,
doing exactly what he wants us to do.

Do you feel like you are constantly trying to figure out what
your life's purpose is? Stop searching and know that you
have purpose right where you are. Your life is significant and
valuable. You don't have to have a six figure salary or beautiful
home to have meaning. Ask God to reassure you of your
purpose tonight.

*Thank you, Father, that you have given me a purpose. You love
who I am and you want me to walk in my purpose, not try to
create a new one.*

How can you embrace your God-given purpose today?

Work of Redemption

In him we have redemption through his blood, the forgiveness of sins, in accordance with the riches of God's grace.

EPHESIANS 1:7 NIV

Have you ever seen anyone at a restaurant insist on paying for a bill twice? Not likely. Nobody in their right mind would pay for a bill that was already paid for in full, would they? It wouldn't make any sense. Yet we all fall into this terrible habit of reminding ourselves of our past mistakes and sins. We allow ourselves to be entrapped in what once was and forget that we are already redeemed. Our sins were already paid for. We are free and clear. Sin free. Debt free.

It doesn't matter who you were or what you did in the past. In God's love for you, in his mercy and grace, not only has he forgiven you, but he has redeemed you from a life of despair. He has taken what was once lost and broken, and transformed it into something beautiful.

God, thank you for the redemptive work you have done in my life. Let it seep into the very core of who I am.

He is so rich in kindness and grace that he purchased our freedom with the blood of his Son and forgave our sins.

EPHESIANS 1:7 NLT

Your history is wiped clean. You are completely free from condemnation, guilt, and punishment. He took all that upon himself so that you could live a new life. That is how much he loves you! In him, you are a new creation. You are no longer tied to who you once were.

God has redeemed you. What a beautiful, undeserved gift it is to walk away from imprisonment and embrace freedom. Accept God's gift of grace—the washing and undoing of sins. Unshackle yourself from the past, and lift your face to the one true King who has set you free.

Father, thank you for redeeming me. Thank you for the beautiful gift of freedom from condemnation, guilt, and punishment. I am so blessed to be called your child.

Do you keep forgetting that you are redeemed?

Directed Hope

Why, my soul, are you downcast?
Why so disturbed within me?
Put your hope in God,
for I will yet praise him,
my Savior and my God.

PSALM 42:5 NIV

As a child you might recall a time when you longed to have a certain new toy and hoped with all your heart Santa would come through! You know the pain of disappointment if it wasn't under the tree and also the joy if it was!

People everywhere are looking for someone or something to put their hope in while unaware that the greatest source of hope is found in Jesus Christ. Place your hope in him this morning and watch how your day turns out.

Lord, conform the longings of my heart—all of my hopes—to the mold you have fashioned for me. My hope is in you and I will wait.

Why am I discouraged?
Why is my heart so sad?
I will put my hope in God!
I will praise him again—my Savior and my God!

PSALM 42:5 NLT

What are you hoping for today? Are you hoping a key person in your life or your circumstances will change? Fulfillment of such a hope cannot be guaranteed. However, when we place our hope in Christ, then every longing we have will be fulfilled!

God knows what we really need, so he may have to tweak our longings a bit to fit his plans. But when our hope and trust are directed toward the God of all hope, we will not be disappointed.

God, I know that all of my desires are known to you and you give me what I really need.

Direct your hope toward the God of all hope today and don't be disappointed!

Naughty or Nice?

He has not left himself without testimony: He has shown kindness by giving you rain from heaven and crops in their seasons; he provides you with plenty of food and fills your hearts with joy.

ACTS 14:17 NIV

Let's be honest—there are times when we try to "behave" so God or others will favor us when we need it. At those times, we look a little like the children of this season, impatiently awaiting the reward of good Christmas presents. They are behaving, yes, but not for the right reasons!

It is true that great rewards await the obedient. Let us not overlook, however, the beautiful kindnesses of the Lord that rain upon us day by day. Thank him for those kindnesses today.

God, thank you for the good gifts you have given me this year. Thank you for your kindnesses I have not deserved.

"He never left them without evidence of himself and his goodness. For instance, he sends you rain and good crops and gives you food and joyful hearts."

ACTS 14:17 NLT

God is good, and he is kind. He meets our needs and gives us joy that overwhelms our souls. His kindness is not dependent upon our behavior, but upon his good nature. Certainly, we are blessed.

Take some time this season to dwell on what God has already given you. If you can be thankful for what you already have, everything else that comes your way will be like bonus blessings!

Father, your tireless labors of love are evident everywhere in my life, and I am so grateful you are with me. Thank you! I love you too.

What are you particularly grateful for this Christmas season?

The Love-Joy Life

*"As the Father has loved me, so have I loved you. Abide in my love.
If you keep my commandments, you will abide in my love, just
as I have kept my Father's commandments and abide in his love.
These things I have spoken to you, that my joy may be in you, and
that your joy may be full."*

JOHN 15:9-11 ESV

Joy comes into our lives through actions of obedience.
Moreover, we may obey God for the sake of righteousness,
but God rewards us for it in baptizing us in his love!

As we abide in this love, we become vessels of joy, spilling
onto dry places in the world around us. That joy will consume
us, becoming a hallmark of his righteousness. Ask God to fill
you with joy today so that you can overflow with joy toward
others.

*Thank you, Lord, for hearing my cry for mercy. You are my strength
and shield.*

"As the Father loved Me, I also have loved you; abide in My love. If you keep My commandments, you will abide in My love, just as I have kept My Father's commandments and abide in His love. These things I have spoken to you, that My joy may remain in you, and that your joy may be full."

JOHN 15:9-11 NKJV

Strength and courage rise in the context of God's joy. We pursue and choose his ways, gaining fortitude to overcome, and we begin to live the supernatural life. In following the faithful one who overcame the world, we become like him, and we overcome as well.

By abiding in God's love, you are able to keep his commandments. When you feel loved unconditionally, it allows you to offer the same love to others. Accept God's unconditional love for you tonight and be filled with joy.

Thank you for loving me, God. Help me to abide in your love tonight.

What does it mean to you to abide in God's love?

Shine Above All

When they saw the star, they rejoiced exceedingly with great joy.
MATTHEW 2:10 ESV

"Rejoiced exceedingly"? With "great joy"? Matthew does not want us to underestimate the power and depth of the wise men's joy! They had traveled far, following Christ's star. When that star stopped over a house in Bethlehem, they were filled with joy because they knew a great king had arrived.

As you spend time with the King this morning, rejoice! His coming has given us a reason to be full of joy.

God, you're amazing. Thank you for inviting me to continually embrace your perspective and enjoy your presence.

When they saw the star, they were filled with joy!

MATTHEW 2:10 NLT

You give people an opportunity for joy, because you carry Jesus in you. He expresses his love through you, and he wants you to shine! Shine in God's presence and goodness, which rest deep within you.

Shine like that star, which announced Christ's presence to the world two millennia ago. His joy, gratitude, and deeds will blaze brightly through your own. So shine!

Father, you live and shine in me, giving me great hope and joy in every circumstance. Help me to blaze bright and give others joy and cause for gratitude.

How can you shine like a star today?

Praise from Joy

The angel said to him, "Do not be afraid, Zechariah, for your prayer has been heard, and your wife Elizabeth will bear you a son, and you shall call his name John. and you will have joy and gladness, and many will rejoice at his birth, for he will be great before the LORD. And he must not drink wine or strong drink, and he will be filled with the Holy Spirit, even from his mother's womb."

LUKE 1:13–15 ESV

Joy results in praise. Though Zechariah was a little slow at first, the end result was praise. "Your prayer has been heard!" Elizabeth had been barren many years; they, as a couple, knew something about waiting!

These faithful people surely expressed to God their longings, sufferings, and grief. They had sincerity and vulnerability before God, and in the end, they had extreme joy and praise. Be sincere and vulnerable with the Lord this morning and ask for it to develop joy in you.

Jesus, I want to share how I feel today. Hear me and know me. Thank you for becoming a vulnerable baby for our salvation.

The angel said, "Don't be afraid, Zechariah! God has heard your prayer. Your wife, Elizabeth, will give you a son, and you are to name him John. You will have great joy and gladness, and many will rejoice at his birth, for he will be great in the eyes of the LORD. He must never touch wine or other alcoholic drinks. He will be filled with the Holy Spirit, even before his birth."

LUKE 1:13–15 NLT

You can trust God with every emotion. Maybe Christmas is hard; you have no joy in your circumstance. Let him know your lament. Maybe it's full of joy, overflowing with praise. Maybe you're too busy to feel anything. If so, spend some time before the Lord in silence (like Zechariah had to!).

Whatever your emotion, God can handle it. There are people holding on to promises, people in grief, people filled with joy, people with hope fulfilled and hope expectant. Reach out to others this Christmas, and let them express their emotions to God.

Father, thank you that you can handle all of my emotions. However I'm feeling today, you embrace me and fill me with joy.

Dance or cry, but whatever you do, be vulnerable and draw near to God.

Seek, then Boldly Proclaim!

They hurried off and found Mary and Joseph, and the baby, who was lying in the manger. When they had seen him, they spread the word concerning what had been told them about this child, and all who heard it were amazed at what the shepherds said to them.

LUKE 2:16-18 NIV

When the shepherds were told about Jesus, they didn't pencil him into their schedules; they ran to him! They ran as fast as their feet could carry them. Who watched over the sheep? Who knows! But in that moment, they knew the importance of the Lord's advent, and they rushed in to Bethlehem, and into his barn stall, to see him.

Are you excited to sit with Jesus today? Tell him what a good and perfect gift he is to you this morning, and then share his goodness with others throughout the day.

Lord, thank you for coming to exchange beauty for ashes, joy for mourning, and praise for heaviness. I sing to the world with all my soul, "Glory to God in the highest heaven!"

They went with haste and found Mary and Joseph, and the baby lying in a manger. And when they saw it, they made known the saying that had been told them concerning this child. And all who heard it wondered at what the shepherds told them.

LUKE 2:16-18 ESV

Once they rushed to him, and experienced him, they rushed to tell of him. God didn't choose earthly leaders to spread the word. He chose messengers who would faithfully carry the good news.

Who is this Lord of ours, that fishermen and ranch hands spread his good news? Hallelujah! Christ has come! Tell your friends! Tell your neighbors! Tell everyone you meet: Jesus is the Lord, and he has come in the flesh! Hallelujah!

God, thank you for the gift of your Son. You sacrificed relationship with your Son so that I might come into right relationship with you. There is no better gift than that. Nothing I received today can even compare!

Reflect on the priceless gift God gave the world all those years ago.

Boxing Day

All who are under the yoke of slavery should consider their masters worthy of full respect, so that God's name and our teaching may not be slandered.

1 TIMOTHY 6:1 NIV

In many countries around the world, the day after Christmas is called Boxing Day: a tradition that began in a time when tradespeople were given Christmas boxes of money or presents to acknowledge good service throughout the year.

While we don't like to think of ourselves as servants these days, many of us are involved in employment or some type of service. As such, we should be full of respect toward our employers. If you're in a difficult work situation, ask God to help you show respect even when you don't feel like it. It goes a long way toward being a good witness.

Lord, remind me that as I serve others I am positively representing your name and your heart. Give me grace and strength to continue.

Let all who are under a yoke as bondservants regard their own masters as worthy of all honor, so that the name of God and the teaching may not be reviled.

1 TIMOTHY 6:1 ESV

The Bible says a lot about those who have shown diligence and respect to those in authority. There is a higher purpose to us respecting our employers. We may not get our Boxing Day reward for recognition of our service, but we will be honoring God's name as a witness of Christian living.

As you go to bed tonight, pray for those in positions of authority over you. Serve and respect them so that God's name is lifted up.

God, thank you for the reminder to persevere in working hard and being respectful. I want your name to be lifted up.

How can you show respect to those in authority over you?

A Priceless Treasure

I patiently accept all these troubles so that those whom God has chosen can have the salvation that is in Christ Jesus. With that salvation comes glory that never ends.

2 TIMOTHY 2:10 NCV

Strong women tend to be problem solvers. They see an issue looming on the horizon and work to get it fixed as quickly as possible. It would be unfathomable to consider accepting trouble into our lives, wouldn't it? And yet, we are told to patiently accept it. Wait, what?

When we are patient in the midst of our trials, we grow in our faith. We begin to see the work that the Lord wants to do in us and the beauty that comes as a result of it. As you spend time with the Lord today, accept the troubles that present themselves—for the sake of bringing others to salvation.

Lord, I will patiently accept my trials so I can see the beauty you have in the refining process. Help me to endure the worst of it!

I am willing to endure anything if it will bring salvation and eternal glory in Christ Jesus to those God has chosen.

2 Timothy 2:10 NLT

We can be thankful for times of trouble when we trust in God because those hardships refine us. And when trouble comes again, as it will inevitably do, we can be patient as we endure. It doesn't mean we can't work to solve problems. Rather, we find our patience to keep going in the middle of the storm.

If there's a storm raging within you tonight, ask God to give you the strength to endure it and the grace to see the beauty that comes from it.

God, thank you for refining me and drawing me closer to you. I need you all the time, but I especially need to feel your nearness when trouble is lurking.

You can endure the trials of life with God at your side.

Chase Wisdom

Teach the wise, and they will become even wiser;
teach good people, and they will learn even more.

PROVERBS 9:9 NCV

The moment a person decides they can't learn anything from someone is the moment they stop learning at all. It is openness to being taught that makes a man wise. The wisest people never stop learning, never stop exploring, seeing, or doing.

Never close yourself off to learning something new—not even from those younger than you. In their moments of frustration or failure, you can learn. You can learn to lead. You can learn to love well. You can learn through exploration and eagerness. Ask God to put someone in your path who you can learn from today.

Teach me daily, Lord. I want to be open to new understanding.
Humble my heart so that I can learn from anyone.

Instruct the wise and they will be wiser still;
teach the righteous and they will add to their learning.

PROVERBS 9:9 NIV

Wise people have an insatiable hunger to be taught. They understand that they are not the experts on everything and that there is always a person with more experience, more knowledge, and more passion.

You can learn from your triumph and your celebration, your failure and difficulty. You can learn to stop putting pressure on yourself, and instead rejoice in lifelong education. Chase wisdom—never arrive at it.

God, help me tonight to chase after wisdom. I don't ever want to stop learning.

Can you think of someone you can learn from?

Ability to Say No

*Do not swear, either by heaven or by earth or by any other oath,
but let your "yes" be yes and your "no" be no, so that you may not
fall under condemnation.*

JAMES 5:12 ESV

Promises are easy to make, but can be hard to keep. Anyone
can make a promise, but it takes a reliable, trustworthy
person to follow through. Sometimes, we can be *yes* people
when we really shouldn't. We might say yes because we don't
want to disappoint our loved ones. Or we say yes because
we are unrealistic with time constraints and try to shove too
many things into a short time span. Or we say yes because it
is too hard to pass up an exciting opportunity.

When you aren't reliable, it reflects on your character. It
is always better to think carefully about a new venture or
opportunity before you commit to it. Measure if you can be
depended on. If you have to say no this time, maybe the next
time you will be able to say yes. There will always be another
opportunity.

*Father, there are so many expectations and opportunities all
around me. I need your wisdom to choose what to say yes to and
what to pass on.*

Most of all, my brothers and sisters, never take an oath, by heaven or earth or anything else. Just say a simple yes or no, so that you will not sin and be condemned.

JAMES 5:12 NLT

Our culture is not one that allows us a lot of down time. We fill up schedules with activities and work, not leaving any breathing room or time to rest. We don't give ourselves permission to say no when we should. We commit, and then we over commit.

The problem with over-committing is that, inevitably, we will burn out. When we fail to deliver, we really fail to be trustworthy. Our intentions may be for the best, but if we make a habit of not following through with our commitments, people around us will begin to see us as unreliable and untrustworthy. Ask the Lord about what you should say no to tonight. He wants us to be rested and whole.

God, I want to be someone people think of as reliable. Help me to show them that I can do what I say I will do. I know I need your help to say no so that this is possible.

How do you think you are seen by the people around you?

Respectful Words

Respect everyone, and love your Christian brothers and sisters.
Fear God, and respect the king.

1 PETER 2:17 NLT

We were given a very powerful tool when God chose to give us the gift of speech. It can be used to bless, encourage, and even worship the Lord. Or it can be used as a weapon to destroy and cause great pain. We have all spoken and heard words being used both ways.

Sometimes we use cutting remarks to point out faults, instead of speaking truth with respect. We need to learn how to truly love others with our words—even when that involves honest evaluation. Ask the Lord to give you the right words to speak today.

God, I want to be respectful of everyone around me. Help me to use my words to bless and encourage, and to speak the truth in love.

Show proper respect to everyone, love the family of believers, fear God, honor the emperor.

1 PETER 2:17 NIV

It feels much better to give and receive loving communication than it does to give and receive destructive communication. When we think about how Jesus used his words, we know that he used them to bless and speak love. We also know that if there was a conflict, he used truth and wisdom to confront those who were being foolish.

Whenever you are tempted to lash out with your words, take a breath and think about how Jesus responded to those opposing him. Make your words match his example so they will truly count.

Father, give me grace to speak kindly to others even when they aren't kind to me. I want to be someone who reflects you in all I say and do.

Take a moment to write down a strategy for speaking respectfully.

Load of Anxiety

Always be full of joy in the LORD; I say it again, rejoice! Let everyone see that you are unselfish and considerate in all you do. Remember that the LORD is coming soon.

PHILIPPIANS 4:4-5 TLB

Carrying anxiety is like over-packing a car for a trip. Gas mileage suffers, companions have a hard time joining you, and blocked vision endangers your car and others on the road. Clearly, you need to unpack anxiety in order to free yourself for a better journey.

What is the key to shaking anxiety from your life? Rejoice in God, and gratefully request his help with your encumbrances. As you think forward to the next year, choose to bring your anxious thoughts to the Lord and let him replace them with joy.

I rejoice in you, Lord! All of my being praises you! You are good; you are kind. You constantly walk with me.

Always be full of joy in the LORD. I say it again—rejoice! Let everyone see that you are considerate in all you do. Remember, the LORD is coming soon.

PHILIPPIANS 4:4-5 NLT

Joy in the Lord is available in all circumstances. It's like a jug of lemonade in your fridge that readily fills your cup. Rejoicing produces refreshment. Your problems become manageable because Jesus is invited into all areas of your life.

Choosing to be full of joy in the Lord leaves no room for anxiety. Joy is your accompanying reality—anxiety can no longer take that seat. Look forward to our Savior's return and all things being made new. He is coming soon!

God, I praise you. I know you are sovereign over my circumstances. They will pass, but you will always be with me. Come and still my heart. Bring me joy.

Can you commit to handing your anxiety over to the Lord in the new year?

BroadStreet Publishing Group LLC

Savage, MN, USA

Broadstreetpublishing.com

From the Rising of the Sun

© 2017 by BroadStreet Publishing®

ISBN 978-1-4245-5550-5 (hard cover)

ISBN 978-1-4245-5551-2 (e-book)

Devotional entries compiled and composed by Michelle Winger.

Design by Chris Garborg | garborgdesign.com

Edited by Michelle Winger | literallyprecise.com

Printed in China.

17 18 19 20 21 22 23   7 6 5 4 3 2 1